Frances Ya-Chu Cowhig's
Three Parables of Glc

Frances Ya-Chu Cowhig (author) is an internationally produced playwright whose work has been staged in the United Kingdom at the Royal Shakespeare Company, the National Theatre, Hampstead Theatre, Trafalgar Studios 2 (West End), and the Unicorn Theatre. In the United States her work has been staged at venues that include the Oregon Shakespeare Festival, Manhattan Theater Club, and the Goodman Theatre. Frances' plays have been awarded the Wasserstein Prize, the Yale Drama Series Award (selected by David Hare), an Edinburgh Fringe First Award, the David A. Callichio Award, and the Keene Prize for Literature. Her plays include *Lidless*, *The World of Extreme Happiness*, *Snow in Midsummer*, and *The King of Hell's Palace*.

Christine Mok (editor and contributor) is Assistant Professor of English at the University of Rhode Island. Her work has been published in the *Journal of Asian American Studies, Theatre Survey, Modern Drama*, and *PAJ: A Journal of Performance and Art*.

Joshua Chambers-Letson (editor and contributor) is Professor of Performance Studies at Northwestern University. He is the author of *After the Party: A Manifesto for Queer of Color Life* (NYU Press, 2018) and *A Race So Different: Law and Performance in Asian America* (NYU Press, 2013).

Frances Ya-Chu Cowhig's China Trilogy: Three Parables of Global Capital

The World of Extreme Happiness
The King of Hell's Palace
Snow in Midsummer

Edited by
CHRISTINE MOK and JOSHUA CHAMBERS-LETSON

methuen | drama
LONDON • NEW YORK • OXFORD • NEW DELHI • SYDNEY

METHUEN DRAMA
Bloomsbury Publishing Plc
50 Bedford Square, London, WC1B 3DP, UK
1385 Broadway, New York, NY 10018, USA
29 Earlsfort Terrace, Dublin 2, Ireland

BLOOMSBURY, METHUEN DRAMA and the Methuen Drama logo are trademarks of
Bloomsbury Publishing Plc

This collection first published in Great Britain 2022

Introduction and afterwords copyright © Christine Mok and Joshua Chambers-Letson, 2022

The World of Extreme Happiness first published by Methuen Drama 2017
Copyright © Frances Ya-Chu Cowhig, 2017, 2022

The King of Hell's Palace first published by Methuen Drama 2019
Copyright © Frances Ya-Chu Cowhig, 2019, 2022

Snow in Midsummer first published by Methuen Drama 2013
Copyright © Frances Ya-Chu Cowhig, 2013, 2022

Frances Ya-Chu Cowhig has asserted her right under the Copyright, Designs and Patents Act, 1988, to be
identified as author of this work.

For legal purposes the Acknowledgments on p. 233 constitute an extension of this copyright page.

Cover design: Rebecca Hessleton
Cover images: Background © Pavel Kosolapov / Alamy Stock Photo; Label © Trevor Smith / Alamy Stock Photo

A catalogue record for this book is available from the British Library.

A catalog record for this book is available from the Library of Congress.

ISBN: PB: 978-1-3502-3437-6
        ePDF: 978-1-3502-3438-3
        eBook: 978-1-3502-3439-0

Series: Modern Plays

Typeset by RefineCatch Limited, Bungay, Suffolk
Printed and bound in Great Britain

To find out more about our authors and books visit www.bloomsbury.com
and sign up for our newsletters.

Dedicated to the memory of Dr. Shuping "Sunshine" Wang
Scientist, truth-teller, whistleblower

October 20, 1959 – September 21, 2019

Contents

Preface

Joshua Chambers-Letson

Frances Ya-Chu Cowhig's plays have a way of undoing you. This makes them fitting offerings for a world that seems as if it is coming undone. The three plays collected in this volume were written over the course of an era bookended by catastrophes: the financial crisis of 2007/8 and the COVID-19 pandemic. Both global in scale, the first crisis began with the collapse of the U.S. housing markets, radiating out to become the European debt crisis, before reaching for the rest of the world. The second began with the emergence of a novel coronavirus in Wuhan, China, billowing into a global pandemic effecting political and economic destabilization globally. Between these events, a host of economic, political, and environmental crises proliferated, including the retrenchment and renewal of economic and racial nationalism, the expansion of authoritarian governance along with the destabilization of a host of seemingly stable democracies (including the United States), accumulating waves of ecological disaster, and the rapid redistribution of capital (and power) upwards. These crises were and are increasingly more entangled with each other.

As we find in Cowhig's plays, today global capital serves and insists upon being the tissue and thread weaving the globe together. As a result, the cycles of crisis inherent to the process of capitalist accumulation render shockwaves that make it feel as if the earth is shaking apart or coming undone. If the question near the dawn of the twentieth century was "What is to be done?", the ballooning catastrophes characterizing life in the first half of the twenty-first leaves one awake at night wondering if anything *can* be done. The plays in this volume are explorations of this very question.

To describe these plays as "parables of global capital" is to suggest that they are teaching a lesson about what is to be done in the face of all this catastrophe. Something people have been doing for maybe as long as people have been doing things is telling stories as a way of making sense of (and making one's way through) a world in crisis. In theatre, people conjure worlds into being through language and action, suggesting at base the mutability and transformability of the world. In one moment, we are seated in a theatre in Chicago's Loop and then, with a shift in lights and the presence of bodies onstage, we imagine that the space in front of us is somehow a factory in Shenzhen, China. Plays aren't just stories about the world's changeability, they are tiny acts of changing the world. Even if this power is weak, imprecise, and only endures for the time of the performance, by allowing us to brush up against this power, Cowhig's plays remind us that something can yet be done.

This volume collects this trilogy of plays and publishes them together for the first time. To support the reader as they work to engage with the many challenging lessons of these three parables, we have included a host of supplemental materials. There is a new introduction by Christine Mok, this volume's co-editor and a leading scholar of Asian American theatre and performance, a series of updated essays on the plays by co-editor and performance studies scholar Joshua Chambers-Letson, a dialogue between Cowhig and the co-editors, and production histories. These three plays are full with a record of profound loss, but they are also threaded through, in even their bleakest moments, with other possibilities for the world and the people who inhabit it. Such possibilities, Frances' work teaches us, emerge through practices of care and compassion, but also by way of collective struggle and sacrifice. This volume is offered as an act of *doing* in the service of that continued struggle.

Introduction

Christine Mok

To everything (turn, turn, turn), there might be a season, but since mid-March of 2020, the theatres in New York and London have been shuttered. Dust gathers on ghost lights dimly illuminating empty stages as the global pandemic of novel coronavirus (2019-nCoV) spreads and surges. The disease has ignored the boundaries fought for and enforced by nation-states. It has thrived by exploiting systemic inequities and structural racism, the force behind these health and social disparities, to push racial and ethnic minorities further along the continuum of morbidity and mortality. What's more, the pandemic is both another chapter in the taut geopolitical dance between the U.S. and China and marks a resurgence in the long history of anti-Chinese and anti-Asian racism and violence in the U.S. and abroad. If theatre were really a plague, as Antonin Artaud provocatively declaimed first in a lecture at the Sorbonne in 1933, then we have learned from neither the theatre nor the plague some crucial insights about the relationship between the two.

Perhaps this is not only an ethical failure but a foundering of imagination as we try to wrench breathing room in the capitalist realism we find ourselves in. As theorist Frederic Jameson wrote, pushing the attribution to another player, "[s]omeone once said it is easier to imagine the end of the world than to imagine the end of capitalism." He continues, "[w]e may now revise that and witness the attempt to imagine capitalism by way of imagining the end of the world."[1] Curious that Jameson's revision is in witnessing the "attempt to imagine capitalism" rather than the attempt to imagine *the end* of capitalism. Perhaps, the sentence enacts the very occlusion and limit point of the imagination of capitalism. Yet, what would happen if we did witness the attempt at a beginning point to capitalism, a starting point to the end of the world—in hopes that we might then imagine otherwise?

Frances Ya-Chu Cowhig is a playwright of the Anthropocene, the geological epoch so named because "human"[2] activity has become the dominant force altering our planet on a geologic scale through the ongoing[3] violence of extractive capitalism. She builds worlds that hold up a mirror to ourselves as the humans in this human

---

1   Frederic Jameson, "Future City," *New Left Review* 21 (May–June 2003): 7.
2   The "human" in the anthro of Anthropocene flattens differential power in that, following anthropologist Zoe Todd, "humans-in-the-world . . . blunts the distinctions between the people, nations, and collectives who drive the fossil-fuel economy and those who do not." Zoe Todd, "Indiginizing the Anthropocene," in *Art in the Anthropocene: Encounters Among Aesthetics, Politics, Environments and Epistemologies* (London: Open Humanities Press, 2015). http://openhumanitiespress.org/Davis-Turpin_2015_Art-in-the-Anthropocene.pdf
3   From 1492 to the present, according to Sylvia Wynter: "The struggle of our new millennium will be one between the ongoing imperative of securing the well-being of our present ethnoclass (i.e., Western bourgeois) conception of the human, Man, which overrepresents itself as if it were the human itself, and that of securing the well-being, and therefore the full cognitive and behavioral autonomy of the human species itself/ourselves." Sylvia Wynter, "Unsettling the Coloniality of Being/Power/Truth/Freedom: Towards the Human, After Man, Its Overrepresentation—An Argument," *CR: The New Centennial Review* 3, no. 3 (Fall 2003): 260–1.

epoch to attend to the capitalist destruction that threatens life and the collaborative survival necessary to make life liveable.

Born in Philadelphia, and raised in Virginia, Okinawa, Taipei, and Beijing, Cowhig draws on her peripatetic childhood between the U.S. and East Asia, to craft theatrical worlds that reveal connections between people, places, events, and encounters, exposing the ties that bind the local with the global. Cowhig received an MFA in Writing from the James A. Michener Center for Writers at UT Austin, a BA in Sociology from Brown University, and holds a certificate in Ensemble-Based Physical Theatre from the Dell'Arte International School of Physical Theatre. She was formerly Associate Professor of Drama at the University of California at Santa Barbara. Her plays have been awarded the Wasserstein Prize, the Yale Drama Series Award (selected by David Hare), an Edinburgh Fringe First Award, the David A. Callichio Award, the Keene Prize for Literature, and a United States Artist Fellowship.

Cowhig began writing plays in undergraduate and remarks, in an interview with fellow playwright Caridad Svich, that "I really found grounding and a kind of rootedness in the process of writing."[4] Her plays include: *Lidless* (2010),[5] which won the Yale Drama Series Award, *410 [GONE]* (2014), which she first wrote in college, *The World of Extreme Happiness* (2013), *Snow in Midsummer* (2017), and *The King of Hell's Palace* (2019), which are collected together for the first time in this edition. With each play, she provides an unflinching look at the consequences of human actions. Her plays are visceral, full up with the stuff of life—blood, flesh, excrement, sweat, tears, dust, ash, and dirt. And, the alchemy that transmuting these materials (Dou Yi's heart buried to nourish the dirt that is a new home for a small willow tree in *Snow in Midsummer*) makes possible.

The three plays in this volume, parables of global capital that ask us what worlds we reap and sow, each dig into the emergence of capitalism in China. *The World of Extreme Happiness* (2013), *Snow in Midsummer* (2017), and *The King of Hell's Palace* (2019) asks its performers, readers, and spectators to imagine capitalism by way of imaging the ending of worlds in and through the China Dream. President Xi Jinping invoked the China Dream in his closing speech of the National People's Congress of the People's Republic of China (PRC) in 2013, as "the dream of the great rejuvenation of the Chinese nation"[6] to orchestrate the rise-of-China that Cowhig's three plays follow. That rise stitches together competing narratives of China's past and present: from epic historical glories as the center of the universe, the Middle Kingdom, to the Qing Empire's defeat in the Opium War of 1840, to the dream of the communist society inspired by the Russian Revolution yet ravaged by its Great Leap Forward into the 1975 Banqiao Dam failure and famine, both catastrophic human-made disasters, to when the Party merged China with global capitalism through an economic reform platform in the late twentieth century. Though global capitalism has been knocking on China's door since before the Opium War, it was the Party that officially ushered it in, setting its people on a collision course with another dream, the American Dream, and its heady mix of manifest destiny with capitalist uplift and consumerism.

---

4   Caridad Svich, "Frances Cowhig: Recovering Trauma," in *The Breath of Theatre* (South Gate, CA: NoPassport Press, 2013), 302
5   I am indicating first publication date in the parentheticals.
6   "President Vows to Press Ahead with 'Chinese Dream.'" *Xinhua News*, March 17, 2013.

Cowhig uncovers national and global histories in her staging of a contemporary China to disentangle rise-of-China rhetorics and the China Dream. The characters, settings, and actions work within and against the very representations circulating through the myths told about China by the West and, by China, about itself, both of which have been overlaid by ideologies about the Other. This field of (differential) power and representational politics is cross stitched in the two epigraphs to Edward Said's 1978 monograph *Orientalism*. The first, "[t]hey cannot represent themselves; they must be represented," is from Karl Marx's essay "The Eighteenth Brumaire of Louis Bonaparte," and the second, from Benjamin Disraeli's novel *Tancred*: "The East is a career."[7] In the representation of the East (by the West) and the colonial occupation of the East (by the West), we see the entangled relations between East and West (Orient and Occident) that orientalism animates. As co-editor Joshua Takano Chambers-Letson elucidates in his afterword to *Snow in Midsummer*, first published in 2017, "[b]y setting the play[s] in the overdeteremined elsewhere of "China," Cowhig consistently deconstructs . . . [and], remind[s] the audience member of the ways in which "China" and "America" (or "East" and "West") are less distinct and coherent identities than mutually implicated, co-constitutive, overlapping, and deeply integrated systems of economic, political, ideological, racial, sexual, territorial, and discursive practice."[8] Thus, her three "China" plays actively engage in an ethics of representation, staging China as method,[9] to show a global matrix of systems.

The China of her plays does not dissolve the West's presence and its related historical and structural inequalities, but instead dislocates the position of her English-speaking audience as and at the center, inviting, and I borrow again from Chambers-Letson, "audiences in Britain . . . and the U.S. to make critical connections to their own surround."[10] Notably absent from her plays, a common trope of both U.S. and British stages, is the (oft white) audience stand-in character who, in traveling to China, gently brings the (oft white) audience along for the exotic ride. Instead, the plays immerse spectators in her contemporary China, positioning the spectator as more than mere observer, voyeur, or tourist. To riff on Jill Dolan's 1988 monograph *Feminist Spectator as Critic*, which unseated the "ideal spectator" of the (white, middle-class, heteronormative) male gaze to theorize reparative and resistant feminist spectatorship and meaning-making, Cowhig's China Trilogy also positions its spectators to engage in critique. Specifically, Cowhig's spectators are positioned to engage in Asian Americanist critique. Coined by cultural theorist Kandice Chuh, Asian Americanist critique offers the approach that "taking Asiatic racialization seriously opens and sometimes compels avenues of inquiry and raises questions and creates archives that would otherwise be unavailable."[11] The questions and avenues spurred by Cowhig's Asian Americanist

7   Edward Said, *Orientalism* (New York: Pantheon Books, 1978), xii
8   Joshua Takano Chambers-Letson, this volume, 222
9   China as Method is a riff on Asia as Method, coined first by Japanese sinologist Takeuchi Yoshimi in a 1960 lecture, "Asia as Method," and further theorized by Kuan-Hsing Chen in his 2010 monograph, *Asia as Method: Towards Deimperialization* (Duke University Press, 2010).
10 Chambers-Letson, this volume, 221
11 Kandice Chuh, "It's Not About Anything," *Social Text 121* 32, no. 4 (Winter 2014): 127. For the most, see Chuh's two monographs: *Imagine Otherwise: On Asian Americanist Critique* (Duke University Press, 2003) and *The Difference Aesthetics Makes: On the Humanities "After Man"* (Duke University Press, 2019).

critique puts pressure on an essentialized Chinese identity and a seamless China Dream (or, for that matter, the American Dream), as manipulated by both Chinese and Western nation-states to their own political and economic ends. By doing so, Cowhig reveals across her plays that the global capitalism that China rushes to not only join but also dominate is twenty-first-century racial capitalism[12] that is both predicated on differential human value and produces racial, gender, and sexual difference necessary for the maximization of profit.

In an interview from 2014, Cowhig notes how her own positionality informs the performative relation of Asian Americanist critique that her plays invite, "because Chinese writers who try to write about social or political truths are often punished by the government, because there aren't many plays about contemporary China, and because there aren't very meaty roles for Asian actors in the U.S. or the U.K., by writing a few plays on China I can address multiple 'gaps' at once."[13] She draws a direct link between her commitment to writing about China from outside of the country, as a member of the diaspora, to writing many dynamic roles for actors of Asian descent. While the characters are Chinese, the actors are transnational Asian American and British East Asian.

"They cannot represent themselves; they must be represented" is the unofficial motto for the history of Asian representation on Western stages. Asian performers have been dispossessed of their own embodiment through performance practices of erasure from nineteenth-century yellowface to twenty-first-century whitewashing. Cowhig's plays refute these erasures. Each of her plays is populated by large casts of multi-generational characters. While the plays offer double casting possibilities to underscore juxtaposition and connection, Cowhig's play worlds are a welcome respite from the winnowing of (American) theatre where budding playwrights are advised to write two-handers and avoid controversial topics or complex emotion in favor of familiar psychological melodrama. Before writing *Snow in Midsummer*, Cowhig embarked on a listening tour with the British East Asian acting community in London, in the aftermath of the casting controversy in the Royal Shakespeare Company's (RSC's) 2012–13 production of the classical Chinese play, *The Orphan of Zhao*. The casting, as well as marketing and promotion, generated international criticism in newspapers and on blogs, with the Asian American Performers Action Coalition (AAPAC) and playwright David Henry Hwang, from across the pond, issuing statements. Soon after, the RSC green lit their Chinese Translations Project, with Cowhig as the first playwright commissioned to adapt a classical Chinese play. In her listening tour, Cowhig was interested not just in how British actors felt about representation, she asked them the kinds of roles they dreamed for themselves, using their wish list to guide her ethics and politics of representation. Given how often her plays hinge on uncovering, visibility is a double-edged sword. Indeed, another important element to Cowhig's Asian Americanist critique is the awareness of who her audience is, for whom her actors are performing for and inviting to be beholden to and apprehended by. Her plays invite us

12 See Cedric Robinson's *Black Marxism: The Making of the Black Radical Tradition* (University of North Carolina Press, 1983).
13 "TALK: Frances Ya-Chu Cowhig on writing impossible plays," *TANK Magazine*. The Complicity Issue #60. Spring 2014. https://tankmagazine.com/issue-60/talk/france-ya-chu-cowhig/

to think deeply within the art of live performance about the interplay between the histories and present politics of racialized bodies beyond the theatre's walls.

Rather than following their production history, the China Trilogy is presented here in an order that moves from what Cowhig, in an interview with the co-editors, noted as the bleakest to the most hopeful—a potential order if the plays were produced as a single day theatre marathon. *The World of Extreme Happiness*, set in rural and urban China in 1992 and 2012, follows an uneducated Chinese girl as its tragic hero to explore the paradoxes of "new" capitalism in China. While Sunny's story is a kind of Everywoman in New China, *The King of Hell's Palace*, based on the true story of the HIV/AIDS outbreak in China, is set in Henan province. Straddling 1992 and 1998, the play focuses again on rural and urban China by exploring the political machinations and medical repercussions of the rush to extract blood plasma from the most vulnerable. 1992 marks "year zero" in the trilogy, for in January and February 1992, the then retired party leader Deng Xiaoping toured Shenzhen (the PRC's first special economic zone), Zhuhai, Guangzhou and Shanghai in what is known as his Southern Inspection Tour. His final political act was a series of statements about China's reform and opening to the world that propelled his vision for new capitalism in a New China. While *The World of Extreme Happiness* and *The King of Hell's Palace* chart the economic, social, and political changes to rural and urban China, with attention to the migrants whose labor and lives made such transformations possible, *Snow in Midsummer* takes an epic view on the aftermath of these changes. An adaptation of Guan Hanqing's classic Yuan drama, *Snow in Midsummer* dramatizes the haunting of past choices, actions, and injustices. Though both previous plays gesture to the mythic (Monkey King's 72 Transformations in *The World of Extreme Happiness*) and the cosmological with a Buddhist hereafter of judgment and reincarnation that remains despite the Cultural Revolution, *Snow in Midsummer* stages that afterlife to create space to reckon with the afterlives of racial capitalism as a necessary process for imagining redemption.

Cowhig has written about her process for the Playwrights Foundation in the following way: "When I think about what I want to write, I think about the things that disappoint, frustrate, anger or excite me, and create a set of constraints and challenges that require that I envision a world in which these emotions are addressed, challenged, or explored."[14] For *The World of Extreme Happiness,* which began as an Emerging Artists open commission from South Coast Repertory in 2010, Cowhig connected her own memories in Beijing of the cardboard shanty towns of migrant workers in the shadow of glass skyscrapers just outside the diplomatic compound she grew up in, with the current statistics that the biggest migrations in the world are internal. She researched what has been called an internal apartheid in China (in part because rural residency permits "lock" migrants into their rural and migratory status). Three texts sparked the play—Leslie T. Chang's *Factory Girls: From Village to City in a Changing China* (2008), Xinran's *Message from an Unknown Chinese Mother: Stories of Loss and Love* (2012), and Liao Yiwu's *The Corpse Walker: Real Life Stories: China From the Bottom Up* (2008)—and provided new lenses into a world unfurling as Cowhig herself was

---

14 Frances Ya-Chu Cowhig, "Playwrights Foundation Blog Post, March 7, 2013." http://playwrightsfoundation.blogspot.com/2013/03/frances-ya-chu-cowhig-world-of-extreme.html

growing up. *The World of Extreme Happiness* had its first workshop (2012) and U.S. production (2015) at the Goodman Theatre in Chicago. Its first U.K. production was at the Royal National Theatre's Shed Theatre, in London in 2013.

Through her father, Cowhig was able to meet and speak with Liao Yiwu, the author of the oral history collection, *The Corpse Walker*, and others who spoke of life in the aftermath of the Cultural Revolution and daily life under accelerated capitalism. She also met Dr. Wang Shuping. Her father initially met Dr. Wang while working for the Environment, Science and Technology section of the U.S. Embassy in Beijing. Dr. Wang, who passed away on September 30, 2019, was the whistle-blower of the rural AIDS crisis in Henan Province. She was a doctor and research scientist who, while working at an Epidemic Control Station in Zhoukou township in Henan province, discovered that government-run plasma stations were contaminated and spreading both hepatitis and HIV. She took great risks to herself and her family to defy Chinese officials and alert the international community. In 2012, Cowhig pitched the idea of writing a play inspired by her life and actions to the Goodman Theatre and received a commission to write the play, which is built from interviews with Dr. Wang. The Goodman produced a workshop in 2016. The first U.K. production was at Hampstead Theatre in London in 2019. The U.S. premiere was programmed, delayed, and then cancelled due to COVID-19. In the weeks preceding the U.K. production's premiere, officials from the PRC Ministry of State Security approached Dr. Wang's family, friends, and former colleagues in Henan and Beijing to shutter the British production through intimidation. "With bullying and censorship, the government has covered up the HCV and HIV epidemics in China very successfully," Dr. Wang wrote in a statement, "[w]hy, in 2019, do they worry so much about a play being produced in London, twenty-four years after the events it depicts?" She continued: "The only thing harder than standing up to the Communists and their security police is not giving in to pressure from friends and relatives who are threatened with their livelihoods all because you are speaking out. But even after all this time, I will still not be silenced, even though I am deeply sad that this intimidation is happening yet again. *The King of Hell's Palace* will go ahead."[15]

Perhaps, the same spirit of persistence in the face of the cruelty of the State drew Cowhig to Guan Hanqing's *Dou E Yuan* (also known as *The Injustice to Dou E* and *Snow in Midsummer*). Commissioned by the RSC as part of their Chinese Translations Project, Cowhig sifted through several golden age Chinese plays before honing in on the story of Dou E. The U.K. premiere was produced by the RSC at the Swan Theatre in Stratford-upon-Avon in 2017. The U.S. premiere was in Ashland, Oregon, at the Oregon Shakespeare Festival in 2018. Cowhig worked with translator Gigi Chang, creating her adaptation from Chang's literal translation of the original play. Because the Yuan stage used minimal formal scenery and props and had a more boisterous audience than is usual today, the play relies on prose to narrate onstage action and the passage of time. For contemporary audiences, *Dou E Yuan* feels repetitive, with characters telling the audience again (and again) who they are and what has happened, even as they also set the audience up for what is about to happen. While this repetitive quality is a

---

15 Shuping Wang, Statement on *The King of Hell's Palace*: https://www.hampsteadtheatre.com/news/2019/september/full-statement-dr-shuping-wang/

function of the form (variety theatre with a rambunctious, not socially distant, audience enjoying food and drink), it is a dramaturgical quirk that Cowhig's play reinforces by connecting who characters are with what has happened to them in order to see what shapes their present and future actions. By returning to the contemporary Chinese factory town in *Snow in Midsummer*, we see the impact of global capitalism on vulnerable populations and ecologies. Cowhig insists upon the interrelation of actions and their consequences, the interpersonal and the institutional, human and geologic, life and afterlives. *Snow in Midsummer* is a ghost story, murder mystery, detective story, and post-apocalyptic, supernatural adventure—all in the pursuit of justice, hope, and future possibility.

It is that future possibility that the China Trilogy ends on. A hope is that by the time you are holding what will undoubtedly be the handsome cover to this collection, the theatres will be open again and that in opening back up something else besides business as usual is happening onstage, backstage, and in the boardrooms where the decisions that shape both happen. If there is a lesson to be learned from the parables Frances Ya-Chu Cowhig offers to audiences, it is that a world has ended; and we are waiting, in the wings, on the brink of another.

The World of Extreme Happiness

The World of Extreme Happiness was first staged at the Goodman Theatre's Owen Theatre (Robert Falls, Artistic Director; Roche Schulfer, Executive Director), Chicago Illinois, on December 9, 2012. The cast for this workshop production was as follows:

Sunny	Marissa Lichwick
Pete / Mr. Destiny / Ran Feng	Kevin Matthew Reyes
Ming-Ming / Xiao Li / Qing Shu Min	Cindy Im
Wang Hua / Artemis Chang	Mia Park
Li Han / James Lin	Daniel Smith
Old Lao / Gao Chen	Ben Wang

Director	Jonathan Berry
Scenic Design	Kevin Depinet
Costume Design	Christine Pascual
Lighting Design	Jesse Klug
Sound Design	Mikhail Fiksel
Dramaturg	Neena Arndt

The World of Extreme Happiness was originally commissioned and developed by South Coast Repertory with support from the Elizabeth George Foundation.

The World of Extreme Happiness was first staged in the United Kingdom by the Royal National Theatre's Shed Theatre (Nicholas Hytner, Artistic Director; Lisa Burger, Executive Director), London, on September 25, 2013. The cast was as follows:

Sunny	Katie Leung
Pete / Ran Feng	Chris Lew Kum Hoi
Ming-Ming / Xiao Li / Qing Shu Min	Vera Chok
Wang Hua / Artemis Chang	Sarah Lam
Li Han / James Lin	Daniel York
Old Lao / Mr. Destiny / Gao Chen	Junix Inocian

Director	Michael Longhurst
Designer	Chloe Lamford
Lighting Design	Philip Gladwell
Movement	Anna Morrissey
Music and Sound Design	Max and Ben Ringham
Fight Director	Bret Young
Company Voice Work	Kate Godfrey

The World of Extreme Happiness had its world premiere at the Goodman Theatre's Owen Theatre (Robert Falls, Artistic Director; Roche Schulfer, Executive Director, Chicago, Illinois on September 13, 2014. This co-production transferred to Manhattan Theatre Club's City Center Stage I (Lynn Meadow, Artistic Director; Barry Grove, Executive Producer), in New York City, on February 3, 2015.

Sunny	Jennifer Lim
Pete / Ran Feng	Ruy Iskander (Chicago)
	Telly Leung (New York)
Ming-Ming / Xiao Li / Qing Shu Min	Jo Mei
Wang Hua / Artemis Chang	Jodi Long (Chicago)
	Sue Jin Song (New York)
Li Han / James Lin	Donald Li (Chicago)
	James Saito (New York)
Old Lao / Mr. Destiny / Gao Chen	Francis Jue

Director	Eric Ting
Scenic Design	Mimi Lien
Costume Design	Jenny Mannis
Lighting Design	Tyler Micoleau
Sound Design	Mikhail Fiksel
Dramaturg	Neena Arndt
Dance Consultant	William Tuekun Wu
Production Stage Manager	Kimberly Osgood (Chicago)
	Winnie Lok (New York)

Characters

Sunny, *18–20. Female. Migrant factory worker.*

Pete, *16–18. Male. Sunny's brother.*
Also plays: **Ran Feng**, *20–36. Coal miner.*

Li Han, *25–45. Male. Sunny's father. Coal miner.*
Also plays: **James Lin**, *51. Factory owner.*

Old Lao, *65. Male. Head of Sanitation at Shenzhen Factory.*
Also plays: **Gao Chen**, *50. Public Security Officer.*
       Mr. Destiny, *60. Self-help guru.*

Artemis Chang, *52. Female. Vice President of Price-Smart China.*
Also plays: **Wang Hua**, *40–60. Midwife turned fix-it woman.*

Qing Shu Min, *26. Female. Police officer*
Also plays: **Xiao Li**, *22. Sunny and Pete's mother.*
       Ming-Ming, *23. Factory worker.*

Place and Time

Rural and urban China, 1992 and 2011–12.

Scene One

*Rural China, 1992. A dilapidated brick house in a town along the Yangtze River. Faded Spring Couplets flank the exterior door. Inside, **Wang Hua** assists **Xiao Li**, who is in labor. Outside, **Li Han** squats by a tin slop bucket, shelling peanuts. He tosses the husks into the bucket. A lit cigarette is perched between his lips. His hands and face are smudged with coal dust. He has a dejected, morose air about him.*

Xiao Li (*screaming*)   Get out of me you son of a turtle!

Wang Hua   Push!

Xiao Li   Get out before you crush my guts!

Wang Hua   Harder!

Xiao Li (*through pushes*)   For nine months you've been eating me like a plague. Robbing my breath. Stealing my blood. (*Gasps.*) Fuccck!

*The labor continues in the house, mostly in the form of pacing and labored breathing. **Li Han** continues to smoke and shell peanuts. **Ran Feng** enters, squats beside **Li Han**, and lights a cigarette.*

Ran Feng   Put all your love in one basket and you live in fear of losing it.

Li Han   Is that why you fuck so many whores?

Ran Feng   What if your favorite gets killed by her pimp? What if she gets pregnant, or hangs herself and stops being such a nice fuck? Spread your love in many places, and you will never experience heartbreak.

Li Han   Go home.

Ran Feng   It's only been a week. Don't lose hope.

Li Han   What if she was kidnapped, or shot down by gangsters? What if I receive a ransom note, strapped to a severed leg?

Ran Feng   That only happens in Taiwan.

Wang Hua   Come out, baby. You have a nice house, and a pretty mom, even though she has the mouth of a farmer.

Xiao Li (*to **Wang Hua***)   Fuck your mother.

Li Han   Yesterday I dreamed Xin Xin came to my bed and sat on my face. As she rocked back and forth, making soft little sounds, I lay still, savoring her warmth on my skin, weeping fat tears of joy because my heart had come back to me. Suddenly, I felt something hot and gooey slide down my cheek. For a moment, I was confused. Then, I realized Xin Xin had laid a turd between my eyes. It mixed with my tears, slid towards my lips, and melted on my tongue. It was salty, and sweet. Like tofu, fermented with black beans. What do you think that means?

Ran Feng   Li Han. She shat on your face.

Li Han   The turd was still warm. That could mean she's alive and trying to get back to me.

Ran Feng   Li Han. She shat on your face and you ate it. The symbolism's obvious. You accepted the shit of your lost pigeon into your mouth and digested it.

Li Han   She can't be lost. It must be a good omen. What if it means—

Ran Feng   If your beloved bird doesn't make it home, I'll give you the offspring of my best breeding pair and you can find your heart all over again.

Li Han   I don't want your second-rate pigeon. I want Xin Xin! If she's not back by evening I'll die in my sleep from heartbreak.

Ran Feng *and* **Li Han** *continue to smoke and shell peanuts. Focus shifts to the inside of the house, where* **Xiao Li** *is doubled over and moaning.* **Wang Hua** *rubs* **Xiao Li**'s *swollen belly.*

Wang Hua   It's crowning!

Xiao Li   Does it have balls?

Wang Hua   PUSH!

Xiao Li (*through pushes*)   What. Is. IT?!

Wang Hua   Say something nice!

Xiao Li   You can be the first son and cherished heir. Everything we have will be yoursssssaiighhiyiyiiyiyiyiyiyahyuhhhhh!

Wang Hua *catches the baby as it comes out.*

Wang Hua   It's done.

Xiao Li   How does his penis look?

Wang Hua *checks the baby's genitals then wraps her in sheets of old newspaper and tucks it under her arm.*

Xiao Li   Sometimes you can't tell. The balls hide in the stomach, and you—

Wang Hua (*interrupting*)   Shut up before you get us in trouble.

Xiao Li   You said that if I ate more meat—

Wang Hua   It's not that simple.

Xiao Li   I can't read. I can't just look in a book and find instructions.

Wang Hua   You want the recipe for boy babies? Lose weight, comb your hair, and get your husband to fuck you. You must have been very bad in your last life to be punished so much in this one.

Xiao Li   I want a son.

Wang Hua   Don't waste your breath wanting. Just make one.

Xiao Li (*screaming*)   I want a son!

Wang Hua *approaches* **Li Han** *and* **Ran Feng**. **Li Han** *lifts the lid off the slop bucket.* **Wang Hua** *drops the newspaper bundle inside.* **Li Han** *hacks a loogie, spits into the slop bucket, and replaces the lid.*

Wang Hua   Make a soup with flour and water. She'll need it to regain her strength.

Li Han   I paid for a son.

Wang Hua   My job is to deliver a child.

Li Han   A boy is a child. A girl is a thing. Five times I've paid for a child. Five times you've given me things.

Wang Hua   It must be fate that all the Li family deserves is things.

Li Han *slaps* **Wang Hua**. *She staggers backwards, pulls a wad of bills out of her pocket and throws them at* **Li Han**.

Li Han   One more "thing" and you'll never work this village again.

Wang Hua *kicks* **Ran Feng**. *Peanuts fly across the floor.* **Li Han** *lights a cigarette.*

Ran Feng   Ma! What the fuck was that for?

Wang Hua   Get up. Grow up. Find a wife.

Wang Hua *spits at* **Li Han**'s *feet, then exits.* **Ran Feng** *follows her out.* **Xiao Li** *whimpers in the next room.*

Li Han   The neighbors are mocking us. If we don't have a son, we'll be the laughing stock of the village. Try harder, okay? The fate of seven generations rests on us.

Li Han *lifts the slop bucket and heads for the door.*

Xiao Li   Three months she's been kicking. She was so fierce. So demanding.

Li Han *doesn't respond. He is frozen by the front door, listening to something.*

Xiao Li   Why would a girl do such things?

Li Han   Do you hear that?

Xiao Li   Hear what?

Li Han   That sound. That beautiful, precious sound.

Li Han *opens the front door. He gasps in delight, and crouches by the door.*

Li Han   My heart! You've come back! Oh no, a broken wing? You must have hopped home, you poor thing. Don't worry. Daddy will fix you up.

Li Han *scoops up the unseen bird and carries her to an offstage pigeon loft.*

Li Han (*offstage*)   Xiao Li! Perfect Girl needs a treat.

Xiao Li   The pig needs to eat.

Li Han (*offstage*)   Have some mercy. She's suffering!

Xiao Li   Look in the slop bucket. There might be some yam scrapings.

Li Han *enters and lifts the lid off the slop bucket.*

Li Han (*screams*)   Aughyiyaiiyah!

Xiao Li   What?

Li Han   It's still alive! And—fuck me! It's smiling!

Xiao Li   Foolish girl. Tell her to die.

Li Han   She's smiling, like I'm the sun on a cold winter day! I've never seen such a pathetic thing.

Xiao Li   Close the lid. She'll die soon enough.

Li Han   What if this is a good omen?

Xiao Li   Horse shit. Girls are bad luck.

Li Han *scoops the soggy newspaper bundle out of the slop bucket and places it into* **Xiao Li***'s arms.*

Li Han (*chuckling*)   Look at that. Born into a bucket of pig slop, and she's smiling like a Buddha. We'll name her Sunny. Heheh.

Xiao Li   I want a son.

Li Han   Then make one.

Li Han *pulls yam scraps from the bucket, then heads to the pigeon loft.*

Li Han   Nurse her. Keep her soft. We'll sell her once she's old enough to fuck. (*To pigeon.*) Here you go, my beauty.

Xiao Li (*to bundle in her arms*)   Stupid girl.

Li Han (*offstage*)   Who's the prettiest birdie?

Xiao Li   Why are you alive?

Li Han (*offstage*)   Who loves you so much?

Xiao Li   And still smiling?

Li Han (*offstage*)   Daddy loves his Perfect Girl. Yes he does.

Xiao Li   Don't you know the lives of girls are full of misery?

Baby Sunny *gurgles.*

Xiao Li (*to baby*)   Once upon a time, on a mountain of flowers and fruit, a pregnant rock released a stone egg, from which hatched the King of the Monkeys. He found a teacher and learned the 72 Transformations, so he could change into any form. One day, Monkey used his powers to break into Hell and erase his name from the Book of Life and Death, stealing immortality. Then he stormed heaven and ate peaches meant for the Queen. Buddha caught Monkey and trapped him under a mountain guarded by the Goddess of Mercy. Five hundred years later he's freed. Monkey makes new friends and joins them on a journey west to retrieve the Lost Teachings. *(Beat.)* Sunny Li. Drink.

Xiao Li *lifts the newspaper bundle to her breast.* **Sunny** *(eighteen) enters, wearing a factory uniform. The next scene assembles around her.*

Scene Two

Shenzhen, 2011. Factory bathroom. **Sunny** *mops the floor.* **Old Lao,** *a grizzled sanitation unit manager sporting thick black glasses, a baseball cap and a green uniform enters carrying a thick binder.*

Old Lao   Who are you?

Sunny *(meek)*   Sunny Li.

Old Lao   Louder.

Sunny   Sunny Li.

Old Lao   Where's the girl who usually works here?

Sunny   She was—um—transferred to—the cafeteria, b-because our section manager—had a bad . . . accident.

Old Lao   You call jumping out an eight-story window an accident? Spoiled brat. If he thought this job was hard he should have seen the public toilets I cleaned in the eighties. Do you know what you're doing?

Sunny *(hesitant)*   I . . . . um . . . . I don't mean to trouble you, but—

Old Lao *(barks)*   What?

Sunny   Bleach!

Old Lao   What about it?

Sunny   I've been uh . . . . using it on toilets—but sometimes it doesn't work.

Old Lao   I bet you're talking about these girl bathrooms. Women have terrible aim. We men know how to shoot straight but you squatting bitches piss all over the place. If the bleach isn't working your solution lacks strength. Triple the concentration and leave it on for an hour. That should do the trick.

He returns to his binder. **Sunny** *mops silently.*

Old Lao   Do you know what you're doing?

Sunny *nods.*

Old Lao   We'll see about that. When I come back, this bathroom better be spotless.

Old Lao *exits.* **Sunny** *mops the floor. Her cell phone, which has a techno-pop ringtone, goes off. She attaches an earpiece and continues mopping.*

Sunny (*into phone*)   Pete! Stop calling during my shifts –

Pete *wearing his school uniform, does acrobatic warm-ups and stretches inside the dilapidated brick house in rural China where* **Sunny** *was born. He is on the phone.*

Pete (*into phone, in Monkey voice*)   "Buddha tricked me," said Monkey, "and trapped me in Stone Mountain five centuries ago. Please, Goddess of Mercy. Use your powers. Rescue me."

Sunny   I'm tired of being Goddess.

Pete (*in Goddess voice*)   "Monkey, your sins were great. How can I be sure that if I release you from Stone Mountain you won't cause more trouble?"

Sunny   Have you done your homework?

Pete   Monkey doesn't talk like that.

Sunny   Watch it, rice bucket. You're asking to be kicked.

Pete (*in Monkey voice*)   "Chop off my arms, I can still strike. Hack of my legs. I can still—"

Sunny   I scrub floors twelve hours a day so you can be in school.

Li Han *enters, covered in coal dust and strips down to white boxers.*

Pete (*into phone*)   Ba's home.

Sunny   My section manager jumped out the window.

Pete   You told me that last month.

Sunny   That was someone else.

Pete *pours hot water into a basin of water for* **Li Han**, *who steps in and washes soot off his body.* **Sunny** *continues mopping.*

Li Han   Too hot.

Sunny   This means there's an open management position.

Pete (*sarcastic*)   Ooooooh.

Pete *pours cold water into the basin.* **Li Han** *continues washing.* **Pete** *hands* **Li Han** *a jar of tea. He takes a sip.*

Li Han   Too cold.

Li Han *dumps the tea in the bathwater.*

Sunny   What did you learn in school?

Pete   Ba thinks I should stop going.

Sunny   That's not his decision. I pay your tuition. Put him on.

Pete *hands* **Li Han** *the phone.*

Pete   What?

Sunny   School's his only way out.

Li Han   He made it to tenth grade. Enough. He'll get stuck up if he goes further.

Sunny   I already paid his tuition.

Li Han   Get a refund. I need new shoes. The house needs new windows.

Sunny   I send you money every month.

Li Han *steps out of the tub, then hacks a loogie into the water.*

Li Han   It's not enough.

Sunny   Stop spending so much on your birds.

Li Han *hangs up the phone, hands it to* **Pete** *and continues washing.* **Sunny** *mops the floor furiously.* **Pete** *calls* **Sunny.** *She answers.*

Pete   I'll work in the mine. It'll be fun. I'll make my own money and buy what I want.

Sunny   They collapse all the time.

Pete   Then come home.

Sunny   No.

Pete   If you don't I'll drink beer for breakfast and spend all my money on hookers and cigarettes.

Sunny   Don't cry to me when your "friend" falls off and you're dying of AIDS, Black Lung and Hepatitis C.

Pete   No one's going to promote you. You can't read. Everyone knows you're a dirty hick and wants to throw rocks at you, spit on your hair, piss on your shoes, flick boogers down your shirt and thinks you're the stupidest person on earth.

Sunny   Why can't I read? Why am I stupid? Who went to the city so you could go to school? (*Beat.*) I'm not moving back. It's ugly. Everyone's trapped.

Li Han *towels off, then puts on a ratty T-shirt and loose cotton pants. He pulls a few cabbage leaves from the slop bucket and exits towards the pigeon loft.* **Pete** *makes sure* **Li Han** *is out of earshot.*

Beat.

Pete   Get me a job in the factory.

Sunny   You're staying in school.

Pete   Sunny—

Sunny (*interrupting*)   Shut up and be glad you were born with a penis.

Sunny puts away the earpiece and mops. **Pete** *and the countryside disappear.* **Old Lao**, *a grizzled man sporting thick black glasses, a baseball cap, and a green uniform enters, carrying a thick binder.* **Old Lao** *looks around, making notes and checking things off.* **Sunny** *eyes* **Old Lao** *a few times, opens her mouth, shuts it, and mops some more.*

Sunny   I'd like to have—I mean . . . um—apply for the open management position.

Old Lao   I'd like to fuck every phone girl in the front office and see who screams loudest.

Sunny   I'd appreciate this opportunity.

Old Lao   I'd appreciate a trip to Paris.

Sunny   I need to make more money.

Old Lao   I need to be a rich American. Maybe in the next life our dreams will come true.

Sunny   You're unit manager. If you wanted to promote me, you could.

Old Lao   How old are you?

Sunny   Eighteen.

Old Lao   How long have you worked here?

Sunny   Four years.

Old Lao   There are men in this factory who've cleaned toilets for decades. What message would it send if I chose you over them? Know what you need to do?

Sunny   What?

Old Lao   Keep your aspirations low and your expectations even lower. That way you'll never be disappointed. Focus on life's little delights. For example—are you listening? When I need to take a piss I wait. For at least thirty minutes.

Sunny   Why?

Old Lao   Because then, for the twenty seconds I'm pissing it feels like the greatest thing I've ever experienced!

Sunny *mops the floor furiously, trying to hide her disappointment.*

Sunny   Thanks for the advice. You changed my life.

Beat.

Old Lao   So you knew him.

Sunny   Who?

Old Lao   The kid who jumped out of Building Seven.

Sunny   He was my section manager.

Old Lao   Did he try any funny stuff?

Sunny   Funny stuff? Like what?

Old Lao   Did he try to make you believe something strange, join a cult or sign your name on some papers?

Old Lao *thrusts a wrinkled document into* **Sunny***'s hand.*

Sunny   What's this?

Old Lao   How should I know? I've never seen it before in my life.

Sunny   But you just—

Old Lao   You say you found it in the bushes, by Building Seven? Looks like the poor kid was in over his head. Good thing you got to it before the police did, or his parents would be extra heartbroken.

Sunny   What are all these signatures?

Old Lao   Sounds like trouble.

Sunny   Did you sign it?

Old Lao   Do I look like a guy that signs political documents?

Sunny   This is a petition, isn't it?

Old Lao   A petition?! Keep that away from me.

Sunny   But you just—

Old Lao (*interrupts*)   Sorry, kid I can't promote you. Come back in ten years, and I'll see what I can do.

Old Lao *walks away, leaving* **Sunny** *alone with the document.*

Scene Three

An urban loft in Shenzhen. **James Lin** *and* **Artemis Chang** *gaze out a high-rise window. Both are well dressed,* **James** *in a suit,* **Artemis** *in heels and a designer dress, her hair in an elegant up-do.*

James   Forty years ago this wasn't a Special Economic Zone. It was just dirt, rice, and country people. More people work in my factory than ever lived in our village, over every generation. On days it's not foggy I can see where your family's house used to be.

Artemis   Times change. Every person has to decide – adapt or become obsolete. Isn't that what you used to tell me?

James   Artemis. I miss the old days.

Artemis   You miss insanity.

James   We were kids down there. Flying kites, running barefoot—

Artemis *unbuttons* **James***' collar and removes his tie.*

Artemis   To the continued partnership of Price-Smart and Jade River Manufacturing. May we keep customers happy, shareholders satisfied– and your workers from committing suicide.

James   We're talking eleven suicides in the past month. Do you really think you can spin that?

Artemis   Suicides happen in clusters. All we're seeing are the problems of similarly sized cities.

James (*not hearing her*)   What if it's not about the money? What if my workers just need better beliefs?

Artemis *takes off her earrings and lets down her hair.*

Artemis   What kind?

James   Suicide rates are lower among Latin American workers. They have heaven to look forward to. Chinese workers have to die, be reborn and suffer all over again.

Artemis   "Price-Smart responds to spate of worker suicides by promising rewards in heaven in exchange for low-wage toil on earth?" Follow the example of Fox-Conn and ask them to sign a no-suicide pledge.

James   The factory isn't the problem. The problem is how the Western press sees us. Rural people have fewer rights. They come to the city, work for me, their lives get better, but when a few fall through the cracks it's my fault?

Artemis   You're saying your factory's a sanctuary.

James   Where my workers have the opportunity to flourish, all expenses paid!

Artemis   It's like one of those reality shows. Young people come from all over, live together and fight to make their lives better. (*Beat.*) How about we make a documentary?

James   A documentary?

Artemis *removes her underwear, leaving her dress on.*

Artemis   About your factory. A never before seen look at the hopes and dreams of young migrants who flood cities in search of better opportunities . . . Compelling factory owners to employ great numbers of the rural poor. Giving them the opportunity to flourish inside a system of rural-urban apartheid.

James *is silent. He considers her idea.*

James   It's about scale. China has four times as many people as the U.S. Western ideas of social welfare have never worked. Factories provide fresh opportunities. It's not college—but they're learning new skills. Jade River's suicides are tragic—

Artemis (*aroused*)   But statistically insignificant.

James   The documentary should have a high profile premiere in Beijing. Invite big foreign investors.

Artemis   Diplos and press too. Get one of your workers to speak. Reporters love "Rags to Riches" stories.

James   It should be a girl.

Artemis   A poor peasant girl. Whose life has been transformed by your factory.

Artemis *dodges* **James** *' kiss and leads him into the bedroom.*

Scene Four

Shenzhen factory, morning. **Sunny** *cleans a bathroom.* **Ming-Ming,** *a factory worker, enters. She wears a robe over her pajamas and carries her toothpaste and toothbrush in a toiletries bucket decoupaged with photographs of* **Artemis Chang**. *She doesn't notice* **Sunny**.

Ming-Ming (*to herself*)   I am the most important person in the world. The things I say and do are important. They are full of meaning. If I wait for success I will fail. Action is the only worthwhile thing.

Ming-Ming *takes a portable cassette recorder out of her pocket and presses "play." She listens to the recording and mimes corresponding hand motions while brushing her teeth.* **Sunny** *continues mopping, but eyes her curiously.*

Tape Recording (*voice of* **Mr. Destiny**)   When shaking hands with a potential employer, first wipe your hand on your clothing to remove any sweat. Failure comes when the palm is clammy. A successful handshake lasts for at least three seconds, but never more than seven. If you hold on for too long you will give the impression of being needy. (*Chimes sound.*) Please assume your Personal Power Position and announce your mantra of the week. (*Chimes sound.*)

Ming-Ming *assumes her Personal Power Position.*

Ming-Ming   "It is my destiny to make lots of money." (*Coaching herself.*) Louder. More conviction. "It is my destiny to MAKE LOTS OF MONEY." (*Coaching herself.*) Push. Dig. Triumph. "IT IS MY DESTINY TO MAKE LOTS OF MONEY!!!" (*Coaching herself.*) Good improvement. Consolidate your gains.

Ming-Ming *holds her hands in prayer and seals it with a loud Om sound.* **Sunny** *clasps her hands in prayer, mimicking her, accidentally dropping her mop in the process. It crashes to the floor, startling* **Ming-Ming**, *who shrieks and whirls around.*

Sunny   Sorry.

Ming-Ming   Ugh. Have you been here this whole time?

Sunny   What's—um . . . what's a Personal Power Position?

Ming-Ming   A scientifically proven way to give yourself courage, conviction and strength.

Sunny   For what?

Ming-Ming   How do we act around city people?

Sunny   Who?

Ming-Ming   Peasants.

Sunny   Like we're small . . . and stupid.

Ming-Ming   We think we're second-class citizens. And because we believe it, it becomes our reality. Action molds character. Character creates destiny.

Sunny   So when you do your Personal Power Position and say your—

Ming-Ming   Mantra of the week.

Sunny   What happens?

Ming-Ming   It reroutes the circuits of my brain and brings me two steps closer to changing my fate. Try it.

Sunny   I'm on duty.

Ming-Ming   No one controls your brain. You can clean tile *and* change your fate.

Sunny (*while mopping*)   It is my destiny to make lots of money.

Ming-Ming   Again.

Sunny   It is my destiny to make lots of money!

Ming-Ming   I don't believe you.

Sunny   It is my destiny to make lots of money!!!

Ming-Ming   Louder!

Sunny   IT IS MY DESTINY TO MAKE LOTS OF MONEY!

Ming-Ming   Again!

Sunny (*top of her lungs*)   IT IS MY DESTINY TO MAAAKE LOTS OF MOOONEEEYYY!!!

Ming-Ming   You just lit a dead part of your brain and activated some junk DNA.

Sunny   Where did you learn this?

Ming-Ming   It's homework, for a self-help class I take each evening.

Sunny   You work a twelve-hour shift then go to school afterwards?

Ming-Ming   It's like Aristotle said—excellence is a habit. We are what we do. Besides. It's fun! When you finish the course you get a framed diploma from any university you want.

Sunny (*pointing to toiletry bucket*)   Who's that?

Ming-Ming   This brave woman is vice president of Price-Smart—the company that sells everything we make in this factory. She was born in the countryside but went to Harvard and Beijing University. Artemis Chang is living proof that we can climb the ladder of success and realize our dreams.

Sunny's *cellphone goes off. She silences it.* **Ming-Ming** *starts to leave.*

Sunny   Can I take the class with you?

Ming-Ming   What makes you think you have what it takes?

Sunny   Because . . . because I believe that I do! And when I believe it, it becomes my reality.

Ming-Ming   A parrot can quote my words back to me. That doesn't make her worthy.

Sunny   Can a parrot pay you twenty kuai?

Ming-Ming   Ninety.

Sunny   Thirty.

Ming-Ming   Eighty.

Sunny   Forty.

Ming-Ming   Sixty.

Sunny   Fifty-five.

Ming-Ming   Meet me by the north gate at 6:40. Don't be late.

Sunny   I won't. Thank you.

Ming-Ming   Thank yourself. You just made your dreams come true.

Ming-Ming *exits.* **Sunny** *tries her Personal Power Position.*

Scene Five

Li Han's *rural home. Night.* **Pete** *cleans bamboo pigeon training baskets.* **Li Han** *holds one of his pigeons and inspects its eyes, feet, and wings.*

Pete   One-eye cold.

Li Han   Treatment?

Pete   Spit in the offending eye—puh! Then feed her oranges for breakfast.

Li Han   Heaving in nest, sad eyes, no appetite?

Pete   Then she is egg-bound.

Li Han   Cause?

Pete   Sudden heartbreak.

Li Han   Reason?

Pete   Separation from mate. Oil vent, massage stomach in a downward direction.

Beat. **Li Han** *coos at his pigeon.*

Li Han   Crusty skin, wobbly walk, pus oozing around new feathers?

Pete   I have a math test tomorrow.

Li Han   I told you to stop going to school.

Li Han *continues to interact with his pigeon.*

Pete   Ba. I promised Sunny—

Li Han (*interrupting*)   Check on the birds.

Pete *exits.* **Li Han** *caresses his pigeon, and sings the love song "My Heart Will Go On." * **Wang Hua** *approaches his front door, pulling her fix-it cart, a portable workshop filled with tools and half-mended household artifacts. A greasy tarp covers half the cart. She wears a heavy apron and fingerless gloves.*

Wang Hua   Li Han? Are you home?

Li Han *opens the door but doesn't let her in. He puts the pigeon in one of the training baskets.*

Li Han   It's late.

Wang Hua   I delivered a mended pot to your neighbor and thought I'd stop by.

Li Han   I'm tired.

Wang Hua   I can't charge as much to mend a pan as I could to birth a boy, but I get by. (*Sighs.*) It's a shame we couldn't save your wife during her final birth. Making a boy took all the strength she had left on earth.

Li Han   Let's talk another time.

Wang Hua   Remember my son, Ran Feng? He went to Shanghai and found work on a construction site.

Li Han   That's a good job.

Wang Hua   It would be—if he kept his head down! The bosses take advantage of the workers. They work eighteen-hour days. Mealtimes and toilet breaks are docked from their pay. It's what we old people expect, but I raised an idiot. (*Whispers.*) He's organizing a strike.

Li Han   Good night, Auntie.

Wang Hua   Talk sense into him. Help him see the big picture.

Li Han   Good night.

Wang Hua *pulls the greasy tarp off her cart, revealing* **Ran Feng**. *His hands and feet are bound, a strip of duct tape covers his mouth. He is fast asleep.*

Li Han   Ran Feng?

Wang Hua   He's my only son. He doesn't have a wife to talk sense into him.

Wang Hua *pours a bottle of water onto* **Ran Feng**'s *face. His eyes fly open. He struggles to free his limbs and mouth but is clumsy, groggy and drunk.*

Ran Feng (*through gag*)   Hugggghh? Whaaaaa??

Wang Hua   Listen up bastard. Li Han has something to say to you!

Ran Feng (*gagged*)   Whuut arrr yuuuu duink mahhhh? Whaaaat duh hellh?

Wang Hua   Go ahead. Tell him!

Ran Feng (*gagged*)   Tellll mee whatuh?

Wang Hua   Tell him why he shouldn't protest! Tell him about the consequences!

Ran Feng (*gagged*)   Fuuuughhht yuuuuu mahhh! Fuuuuuuugck yuuuu!

Li Han   Tell him yourself.

Wang Hua   I don't have direct experience. Why would he listen?

Ran Feng (*gagged*)   Li Huhannn! Li Huhann! Huellpp!

Wang Hua   Tell him about your brother.

Li Han   I don't have a brother.

Wang Hua   Tell him why you don't!

Li Han   Go home.

Ran Feng (*gagged*)   Yaaah mahh! Ets goh hohme!

Li Han *silently cleans pigeon baskets.*

Wang Hua   Your wife told me what happened when you went to Beijing after June Fourth. And how you behaved for months after.

Li Han   (–)

Wang Hua   Silent. Sleeping on straw. Interested in nothing but your dead brother's pigeons.

Li Han   (–)

Wang Hua   I never told Xiao Li, but I knew your grief was the reason she couldn't make sons.

Li Han *coughs, hacks into the slop bucket, takes the pigeon baskets and heads to the pigeon loft.*

Wang Hua   Please, Li Han! Tell him not to protest. You saw Li Chen's body. You know what can happen. Tell him not to protest.

Li Han   Don't protest.

He exits.

Ran Feng (*gagged*)   Wuuhhgd duh hellll mah!? Wahh deh fuggggh?

Wang Hua   You heard him! Don't protest. Don't protest!!!

Wang Hua *smacks* **Ran Feng**, *covers him with the greasy tarp, grabs the handles of her pull-cart and exits.*

Scene Six

Shenzhen auditorium, night. **Sunny** *and* **Ming-Ming** *stand together, dressed in aspirational office-worker clothing. They have different hairstyles than before. Unseen around them are thousands of other peasants, who, with* **Ming-Ming**, *are the voices listed as "Unison."*

Unison (*chant*)   Wealth. Wealth. Wealth. Wealth. POWER. POWER. POWER. POWER. FAME. FAME. FAME. FAME. Honor. Honor. Honor. Honor.

Announcer (*offstage*)   Ladies and Gentlemen presenting. . . . The One . . . The Only. . . . Mr. . . . . . DESTINY!!!!

Mr. Destiny *enters, dressed in faux-Victorian attire. He carries a cordless microphone. The crowd roars.*

Mr. Destiny   What do you deserve?

Unison   MONEY!

Mr. Destiny   When do you need it?

Unison   NOW!

Mr. Destiny   What do you have?

Unison   POWER!

Mr. Destiny   When will you use it?

Unison   NOW!

Mr. Destiny   Two, four, six, eight—

Unison   NOW'S THE TIME TO CHANGE OUR FATE!

Mr. Destiny   Five, seven, nine, eleven—

Unison   WE WILL MAKE THIS LIFE OUR HEAVEN!

Mr. Destiny   Eight, seven, six, five—

Unison   It is time to feel alive!

Mr. Destiny   Seven, eight, nine, ten—

Unison   We will not be crushed again!

Mr. Destiny   WEALTH!

Unison   POWER!

Mr. Destiny   FAME!

Unison   HONOR!

Thunderous applause.

Mr. Destiny   Is there anyone new in this house tonight? Anyone desperate to change their life?

Ming-Ming *nudges* **Sunny**. *She shakes her head, embarrassed.*

Mr. Destiny   If not now, when? How will you change your life if you can't admit your needs to friends? Success is available to everyone.

Ming-Ming   Raise your hand.

Sunny   I just want to watch.

Mr. Destiny   This is the moment you've been waiting for. This is your first test.

Ming-Ming   A city person would reach for this opportunity, take it, and never look back.

Mr. Destiny   You have the power to Change Your Life. All you need to do is Raise Your Hand!

Ming-Ming *grabs* **Sunny***'s hand and raises it.*

Sunny   Stop! Please! I'm not—

Mr. Destiny   You in the back! What's your name?

A spotlight lands on **Sunny**.

Ming-Ming   Say your name.

Sunny   He's not talking to me.

Ming-Ming   Say it!

Sunny   Sunny Li.

Ming-Ming   Louder!

Sunny   SUNNY LI!

Mr. Destiny   Let's hear it for Sunny Li, for taking her life into her own hands!

Thunderous applause.

Unison   SUNNY! SUNNY! SUNNY! SUNNY!

Ming-Ming *pushes* **Sunny** *to the stage. She stands before* **Mr. Destiny**.

Mr. Destiny   Tell us, Sunny, what brought you here tonight?

Ming-Ming   You want a promotion.

Sunny (*softly*)   I want a promotion.

Ming-Ming   They can't hear you.

Sunny (*louder*)   I want a promotion!

Mr. Destiny   Do you want a promotion, or do you *need* a promotion?

Sunny   I *need* a promotion.

Thunderous applause.

Mr. Destiny   And why do you need a promotion?

Sunny *turns to* **Ming-Ming** *for help.*

Ming-Ming   You deserve it.

Sunny   Because I deserve it!

Mr. Destiny   What else?

Sunny   I want . . . no, I *need* to—move up in the world. Higher and higher. And make more money and have more power.

Mr. Destiny   What will you do with that money and power?

Sunny   Spend it! And get more power! And buy nice things and a good education for me and my brother.

Mr. Destiny   Say more.

Sunny   Then I'll go back to the countryside and laugh at everyone who's still poor . . . and living in dirt. Then I'll move back to the city, buy an apartment, improve myself, learn to read every story about the Monkey King and Get Even Stronger!!!

Unison (*chant*)   WEALTH. POWER. FAME. HONOR. WEALTH. POWER. FAME. HONOR—

Mr. Destiny   Quiet!

A hush descends. A cordless microphone appears near **Sunny**. *She takes it.*

Mr. Destiny   Okay, Sunny. We're listening. Tell us your sad story.

Sunny (*to* **Ming-Ming**)   My what?

Mr. Destiny   Something is keeping you from getting that promotion—and it's not something out here—it's inside you. It happened when you were young. Before you could defend yourself. That day, something broke inside you, and even today makes you feel worthless.

Loud booing.

Mr. Destiny   Tell your friends what happened. Get that shame, that burden, off your chest. Let it out, and be free forever.

Long silence.

Sunny   I can't.

Mr. Destiny   Sunny Li. Why do you like stories about the Monkey King?

Sunny   Because he can change. Into anything.

Mr. Destiny   Monkey hatches from a rock. When he opens his eyes he sees riches that could be his with the Right Dream. He finds a teacher and learns the Seventy-Two Changes. With these powers Monkey bursts into Heaven and puts the food and drink of Gods in his stomach. Sunny Li—you deserve those Riches. To get them take the first step and SPEAK!

Long silence. **Ming-Ming** *takes* **Sunny**'s *hand.*

Sunny   When I was born my parents threw me in a bucket of pig slop and left me there to die.

Loud booing.

Sunny   I survived, then my mother died giving birth to my brother. I had to take care of him—and the house—and vegetables and chickens and pig. I wanted school, but we were too poor until I came to the city and found work in the factory. Now he's a student but all I've learned is how to bleach toilets and scrub floors.

Mr. Destiny   Sunny Li believes she was born into a bucket of pig slop. She never feels good enough. She eats less than her share at dinner. She dresses so no one will notice her. Some days she wonders whether anyone would care if she disappeared altogether.

Sunny   How did you know that? How did you—

Mr. Destiny (*interrupting*)   I'm here to tell you that bucket of pig slop never happened. When you were born your mother hugged you and thanked the heavens for your birth. She kissed you all over, rubbed sesame oil into your skin, massaged your hands and feet and said—"Welcome to the world, Sunny. You're exactly what I wanted. I'm so happy to finally meet you."

Sunny   She didn't want me. The only reason I lived was—

Mr. Destiny   Forget who you were. Imagine who you can be in another time—like this one. In another place—like the one you're standing in. If you were speaking to that new Sunny now, would you want her to think she was born into a bucket of pig slop?

Sunny   No.

Mr. Destiny   What would you want her to believe?

Sunny   That she was loved. And wanted.

Mr. Destiny   Just like you.

Sunny   Just like me.

Ecstatic applause.

Sunny   My mother loved me. She wanted me to succeed. I'm all she ever wanted. Her happiness is me.

Mr. Destiny   It is up to us to rewrite our stories. Up to us to build new roads to walk down.

Unison (*chanting low, through end of scene*)   Wealth. Power. Fame. Honor. Wealth. Power. Fame. Honor.

Mr. Destiny   Everything starts with a Dream. Fight, Sunny. Reach out, grab your dreams by the balls and don't let go, until they become your reality. Go back to work. Talk to your boss. And CHANGE YOUR DESTINY!

Loud cheering. Techno music thunders through loudspeakers. Lights flash. Confetti falls from the sky. **Sunny** *and* **Ming-Ming** *dance triumphantly with unseen thousands.*

Scene Seven

The countryside. **James** *is outside at sunrise. Muddy rubber boots are pulled over his city clothes. The sounds of birds, grasshoppers, roosters and running water.* **Artemis** *enters.*

Artemis   That fucking rooster's been screeching since midnight.

James   Crickets sang outside my window. All night long. At dawn it was so foggy, when I held my hands in front of my face I couldn't see them. I should have woken you up.

Artemis   The documentary crew's been shooting this "hopelessly impoverished countryside" since sunrise. I'm sure I'll see footage.

James   Remember when we used to catch king grasshoppers, and bring them to your mother to roast?

Artemis   Nope.

James   It wasn't all bad.

Artemis   Not for the son of a farmer. Now—guess where we're having the premiere?

James   The Grand Hyatt?

Artemis   Think populist. Iconic. Stately.

James   The Summer Palace?

Artemis   Think giant bronze doors, facing the eastern skies. A banquet hall that seats six thousand.

James   Absolutely not.

Artemis   McDonalds did it.

James   It's too much exposure.

Artemis   We're positioning your factory as an institution of social welfare that lifts peasants out of poverty. It's the perfect venue. You're a Party member in good standing. What are you worried about?

James   I didn't become owner of Jade River by sticking my neck out.

Artemis   If we don't spin this your head will roll.

James   Anything but the Great Hall.

Artemis   We need every eye on us.

James   Not *every* eye.

Artemis   When I say the word "Foxconn"—what comes to mind?

James *is silent.*

Artemis   Worker suicides. Reputation is everything. If you don't do this, you will lose control over your public image and Jade River will fall apart.

James   The Great Hall of the People.

Artemis   And in it Jade River will rise from the ashes.

James   You still want a factory girl to intro the film?

Artemis   A cute, rosy-cheeked one who is earnest, serious and stoic. Have a contest. Girls love to win. Make up a prize. Something they really want.

James   An office position?

Artemis   Brace yourself, James. Everything's about to get better.

Artemis *kisses* **James** *on the cheek and starts to exit.*

James   Stay for breakfast. The farmer's wife is making congee—with sweet potatoes. When was the last time you had a sweet potato?

Artemis   I don't eat them. They remind me of famine.

Scene Eight

Beijing International Airport. **Artemis** *emerges from the domestic terminal. She wears an elegant fall coat and pulls a sleek suitcase behind her. She's on the phone.*

Artemis (*into phone*)   That's fine. Read me the press list. (*She listens.*)

Qing Shu Min *approaches. She wears non-descript clothing, and smiles pleasantly.*

Qing Shu Min   Are you Artemis Chang?

Artemis (*back into phone*)   Add CNN, Al-Jazeera, *Southern Weekend, South China Morning Post,* and the *Beijing Youth Daily*. Keep working on Central Television coverage.

Qing Shu Min   Are you Artemis Chang, Vice President of Price Smart?

Artemis *puts away her phone.*

Artemis   Where's your sign?

Qing Shu Min   My sign?

Artemis   My driver should hold a sign with my name on it. So I can approach *her* when I'm ready.

Qing Shu Min   My apologies. Welcome to Beijing.

Artemis   Where are we parked?

Qing Shu Min   Right this way.

Qing Shu Min *takes* **Artemis**'*suitcase and leads her towards a parking garage.*

Artemis   It seems smoggier than usual.

Qing Shu Min   For a price, the weather bureau can seed the clouds to make it rain, so your event can happen on a blue sky day.

Artemis   That won't be necessary.

Qing Shu Min   I've been following your career for some time. It's nice to finally meet you. Not many women of your age have received such a prestigious education. Your parents must be very proud.

Artemis   What happened to the guy who usually gets me?

Qing Shu Min   His daughter has a piano recital.

Artemis   Where's the car?

Qing Shu Min   Just around the next corner.

Artemis   I need to go straight to Tiananmen.

Qing Shu Min   You don't want to freshen up at your hotel first?

Artemis   If I did I would request it.

Qing Shu Min   As you wish.

Artemis   We're on the wrong floor. There isn't a single vehicle in this section.

Qing Shu Min   How strange. I'm sure it's around here somewhere.

Artemis   Forget it. I'll call a cab.

She takes her suitcase and heads towards the terminal.

Qing Shu Min   It must be up one level. The numbers are very confusing.

Artemis   If you want to stay a driver get your shit together.

Qing Shu Min   A driver?

Artemis   Chauffer, transport technician, director of motor vehicle movement, whatever you people want to call it.

Qing Shu Min   I'm not any of those things.

Artemis   What?

Qing Shu Min   In the future, please be more careful about who you follow into dark corners.

Artemis *hesitates, looks around and starts to run towards the terminal.* **Gao Chen** *emerges from the shadows, thrusts a black hood over* **Artemis'** *head, and tightens it. He drags her offstage, muffling her screams.* **Qing Shu Min** *follows, pulling* **Artemis'** *suitcase behind her.*

Scene Nine

The banks of the Yangtze River, morning. **Li Han** *and* **Pete** *walk along the river. Each carries a pigeon-training basket in each hand. A cloth cover tied around each basket obscures the young pigeon within. They swing the baskets back and forth as they walk.*

Li Han   As soon as Taiwan and China are reunited we'll enter their races and win billions. Can you see it? A father-son team, training world class racers.

Pete   I'd rather be poor and perform Monkey in teahouses—

Li Han (*interrupting*)   Yesterday in Taiwan a single pigeon was auctioned off for half a million. Imagine—one bird, worth more than a Mercedes. In the races last June no one knew she was special, then in the last six seconds of her seventh race she surged ahead—

Pete (*interrupting*)   My teacher told me about a school in Beijing where you learn the Monkey King—

Li Han (*interrupting*)   Tomorrow we'll start outdoor training.

Pete   —maybe, if I go to the factory with Sunny and make enough money—

Pete *follows too closely. His pigeon baskets crash into* **Li Han***'s.*

Li Han   Worthless shit!

Pete   I'm sorry—

Li Han   Sorry doesn't soothe their panic. Sorry doesn't mend a broken wing.

Li Han *sets down his baskets, then motions for* **Pete** *to do the same.*

Pete   Is she hurt?

Li Han   Put them down!

Pete *sets the baskets down, more roughly than he should.* **Li Han** *pushes* **Pete** *to the ground.*

Pete   You said to swing the baskets.

Li Han   To give them air. To strengthen their wings. Not break them! They're young. They only know what we show them. If I released them and they had fear, they'd quake in their baskets and never go anywhere.

Pete   That's less idiotic than flying home.

Li Han   Racing birds defect all the time. Some guys lose their whole flock after one race. Do you know why mine return?

Pete   Because they're idiots.

Li Han   Rebellious birds don't become breeding stock. My line will yield champions. Spend more time in the loft. You'll inherit world-class racers.

Pete   I don't want world-class racers. I want to go to the factory. With Sunny—

Li Han (*interrupting*)   Your sister's a bad influence. It's time for her to come home.

Pete   You don't think she's a bad influence when you're spending her money

Li Han   On birds you will inherit!

Pete   I don't want them.

Li Han   These pigeons are descended from birds bred by my brother.

Pete   You don't have a brother.

Li Han   Take care of our pigeons. Go home and let my birds keep you from trouble.

Li Han *coughs up blood.*

Pete   Let me help you carry the—

Li Han (*interrupting*)   Go!

Pete *exits.* **Li Han** *wipes away the blood, checks the pigeons, then, carrying two baskets in each hand, continues along the path.* **Wang Hua** *enters pulling her cart.*

Li Han   Auntie Wang?

Wang Hua (*blunt*)   Fuck off.

Li Han   How's Ran Feng?

Wang Hua   You wouldn't talk him out of the strike. He was struck by a bulldozer during the night.

Li Han   Is Ran Feng—

Wang Hua (*matter of fact*)   I only had to try once. I had a boy so easily. This is my punishment for killing girl babies.

Pete *enters, hanging back. Neither* **Li Han** *or* **Wang-Hua** *see him.*

Li Han   Are they offering you a compensation package?

Wang Hua   Eighty thousand, if I sign a waiver. Forty years of life, and that's what he's worth? (*Beat.*) He's all alone now. No children. No wife. When I'm gone who will care for his afterlife?

A beat, as **Li Han** *checks on his pigeons.*

Li Han   Forgive me Auntie, but my daughter's not married, and your story is very heartbreaking.

Wang Hua   Ghost marriage? To a living woman?

Li Han   Ran Feng needs a young wife to care for his spirit.

Wang Hua   The wife of my son should care for me too.

Li Han   Sunny's been in the factory long enough. She needs to find the right husband.

Wang Hua   How much?

Li Han   Sign the waiver.

Wang Hua   Can she cook?

Li Han   Like the masters.

Wang Hua   What dishes?

Wang-Hua *packs up her cart and starts to exit.*

Li Han   You name it, she'll make it. Twice-cooked pork, stinky tofu, dan-dan noodles, steamed fish—

Wang Hua   Dan-dan noodles were Ran Feng's favorite.

Li Han   Sunny's are the best in the province.

Wang Hua   Sunny was two when Xiao Li passed. Who taught her?

Li Han   My mother.

Wang Hua   Liar. Your mother couldn't make ice cubes.

Li Han   Sunny will be home for New Year's. We'll marry them then. The first week of the New Year is a lucky time for a wedding.

Li Han *follows* **Wang Hua** *off.* **Pete** *takes out his phone and makes a call.*

Scene Ten

Factory bathroom, morning. Light streams through barred windows. **Sunny** *wears her factory uniform.* **Ming-Ming** *freshens* **Sunny**'s *hair and excessive makeup. Both have new hairstyles.* **Sunny**'s *phone rings. She silences it.*

Ming-Ming   Look him straight in the eye.

Sunny *starts to speak.*

Ming-Ming   Don't smile right away—you'll seem too agreeable.

Sunny *starts to speak.*

Ming-Ming   Don't use your high voice—it weakens your position.

Sunny (*in a deep voice*)   "I've been a level one sanitation technician for fifty months. I've done superior work and never failed an inspection."

Ming-Ming   If you stick with that delivery you will definitely get promoted.

Sunny   Thank you, Ming-Ming.

Ming-Ming   Thank yourself.

Sunny   No—really! If I hadn't met you, I wouldn't have taken the course, and I wouldn't have a diploma that says Harvard University!

Ming-Ming   Our brain circuits are rewired and our junk DNA is lit.

Sunny   I should burn incense for the dead section manager—if he hadn't jumped out the window there wouldn't be an open management position.

Ming-Ming   It's like Charles Darwin said—"Only the strong survive."

Sunny   You're strong. That's why you've lasted so long.

Ming-Ming   In a year I'll be twenty-four and all my capital will be used up. If I don't make it to an office position soon they'll replace me with a fourteen-year-old with better eyes and faster fingers.

Sunny   They'd be idiots to do that. You have the best quality control in your unit.

Ming-Ming   This is your day. We'll work on my "Factory Girl" audition after you get promoted. Take a deep breath. Find your center.

Sunny *assumes her Personal Power Position.*

Ming-Ming   You are beautiful.

Sunny   I am beautiful.

Ming-Ming   You are perfect.

Sunny   I am perfect.

Ming-Ming   You deserve this promotion.

Sunny   I deserve to get promoted, live in the White House and be a princess.

Ming-Ming   It's like Malcolm X said: "By Any Means Necessary."

Ming-Ming *exits.* **Sunny** *assumes her Personal Power Position. Her phone rings. She turns it off.* **Old Lao** *enters with his clipboard and begins a routine quality inspection.* **Sunny** *reaches for the mop and cleans furiously.*

Old Lao   You lost your color. Your eyes are sunken. Are you sick?

Sunny   It's called makeup.

Old Lao   You look like a corpse of a whore given black eyes by her pimp.

Sunny   I appreciate your feedback. I'll evaluate this information and use it to improve my appearance so I can do a better job representing this factory and our glorious country.

Old Lao   Heheheh.

Sunny (*takes a deep breath, finds her center*)   Good morning.

Old Lao   Bad morning. There were worms in the congee.

Sunny   You should file a complaint.

Old Lao   Someone's getting ideas from a fancy petition.

Sunny   I'm not a political person. I'm just a person who deserves to be promoted to section manager.

Old Lao   Here we go again.

Sunny (*drops into her low voice*)   I've been a level one sanitation technician for fifty months. I've done superior work and never failed a—

Old Lao (*interrupting*)   You are the most important person in the world. Your bowel movements are radiant. Full of meaning. If you wait for success you'll die in a sewer. Being a spoiled brat is the only worthwhile thing.

Sunny   I need a promotion.

Old Lao   I need to be hung like a donkey.

Sunny   Give me the job!

Old Lao   Give me a naked KTV waitress.

Sunny   Why are you so allergic to my success?

Old Lao   Why is every young person an idiot?

Sunny   Maybe we'd excel if we had more opportunities.

Old Lao   I gave you an opportunity three months ago.

Sunny   That wasn't an opportunity—that was a one-way ticket to jail.

Old Lao   So you read it!

Sunny   Don't change the subject.

Old Lao   Old Lao is slippery. Like a fish.

Sunny   Promote me.

Old Lao   No.

Sunny (*in her low voice*)   Promote me!!!

Old Lao   You young people are so brain damaged.

Sunny   I deserve this opportunity for success.

Old Lao   I don't care what stupid sorrows you think you've lived through, compared to the past this is paradise. The Great Western Heaven.

Sunny   Last chance.

Sunny *takes a rubber cleaning glove off her right hand and advances towards* **Old Lao**.

Old Lao   What are you going to do? Hit me?

Sunny   It's like Malcolm X said—"By Any Means Necessary."

Sunny *slips her hand into* **Old Lao***'s pants and gives him a hand job.*

Old Lao (*strangled*)   Huhhhhhh . . .

Sunny   Promote me.

Old Lao   Oh fuckkkk . . . fuck me fuuuuck meeee—

Sunny   Say it.

Old Lao   Oh God yes. Yesss . . .

Sunny   Say I'm promoted.

Old Lao   I'm promooooteddd—

Sunny   Tell me *I'm* promoted. "You're promoted, Sunny. You're promoted." Say it.

Old Lao   Shaddup shaddup don't get in the way of my huhhhhhh . . .

Sunny   I'm the best. The most qualified. I deserve this position.

Old Lao   Huhh huhh huhh huhh huhhhh—

Sunny   "You're promoted." "You're promoted." Say it or I'll stop. Say it or I'll stop.

Old Lao   Don't stop—please please please don't stop ohh God dooooon't stoppppp . . . .

Sunny *strokes him harder. Her phone rings again. The frenzied techno-pop love ballad plays over the next section.*

Sunny   Say it or I'll stop! I'm going to stop! I'm stopping—

Old Lao   You're promoted! You're promoted! You're—you're—
Huhhheehhheeeeuuiihhhh-yuhhhhhh-huhhhhhhhhhhh!

Old Lao *shudders and heaves into* **Sunny**'s *hands, knocking his glasses onto the floor.* **Sunny** *calmly removes her hand from his pants, wipes it on a towel, sprays it with a bleach solution, wipes it again, puts her glove back on, silences her phone and resumes cleaning the bathroom.*

Sunny   Thank you for this opportunity. I'll start tomorrow.

Old Lao *finds his glasses, puts them on, stares at* **Sunny**, *then staggers off.* **Sunny** *contains herself until he exits, then repeats her Personal Power Position.*

Scene Eleven

An interrogation room at a Beijing police station. **Artemis** *sits at a table.* **Qing Shu Min** *enters. She carries a tray containing a metal teapot and disposable clear plastic cups. She pours three cups of tea, then smiles.*

Qing Shu Min   Have some tea.

Artemis   We could have settled this at the airport. How much do you want?

Qing Shu Min   Unfortunately, not everyone's for sale. Some people have values they refuse to abandon.

Qing Shu Min *motions to the tea.* **Artemis** *ignores it.*

Qing Shu Min   It's not polite to refuse what your host offers. Didn't they teach that at Harvard?

Artemis *sips the tea.*

Artemis   What's this about?

Qing Shu Min   Your past. Catching up with you.

Artemis   I haven't broken any laws.

Qing Shu Min   But in China you aren't just you. You are your family, too.

Qing Shu Min *drops a folder on the table.* **Artemis** *opens it and finds a collection of black and white photographs.*

Qing Shu Min   Let the past be a fleeting storm cloud, forgotten once the sun emerges. Why waste strength carrying umbrellas on blue-sky days? Or do you cling to the memory of the storm, afraid you might not know who you are without it? Do you want it to rain, Ms. Chang?

Artemis   What is this?

Qing Shu Min   You don't recognize them? (*Clicks tongue in disapproval.*)

Artemis   I know who they are. What I don't know is why I'm in a police station, with Public Security Officers, drinking bad tea.

Qing Shu Min   This tea was a gift from the *Governor* of Taiwan. Take smaller sips and swish it through your mouth before swallowing. Be patient. Give your taste buds a chance to receive the full flavor.

Artemis *takes another sip of tea.*

Qing Shu Min   Now, please. Identify the people in the pictures.

Artemis   This is my uncle and aunt on their wedding day. This is my grandfather, holding me after my naming ceremony. (*Beat.*) These are my parents.

Qing Shu Min   Where are your relatives now?

Artemis   They're dead.

Qing Shu Min   All of them?

Artemis   I don't know what happened to my mother.

Qing Shu Min   But the rest?

Artemis   The rest were executed.

Qing Shu Min   You had a secret room in your house where your grandfather hid his books. A neighbor found out and reported your family to the village committee. You were never punished.

Artemis   I was six.

Qing Shu Min   But now you're an adult, and know better.

Artemis   If the past is a fleeting storm cloud you haven't felt a drop of rain in your life.

Qing Shu Min *pulls a large photo out of an envelope and places it face down in front of* **Artemis**. **Artemis** *starts to turn it over.* **Qing Shu Min** *stops her.*

Artemis   Why am I here?

Qing Shu Min   How about we trade intelligence?

Artemis   About?

Qing Shu Min   The business venture that resulted in the daughter of counter-revolutionaries staging an event inside the Great Hall of the People.

Artemis   This is about the premiere?

Qing Shu Min   You are conducting a high profile event in a symbolic building located on the most politically sensitive public space in the nation.

Artemis   It's a PR stunt, designed to improve the corporate image of my company and our largest supplier.

Qing Shu Min   Subversives are sent to asylums for the politically insane. They are medicated and given electric treatments until their condition is stabilized.

Artemis   I'm vice president of a multinational corporation. All I care about is money.

Qing Shu Min   I hope I don't need to explain the importance of maintaining stability and social harmony so that we can pursue economic success and improve our gross domestic happiness.

Artemis   You could improve that appearance and how the world sees you by choosing less violent tactics.

Qing Shu Min   Why would we change when everyone wants to sleep with us just the way we are?

Artemis   If you were comfortable with your PR image I wouldn't be here.

Qing Shu Min   This is not a time for protest, proclamation, or any kind of dissent. Here's my card. (*Hands it to her.*) Notify me immediately if you come across anything suspicious.

Qing Shu Min *takes the folder of photos. She leaves one in front of* **Artemis**.

Artemis   Is there something else you would like me to look at?

Qing Shu Min   It's your mother.

Artemis   My mother?

Qing Shu Min   Yes. At the moment of her death.

Qing Shu Min *exits.* **Artemis** *puts on her coat, takes her suitcase and starts to exit. She pauses, takes the photograph, and exits, without looking at it.*

Scene Twelve

Li Han's *rural home.* **Sunny** *enters, carrying the covered slop bucket. She wears an embroidered red qipao style wedding dress. Her hair and make-up have been elaborately styled. She sets the slop bucket in its usual position.* **Pete** *enters and clears his throat.*

Pete
 A butt ugly peasant named Sunny
 Knew breathing men found her face funny
 She married a ghost
 Who'd been crushed on the coast
 And made her dear Ba lots of mon—

Sunny (*interrupting*)   Go die in the street.

Pete   Go marry a corpse—wait.

Sunny   Shut up and give me a reading lesson.

Sunny *hands* **Pete** *the petition.*

Pete   Ask your new husband to help you—

Sunny *punches* **Pete**.

Pete   Ow!

They settle in to read the petition.

Sunny (*reads, halting*)   "We, the undersigned sanitation workers of Unit 27 are— dissatisfied?"

Pete   "Angry."

Sunny   "Angry and—"

Pete   "Disgusted." Where did you get this?

Sunny   From my unit manager.

Pete   Why?

Sunny *shrugs.*

Sunny   "We are tired of being treated unfairly. If you don't meet our—"

Pete   "Demands."

Sunny   "We will go on a—"

Pete   "Strike."

Sunny   "We will go on a strike and put a video on the—"

Pete   "Internet."

Sunny   "That tells the whole . . . world about our—"

Pete   Protest.

Sunny *crumples the petition and throws it at* **Pete**. *He picks it up, smoothes out the pages and reads it.*

Sunny   Idiots. Workers don't need a different life—just a new perspective.

Pete   What kind?

Sunny   The tragedy isn't that you don't have a Mercedes Benz. The tragedy is that you don't dare to long for one. Don't forget—I used to be a bumpkin too. I didn't think I could change my life until I heard that sentence in a talk by the pioneer of success studies.

Pete   You're still a janitor.

Sunny   I'm a sanitation technician. It's temporary. Soon I'll be promoted to an office position. I'll sit in a nice chair all day and rely on my brains—

Pete (*interrupting*)   Then go home and make rice for a ghost.

Sunny   If you miss your cue and I get married by mistake I will wring your neck and turn you into soup.

Li Han *and* **Wang Hua** *enter.* **Li Han** *carries a foldable altar table.* **Wang Hua,** *who is dressed in gaudy rural fashion, carries a framed photo of* **Ran Feng** *and an urn full of his ashes. They create a makeshift altar in the center of the room, and decorate it with a string of blinking lights.* **Sunny** *places a platter of breaded, deep fried meat on the altar, lights a stick of incense, then approaches* **Wang Hua.**

Wang Hua   To avoid paying a marriage tax, we'll marry you in the old style. The bride and groom will face each other and say "I marry you" three times.

Sunny   Ran Feng's dead. How will he speak?

Wang Hua   I'm his mother. I will say his words for him.

Sunny   Goodbye, Ba. After this I won't be your daughter.

Wang Hua *pulls a "red envelope" out of her purse and gives it to* **Li Han.** *He pockets it*

Li Han   Work hard. Listen to Auntie. Make sure she gets good value for her money.

Wang Hua (*to* **Sunny**)   Face your husband.

Sunny (*motioning toward meat*)   Ba promised I could cook. Quality inspection's important.

Wang Hua   Wait 'till the incense is burnt. Ran Feng should try it first.

Li Han *takes a piece and bites into it.*

Li Han   Go ahead, Auntie. Sneak preview.

Wang Hua *takes a spicy wing and eats it.* **Sunny** *has one too.*

Li Han   Pete. Celebrate your sister.

Pete   I'm not hungry.

Wang Hua   You pass Quality Inspection. Now—

Wang Hua *takes the framed portrait of* **Ran Feng** *off the altar and holds it in front of her face.*

Wang Hua   Face your husband.

Sunny *faces the portrait of* **Ran Feng.**

Wang Hua (*deep voice*)   Sunny Li, this is Ran Feng speaking. Take good care of my mother. Cook her fresh congee each morning, beef noodles for lunch, and fish and vegetables for supper. Clip her nails, rub her feet, pick wax out of her ears and when she is too old to trim her nose hairs, do it for her. If you fail to perform these duties I will haunt you in this life and beat you in the next. I marry you. I marry you. I marry you.

Sunny *makes eye-contact with* **Pete.**

Wang Hua   He's done. Say your part.

Pete *tosses a single pigeon feather on the floor. No one but* **Sunny** *sees him do it.*

Sunny   What's that?

Sunny *picks the feather off the floor and examines it.*

Wang Hua   Finish your wedding.

Sunny   I marry you. I marry you. I—

Pete *tosses a handful of pigeon feathers onto the floor. Only* **Sunny** *sees it.* **Sunny** *picks up the feathers.*

Sunny (*to* **Ran Feng**)   What are you trying to say?

Wang Hua   He's saying finish the marriage, slow-poke, my mother's getting angry!

Sunny   Maybe he's saying he doesn't want to marry me.

Wang Hua (*deep voice*)   Sunny Li, this is Ran Feng speaking. Again. Finish marrying me at once.

Sunny   Ran Feng, you keep sending me feathers. Maybe you want pigeons in the afterlife, not me.

Li Han *examines the feathers, then heads to the loft.*

Wang Hua   Can a pigeon clean my mother's ears? (*Deep voice.*) Can it cook her crispy eggplant?

Li Han *storms in.*

Li Han   What is this? What is the meaning of this?

Wang Hua   Finish the ceremony.

Li Han (*to* **Sunny**)   Where are my birds? Where are my babies? Where did they go? Tell me—tell me!

Sunny   I don't know. Maybe they went where all babies go. Correction. Not all babies. Just the ones you don't want.

A long silence. **Li Han** *approaches the closed slop bucket. He lifts the lid, reaches into the bucket, pulls out a giant mound of pigeon feathers, and sinks to his knees, cradling the feathers in his arms.* **Pete** *makes eye-contact with* **Sunny**, *then exits.*

Li Han (*to feathers*)   My heart. My darlings.

Sunny   You never asked me the name of my dish.

A beat. **Li Han** *stares at* **Sunny**.

Sunny   It's called "Pigeons Coming Home to Roost." Dark meat. Fatty skin. That's why it's so succulent.

Sunny *places the platter of meat in front of* **Li Han**.

Sunny   Get it while it's fresh. We really shouldn't waste it.

Pete *enters and hands* **Sunny** *a giant denim backpack.* **Sunny** *puts it on and exits.* **Pete** *follows her out. After a beat,* **Wang Hua** *sighs and turns to* **Li Han**.

Wang Hua   Your brother had a beautiful laugh. I will never forget its sound.

Wang Hua *reaches into* **Li Han** '*s pocket and retrieves her 'red envelope' full of money. She sets the string of blinking lights on the ground, collapses the altar table, then exits with the table, framed photo of* **Ran Feng** *and urn.* **Li Han** *remains on the floor, beside a string of blinking lights, his arms full of feathers.*

Scene Thirteen

Night on the banks of the Yangtze River. **Sunny** *enters, accompanied by* **Pete**. *Each carries one side of a large denim duffel bag.* **Sunny** *is still wearing the silk wedding dress.*

Pete   We got off at the wrong stop.

Sunny   Old people were crushing me! If we'd stayed on another minute I would have fainted.

Pete   Next time elbow them.

Sunny   That wouldn't have helped. We were at the front of the line and they pushed past us, like it was the last bus on earth.

Pete   They're old. Maybe they remember a time when there wouldn't be another bus.

Sunny   It's not that time now. They need to change their perspective and dare to be braver.

Pete   I'm tired. My shoulder hurts.

They set down the bag.

Sunny   If you worked in the garden you'd be stronger.

Pete   You leave all the time and I'm stuck here.

Sunny   You're not stuck, you're going to school.

Pete   I can't go back.

Sunny   You're almost done.

Pete   I'm not learning anything.

Sunny   Just one more year of high school. You have to finish.

Pete   All my friends have left for the city. It's just me and a bunch of babies.

Sunny   Even if I had money I couldn't take you—train tickets have been sold out for weeks.

Pete   Nothing's impossible if you believe in your heart you can succeed.

Sunny   Don't quote my inspirational sayings back to me.

Pete *opens one of* **Sunny***'s duffel bags and dumps out the contents, strewing clothes, blankets, Pringle canisters, and Snickers bars on the ground.*

Sunny   Fucking rice bucket! What the hell are you doing?

Pete   Believing.

Pete *steps into the duffel bag, curls up tight, then tucks his head in. He barely fits.*

Sunny   It's thirty hours to Shenzhen. You can't stay in there for that long.

Pete   I need money for opera school. My life is wasted here. It is my destiny to perform Monkey King.

Sunny   Suck in your stomach.

Pete   I'm not fat.

Sunny   I will leave a blanket on the banks of this river, but I'm not going to Shenzhen without my snacks.

Sunny *pushes her food back into the bag.*

Pete   Ow! You're scraping me!

Sunny   You should have thought about that before changing your destiny.

Sunny *shoves* **Pete***'s head into the bag, and zips it up.*

Sunny   Can you breathe?

Pete   Barely.

Sunny   What's in your mouth?

Pete (*muffled*)   Nothing.

Sunny *unzips the bag and finds* **Pete***'s mouth is crammed full of Pringles.*

Sunny   My chips!

Pete (*mouth full*)   Barbecue. My favorite.

Sunny   Walk to the train station, then get in my bag. Eat more of my snacks, and I'll dump you on the tracks.

Pete *gets out of the bag and bows profusely, still chewing his chips.*

Pete (*mouth full*)   Thank you. You won't regret this. Thank you. Thank you!

Sunny   In the city, everything moves really fast. You won't have time to think. All that matters are the movements you make with your body.

Pete   I can be a good worker.

Sunny   Then you have to change, and leave your lazy ways behind.

Pete (*as Monkey*)   "Please, Goddess of Mercy. Release me from Stone Mountain. Use your powers. Rescue me!"

Sunny   Close your eyes.

Pete *complies.*

Sunny   Imagine everything you don't need flying out of your fingers and toes, back into the dirt and sky. Empty your mind. Become a machine. When you open your eyes, you will be a new person. Your life will be wide open with possibility. It will be beautiful and blank. Things will be hard. You will get tired. But if you believe in yourself, you can do anything. Do you believe in yourself, Pete?

Pete   Yes. I believe.

Sunny   Let the countryside fade away. Let go of your past. Face your future with clear eyes, and a strong body. Are you ready?

Pete   I'm ready.

Sunny   Then take a deep breath. (*They do this together.*) Now, change.

They open their eyes and gaze forward.

Scene Fourteen

Factory office, waiting room. **Ming-Ming** *dressed in office clothing, sits in a row of metal folding chairs. She is wearing a lot of make-up and jewelry.* **James Lin** *enters from his office and heads towards the door. He's on his phone.*

James (*into cell phone*)   Try her hotel again. Then the Beijing office. I must speak with Artemis immediately.

James *puts away his phone and starts to exit.* **Ming-Ming** *intercepts him.*

James   Yes?

Ming-Ming   Hello, sir. It's an honor to meet you. My name is Ming-Ming Chen and I'm here for the "Factory Girl" audition.

James   I'll let you know when we're ready.

Ming-Ming   Thank you sir. I look forward to sharing my strengths and meeting Artemis Chang, who has been my True Image of Success ever since I started work in this factory.

James   Good luck.

James *exits.* **Ming-Ming** *adjusts her clothing and returns to her seat. She takes out a small mirror and refreshes her hair and make-up.* **Sunny***, dressed in her factory uniform, enters.*

Ming-Ming   Sunny!

Sunny   Ming-Ming! I almost didn't recognize you.

Ming-Ming   I'm here for the audition.

Sunny   Me too!

Ming-Ming   You're auditioning?

Sunny   The reward's an office position, isn't it? Were we supposed to dress up?

Ming-Ming (*beat*)   If you look like the people you want to become, your chances of being accepted will improve by sixty-nine percent.

Sunny   I look stupid. I should change.

Ming-Ming   Don't worry about it. Just be yourself.

Sunny   What have you gone over?

Ming-Ming   The things I'm learning in night school.

Sunny   You're re-taking the course?

Ming-Ming   That was just level one self-improvement. You can never stop learning and improving yourself. The minute you do, you give up.

Sunny   What are you studying now?

Ming-Ming   Public Speaking. Centering Methods. Theories of Eye Contact . . . and Smile Dynamics.

Sunny   Smile Dynamics?

Ming-Ming   There's an optimal number of seconds to wait before smiling, depending on the status of the recipient.

Sunny   How many seconds should I wait with these bosses?

Ming-Ming   It's too late to think about that. Whatever I say will confuse you.

Sunny   What about eye-contact?

Ming-Ming   You took the level one class. Go over what they taught you.

Sunny   There wasn't anything on Eye-Contact Theory!

Ming-Ming   You established Eye Contact with your unit manager in order to get the promotion, didn't you?

Sunny (*lowers voice*)   I used other methods.

Ming-Ming   Other methods? What do you mean?

Sunny whispers into **Ming-Ming**'s ear.

Ming-Ming   That wasn't in the class. Where did you learn that strategy?

Sunny   From a tape.

Ming-Ming   What tape?

Sunny   Advanced . . . Negotiation Tactics.

Ming-Ming   Show me the technique. Step by step.

Sunny   There's not enough time. Whatever I say will confuse you.

Ming-Ming   Fuck your ancestors.

James *enters.*

James   Hello, ladies. I'm afraid Ms. Chang—

Artemis *strides in, looking more poised than ever.*

Artemis (*to girls*)   Line up please. Look left. Look right. Look at me. Smile.

They follow her directions.

Artemis   Repeat after me "Ladies and Gentlemen, Welcome to the Great Hall of the People."

Sunny / Ming-Ming (*stumbling over each other*)   Ladies and Gentlemen, Welcome—

Artemis (*to* **Ming-Ming**)   You first.

Ming-Ming (*like airline hostess*)   Ladies and Gentlemen, Welcome to the Great Hall of the People.

Sunny (*like cheerleader*)   Ladies and Gentlemen, Welcome to the Great Hall of the People!!!

Artemis (*to girls*)   Thank you. That's all.

James *and* **Artemis** *start to exit.* **Sunny** *approaches them.*

Sunny (*earnest, simple*)   Ladies and Gentlemen, Welcome to the Great Hall of the People.

Ming-Ming (*copying* **Sunny**'s *tone*)   Ladies and Gentlemen, Welcome to the Great Hall of the People.

James *and* **Artemis** *turn around.*

Artemis   Relax. Act natural.

Sunny   It's such an honor to stand before you magnificent, kind people—

Ming-Ming   —and share my humble story—

Sunny   —working at Jade River Manufacturing has made my life a success—

Ming-Ming   If it wasn't for the management's generous spirit and benevolent behavior, I wouldn't have been able to—

Sunny / Ming-Ming (*in unison*)   Change My Destiny.

James *pulls out his phone, takes a photo of them and examines it. He points to the screen.* **Ming-Ming** *subtly imitates* **Artemis**' *body language.*

James   Too Western.

Artemis   The message should be "grateful peasant."

Ming-Ming   Hello, madam. My name is Ming-Ming Chen. Please allow me to share my resume, which highlights my qualifications.

Artemis   That won't be necessary.

Ming-Ming   Please, kind lady, allow me to point out the number of years I've worked, which illustrates my commitment—

Artemis (*interrupting*)   We've made our decision.

Ming-Ming *turns to* **James**.

Ming-Ming   Nice to see you again, sir. My name is Ming-Ming Chen and I am the worker with the right qualifications.

James   We've made our decision.

Ming-Ming *snaps into her Personal Power Position.*

Ming-Ming   It is my destiny to make lots of money.

Ming-Ming *lunges towards* **James**' *crotch in an attempt to give him a hand-job. He pushes her away. She stumbles and falls to the floor.*

Artemis   Leave before we call security.

Ming-Ming (*about* **Sunny**)   She's an idiot. She can't even read. The only reason she's here is because I took pity on her. I have experience—I'm the best worker.

James   You're fired.

Ming-Ming (*to* **Sunny**)   I taught you how to behave. I lit your junk DNA.

James   Go.

Ming-Ming   I'm too old. I don't have enough capital to start over. If I leave I'll have to go back to the countryside, marry an idiot farmer and spend my life making children.

James *opens the door.* **Ming-Ming** *exits.* **Artemis** *hands* **Sunny** *a typed-out sheet of paper, written in Chinese characters.*

Artemis   Here's your speech. His secretary will help you memorize it and make it more personal. You'll deliver it in Beijing in June. Do a good job and we'll promote you to a front office position.

Sunny *shakes* **James** *and* **Artemis**' *hands then exits.* **Artemis** *sighs and turns to* **James**.

Artemis   I need a drink.

James   Where have you been?

Artemis   Working out of my hotel room.

James   For two months?

Artemis   Everything's in place. You'll get your premiere.

James   Public Security detains people all the time. The only surprising thing is that you didn't see it coming.

Artemis   James Lin, the obedient Party member knows everything that happens behind closed doors.

James   If you hadn't been so concerned with being right—

Artemis (*interrupting*)   What is it you need me to say to you?

James   That my company is your top priority.

Artemis   Is that all that matters?

James   Until the premiere's over? Yes.

Artemis *takes a black and white photograph out of her purse and offers it to* **James**.

James   Don't bother me with details.

Artemis   Open it.

James *takes the photo. A beat.*

Artemis   A young woman with a long black braid kneels in front of a fence. She's wearing a white shirt and dark pants. Her eyes are open. Her face is calm. She's flying and falling all at once. What do you suppose she's thinking, as that bullet's exiting her head?

James   Maybe she's thinking about you.

Artemis   Remember when I wanted to be a teacher?

James   Like your mother.

Artemis   Or an intellectual, like my grandfather. But then—. Then I wanted to be very rich.

James   So you could take care of yourself.

Artemis   If they'd lived there'd be pressure to have children. Trips home to read classics to my father and cook fish for my mother. I would have caved in, gotten married, and wondered what I might have done if I wasn't living under some man's thumb.

James   You're free.

Artemis   To close my eyes, make money and spend it on pretty things. There are only two roads to walk down. There were only ever two choices. I can see the truth – and always be in pain. Or I can look away and be rich. And safe. And happy.

Artemis *exits.* **James** *is left standing there, holding the photograph.*

Scene Fifteen

Factory bathroom. **Pete** *mops the floor. A janitor's cart is nearby.* **Sunny** *saunters in.* **Pete** *ignores her.*

Sunny   I won the audition! I'm going to Beijing!

Pete   To talk to stuck up city people.

Sunny   Before, my future was a food stall in a dusty alley, that sold steamed buns to a few customers. Now it's McDonalds—clean. Bright. Highly efficient.

Pete   Who's writing your speech?

Sunny   It will be my face on television, representing the workers. My mouth, saying the words. Help me with some characters. I'll say your name on TV as special thanks.

Pete   I'm busy.

Sunny   How about after your shift?

Pete   How about you read this?

Pete *pulls the petition out of his pocket and holds it out to* **Sunny***, who snatches it and shoves it into her pocket.*

Sunny   That's an illegal petition!

Pete   You said you want to represent the workers. You already know all the characters.

Sunny   They'd lock me up forever and send you the bill.

Pete   The countryside was fine.

Sunny   You hated it.

Pete   You made me hate it. I had time there. People looked at my face when I passed them.

Ming-Ming *enters from a shower stall, wearing a robe over her clothes. She is in a dissociative state.* **Sunny** *and* **Pete** *don't notice her, and continue speaking.*

Sunny (*sarcastic*)   "Please, Goddess of Mercy. Release me from Stone Mountain."

Ming-Ming (*to herself, softly*)   Excellence is a habit.

Pete   I know what your problem is. I've finally figured it out.

Ming-Ming (*to herself*)   We are what we do.

Sunny   "Use your powers. Rescue me."

Ming-Ming (*to herself*)   One who feels failure limits her activities.

Pete   You think you're the only person who has dreams and wants things.

Ming-Ming (*to herself*)   Success is dependent on effort.

Sunny   Go home. Mine coal. Make sons.

Ming-Ming *approaches* **Sunny***, but sees someone else.*

Ming-Ming (*dazed*)   Hello, madame. My name is Ming-Ming Chen. It is such a pleasure to meet you.

Sunny   Ming-Ming. You know me.

Ming-Ming (*to* **Pete**)   Good day, sir. It's an honor to make your acquaintance.

She offers **Pete** *her hand. He shakes it and finds his hand covered in blood.* **Sunny** *pushes up the sleeves of* **Ming-Ming**'*s robe and finds long cuts along her arms.*

Ming-Ming (*still detached*)   Louder. Dig deeper. You die in a field if you fail to commit.

Sunny   Get help.

Pete *exits.* **Ming-Ming** *assumes her Power Position.* **Sunny** *tries to comfort her.*

Ming-Ming   I am the most important person in the world. The things I say and do are important.

Sunny / Ming-Ming   They are full of meaning. If I wait for success I will fail. Action is the only worthwhile thing. I am the most important person in the world. The things I say and do are important. They are full of meaning. If I wait for success I will fail. Action is the only worthwhile thing.

Old Lao *enters with a first-aid kit.* **Pete** *follow him in.*

Old Lao   The only thing worse than a factory worker killing herself is one who can't finish the job.

Sunny   She's bleeding. We have to bandage her cuts.

Old Lao   So she can try it again in a week? No. Even the hell she'll go to will be better than what we lived through in the fifties.

Sunny (*to* **Pete**)   Keep her arms above her heart.

Sunny *tries to wrench the first-aid kit from* **Old Lao**. *He resists.*

Old Lao   I've watched you kids moan through this factory for decades. None of you eat bitterness. None of you know pain.

Sunny   You don't know us.

Old Lao *pushes* **Sunny** *away. She returns to* **Ming-Ming**'*s side.*

Old Lao   You don't know how quiet it gets when there's no animals around. No insects because all the plants are dead. No children crying because they don't have the energy. Do you know what I'm talking about? Are you listening?!

Sunny   If you want me to listen—help!

Old Lao *takes over* **Ming-Ming**'*s first aid.*

Old Lao   In the Fifties and Sixties Mao wanted to become the most prosperous nation—by exploiting his "greatest natural resource."

Sunny   Coal.

Old Lao   Peasants. We took apart our houses and melted down our tools. We gave away our clothes, lived in communes, and carried the nation to prosperity. On our backs. "By Any Means Necessary."

Sunny   Did it work?

Old Lao   Shut up! Clean mess. (*To* **Ming Ming**.) You're fine. You didn't cut deep enough.

Sunny *mops the floor.* **Pete** *hangs back and listens quietly.*

Old Lao   To increase grain production, Mao made us kill all the sparrows. He thought they were eating the grain.

Pete   Sparrows don't eat grain.

Old Lao   They eat the locusts that eat the grain. By the time Mao changed his policy—it was too late. All the crops were gone. Local officials staged photos to prove how full and happy we were.

Sunny   Why didn't *you* starve?

Old Lao   I had a little brother. Pang-Pang. One minute he was beside me. Too hungry to move. Then my mother carried him to our neighbor. We got their youngest son in return. I watched my father's hands shake as he held a curtain over that little boy's head. So the gods couldn't see us. My mother slit his throat. I caught his blood in a bowl. We made stew and pudding and bone soup. So nothing would be wasted. Hitler killed eleven million and the world still feels bad. Mao killed five times that many—of his own people—and what do foreigners want when they come to China? His little red book, and a shirt with his face on it. If you kids want to kill yourselves be my guest – but do it because you understand what has happened. Not because you missed some made up opportunity for success.

Sunny *helps* **Ming-Ming** *stand and walk towards the door.*

Old Lao *exits.*

Ming-Ming   Mr. Destiny lives in a shack lined with cardboard and plastic bags. It's not even his own shack—he shares it. It's worse than our dorms.

Sunny   You don't know that—

Ming-Ming   Last week I followed him home. He's a peasant. Like us. He just wears a different uniform.

Sunny   Rest at home. Come back to the city when you feel stronger.

Ming-Ming   Don't worry. Next time I'll commit. I'll succeed. Satisfaction guaranteed.

Ming-Ming *exits.*

Scene Sixteen

A video-game arcade in Shenzhen. **Pete**, *dressed in street clothes, plays a shoot-em-up game in two-player mode. He has a gun in each hand and is completely engrossed.* **Sunny** *enters.* **Pete** *ignores her.*

Sunny   Pete, I've been trying to call you for two weeks.

Pete   (–)

Sunny   I went to your dorm. Your roommates said you'd moved out.

Pete   (–)

Sunny   I'm going to Beijing tomorrow. Wish me luck.

Pete   (–)

Sunny *wrenches one of the guns out of* **Pete***'s hands and plays alongside him.*

Sunny   Get the energy-pack.

Pete   Get your own energy-pack.

Sunny   I have full strength.

Pete *shoots* **Sunny***'s avatar.*

Sunny   Pete!

Pete   Get the energy pack.

They focus on shooting zombies.

Sunny   Why did you leave?

Pete   Behind you.

Sunny   I'm out of ammo—

Pete   Reload.

Sunny   I memorized my speech.

Pete   Get that guy—

Sunny   That's a girl, I'll lose points—

Pete   She's a zombie—GET HER!

Sunny   Are you sure?

Pete *tries to grab his second gun back from* **Sunny***. He is unsuccessful.*

Pete   I'm fine on my own. I don't need your stupid help—it's not help. It's just bad advice. And poison.

Sunny   Shut your fucking face. You're distracting me.

Silence. They play.

Pete   City people play a computer game where they pretend to be farmers. They plant seeds, harvest vegetables and get points for stealing crops.

Sunny   You made that up.

Pete   A doctor messed up a heart surgery because he'd stayed up guarding his computer vegetables and didn't get enough sleep.

Sunny   Why do they want to be farmers?

Zombie attack from all sides. The game gets really intense, fast and furious. **Sunny** *and* **Pete** *go into shoot-em-up overdrive.*

Pete   They're fake farmers. Growing vegetables they can't even eat.

Sunny   They're crazy.

Pete   You want to be a fake city person.

Sunny   Monkey King wasn't fake just because he had lots of transformations.

Pete   His transformations were temporary, idiot. As soon as the danger was gone he turned back into himself. Even when Monkey turned into a rock, the rock had a monkey's tail. You always knew it was him.

Sunny   Reload.

They play the game.

Pete   You could live and die here with no rights and nothing a city person's guaranteed—

Sunny   Use the flame thrower. Where do you sleep?

Pete   Train station.

Sunny   Why did you leave the factory?

Pete   I was riding the bus. A group of city kids got on and tried to make me give up my seat. None of the other peasants were in seats. They were squatting on the floor.

Pete *focuses on playing the game.*

Pete   When I got off at my stop they followed me.

Pete *focuses on playing the game.*

Pete   They dragged me to an alley and threw me into a pile of bricks. They kicked me until I was covered in dirt, then stopped and said I was too filthy to touch their shoes.

They play the game.

Pete   Before they left, they took turns pissing on me.

Sunny *stops playing.*

Pete   Know why I like the train station?

Sunny   (–)

Pete   It's full of peasants who act like peasants.

Sunny   (–)

Pete *lowers the gun.*

Pete   They ate our brains.

Sunny   What?

Pete (*motioning to screen*)   Game over.

He exits, limping.

Scene Seventeen

*The Great Hall of the People. Three stylists dressed in sleek black urban attire approach **Sunny** and transform her into a "model peasant." They remove her street clothes and replace it with a stylized peasant outfit, complete with rosy cheeks and headscarf. **Artemis** enters and inspects **Sunny**. She nods her approval. The stylists bow and exit. **Sunny** follows **Artemis** to a podium that has dozens of press microphones mounted on it. Lights shift.*

Artemis (*into microphone*)   Ladies and gentlemen, foreign dignitaries, members of the press and business community—welcome to the Great Hall of the People. Every year millions of migrant workers leave impoverished homes and endure epic journeys in search of better lives. Here to introduce the world premiere of "Factory Girl" is one of these heroes. Please welcome nineteen-year-old Sunny Li.

Artemis *exits.* **Sunny** *takes the podium. Dozens of camera flashes illuminate her face.*

Sunny (*into microphone*)   Ladies and gentlemen, esteemed foreigners, press and business people – good morning. My name is Sunny Li, and I am here to tell you how leaving the countryside to work in a city factory gave me the opportunity to transform my life, support my father and the education of my little brother. Pete.

Life in the countryside was lonely and hard. Factory life is exciting and full of new challenges. I have hundreds of friends. We go everywhere together. Thanks to me, my brother graduated high school. My father treats me like a son, and is so proud I'm supporting our family. I'm so grateful to Jade River Manufacturing for improving the lives of so many peasants, including me, and my best friend. Ming-Ming.

She looks up. Short pause.

When I first got to the factory I didn't like—I hated who I was. I thought the problem was me. So I went to night school and studied self-improvement. I put marbles in my mouth. Bleach on my skin. Every month I tried a new hair color. One day—I was walking past a building covered in shiny windows, and saw the reflection of a city girl in it. It was me! Then two people from Beijing asked me for directions. It felt like the beginning of success—even city people thought I was one of them. I didn't know it wouldn't matter how much I looked like a city person—or how many people I tricked, because my ID card said peasant.

Artemis *enters and whispers into* **Sunny**'s *ear.*

Sunny   City people. They think they can burn through peasants. Like a—a natural resource. To them we're coal. We don't have the same rights, but. . . . we're supposed to make them rich.

Artemis *exits.*

Sunny   I want to say, to my fellow migrant workers—I am sorry for trying to be different. I thought—I thought it was the only way I could—save myself. And change my destiny. But destiny—it's not something one person can change. We have to work together and make—demand—change. For all of us.

Qing Shu Min *enters and turns off* **Sunny**'s *microphone.*

Sunny   My section manager jumped out a factory window. There was a—petition by his body. Filled with hundreds of signatures. Every name was a protest.

Gao Chen *leads* **Artemis** *onstage.* **Artemis** *carries a cordless microphone.*

Artemis   Thank you, Sunny. Ladies and gentlemen, the world premiere of "Factory Girl" will begin in ten minutes

Sunny *steps away from the podium and speaks directly into the audience.*

Sunny   I protest—and I ask you to protest with me. Demand you get the same rights as people born in the city. Go on strike. Stop working. And if they still say no—go home.

Let city people try to live for a single day without us. Stop selling them food and sewing their clothes. Let the city people go hungry. Let them walk naked on the street. Without shoes. And live in houses with broken windows and—

Lights shift. She is alone onstage.

(*Inward, to herself.*) Chop off my arms—I can still strike. Hack off my legs—I can still walk. Rip out my heart—I will mysteriously recover. I can bathe in boiling oil and come out cleaner than I went in.

Gao Chen *places a black hood over* **Sunny**'s *head.*

Scene Eighteen

Li Han's *rural home.* **Li Han** *sits in a chair. There is a stapled document on his lap and an earphone in one ear.* **Qing Shu Min** *is in the next room, listening in on a headset. She holds a walkie-talkie in one hand. A video camera is aimed at* **Li Han**.

Li Han (*into camera*)   I . . . am . . . Li Han. The father of Sunny Li—the . . .

Qing Shu Min (*into walkie-talkie*)   —politically insane worker activist.

Li Han   Politically insane worker activist.

Qing Shu Min   Focus.

Li Han   I have been told that some—some . . .

Qing Shu Min (*interrupting*) Uninformed internet bloggers.

Li Han —people believe Sunny's actions were motivated by the—

Qing Shu Min (*interrupting*) Untimely death.

Li Han —by what happened to my brother. Li Chen. When he took part in—

Qing Shu Min (*interrupting*) A counter-revolutionary riot.

Li Han —student demonstrations—during the—

Qing Shu Min Period of **Li Han** —Eighty-nine Democracy
political turmoil. Movement.

Li Han At home Sunny never caused trouble. Only when she went to the factory
and was exposed to . . . political agitators and—urban intellectuals did her—

Qing Shu Min (*interrupting*) Mental illness.

Li Han —problems develop. I am not suited to care for Sunny's illness. So. . . I am
relinquishing Sunny's guardianship to the state. So she can . . . receive the—medical
attention she needs.

Qing Shu Min Apologize to the country.

Li Han *takes the pen and signs the document on his lap. He bows towards the camera.*

Li Han Forgive me for raising a Bad Element.

Qing Shu Min *hands* **Li Han** *a document.*

Qing Shu Min Sign the waiver. By accepting this compensation you agree not to
sue the factory.

He does, and returns the document to **Qing Shu Min**. *She takes out a stack of
one-hundred yuan notes and offers it to* **Li Han**.

Li Han She's just a girl.

Qing Shu Min It's time to forget the past and face a brighter future. You deserve a
chance at happiness. Don't you agree?

Li Han *stares at the money, but doesn't take it.* **Qing Shu Min** *drops it on his lap,
then she and* **Gao Chen** *exit.*

Scene Nineteen

Beijing Ankang Psychiatric Hospital. **Sunny** *sits on a metal chair in an otherwise
empty space, dressed in dirty white pajamas. Months of torture and medication have
made it difficult to recognize names and faces. Her body is there, her mind nearly
destroyed. Her arms, legs and face are covered in bruises. For the entire scene, her
head dangles limply to the side, her mouth hangs open and her bulging eyes stare
vacantly at the ceiling.* **Pete** *enters, dressed in a blue janitor's uniform.*

Pete   Sunny?

No response from **Sunny**.

Pete   Sunny, it's me. Can you hear me?

Sunny   (–)

Pete   I was worried you might not recognize me because of all the—(*He looks around, suddenly fearful.*) You know who I am. You recognize me. Don't you?

Sunny   (–)

Pete   I got a job as a janitor so I can see you whenever I want. I had to go to the labor market every day for three months. But I'm here now. Are you happy to see me?

Sunny   (–)

Pete   Last month I met a man who used to perform Monkey King in teahouses— look what he's taught me—

Pete *executes a sequence of fluttering, staggering movements—the Drunken Monkey sequence, from Peking Opera.*

Pete   It's "Drunken Monkey." I learned it for you. (*Still moving.*) Monkey moves like this after getting drunk on the wine of immortality he steals from the Emperor of Heaven. Remember? They sentence him to death, but when they try to chop off his head the blade breaks, and the fire they burn him with—

Sunny (*interrupting*)   Ahhannngeeeeehmeeee.

Pete   What?

Sunny   (–)

Pete   The fire they burn him with tickles. Even the golden arrows can't—

Sunny (*interrupting*)   Aaaange me.

Pete   Aaange you?

Sunny   Change me!

Pete   Change you? Into what?

Sunny   (–)

Pete *pulls out his cellphone and shows* **Sunny** *a video recording of her speech.*

Pete   You're a hero. A peasant hero. Your speech is on the internet. Millions of people watched it and guess what? All the workers in our factory went on strike. Even miners and construction workers heard you. Everything's stopped.

Sunny   (–)

Pete   Two months ago the factories closed and now all the pollution is gone. A week ago there was rain—now the skies are bluer than anyone can remember. Last night in Beijing you could even see stars. The city slickers were scared—they had never seen such a bright sky. They thought the stars were American missiles coming to wage World War Three on us.

Sunny (–)

Pete Peasants are going back to the countryside to make their own jobs, start their own schools and take care of each other. It's the Sunshine Revolution! After you! The countryside had an election to choose a new leader. There was no corruption, murders or bribes—and guess who they chose?

Sunny (–)

Pete *exits and returns with an office chair, the kind that rolls and swivels.*

Pete You're Chairlady Sunny, and until we figure out a perfect society and get rid of money your face will be on all the bills. It's only an honorary title because people will rule themselves, but look what they asked me to give you—

A chair, for your new office position!

The Citizens of the Countryside have authorized me to remove you from this hospital.

Pete *moves* **Sunny** *to the office chair. She whimpers, her body jerks and spasms, then comes to stillness when he sets her down.* **Pete** *pushes the chair through the space. Faster and faster, in spirals.* **Sunny** *remains limp and motionless.*

Pete Ladies and gentlemen, presenting the face of the Sunshine Revolution, Chairlady Sunny! Whee!

They come to a stop. **Sunny** *is the same as before.*

Sunny Change me.

Pete Later, as punishment for making outrageous claims and trying to cross the universe in one leap, Buddha made a Stone Mountain and trapped Monkey in it. Monkey would have been stuck there, but—

Sunny Change me.

A long pause, as **Pete** *silently struggles through, then finally accepts, what his sister is asking him to do.*

Pete She was freed. Monkey was freed from Stone Mountain by—the Goddess of Mercy.

Pete *clamps his hands over* **Sunny**'s *nose and mouth, suffocating her. He holds her as her body rebels, thrashes, pleads and struggles for life.*

Pete Imagine everything you don't need flying out your fingers and toes. Back into the dirt and sky. When you open your eyes, your life will be wide open with possibility. It will be beautiful and blank. Let go of your past. Face your future with clear eyes and a strong body. Change, Sunny. Change. Change. Change.

Sunny *goes limp, and collapses into her brother.* **Pete** *exits.* **Sunny** *remains in the chair. Her eyes are still open. She stares blankly at the audience. A long stillness.*

End of Play.

Afterword

Joshua Chambers-Letson

The People, the so-called People, are simple-minded loafers who linger on in
any steadily worsening situation, people who have been dulled and forsaken by
the deceptions of culture, their personalities deprived and lost, they are people
who have abandoned their rights and responsibilities, who walk like ghosts on
the ever-widening streets, and whose true emotions, dreams, and homes are
long lost. They will no longer feel warmth in the night, no longer have
expectations, and they shall not dream again.

(Ai Weiwei)[1]

Frances Ya-Chu Cowhig's *The World of Extreme Happiness* begins as Li Han, a coal
miner in rural China and the father of the play's principal protagonist, describes a
dream. Xin Xin, whom one could at first assume is a prostitute, comes to his bed and
sits on his face. While "savoring her warmth on my skin," Li Han is surprised to find
"something hot and gooey slide down my cheek." When he realizes that Xin Xin has
"laid a turd between my eyes," instead of responding with revulsion, he describes it as
"salty, and sweet. Like tofu, fermented with black beans." There is an uncomfortable
disconnect for the audience, being asked to imagine a seemingly abject occurrence
(human feces falling onto one's face and into an open mouth) as nourishing, if not
sexually arousing. Li Han's friend, Ran Feng, interprets the dream thus, "You accepted
shit into your mouth and digested it." A few moments later we learn that Xin Xin is not,
in fact, a woman, but one of Li Han's beloved racing pigeons. While his fecophilic
dream may seem no less unsettling to some in the audience, Li Han's metaphor of
fermented tofu with black beans still asks us to imagine "shit" as something that is not
only digestible, but potentially delicious.

Ran Feng's explanation of Li Han's dream seems to resonate with an Ai Weiwei
quote Cowhig chose as an epigram to an earlier edition of the play. The "people" have
come to swallow shit ("the deceptions of culture") and learned to digest it as they've
"abandoned their rights and responsibilities." But just as Xin Xin's identity is unstable
in the opening scene (is she a prostitute, or a bird?), what it is that constitutes "the
people" and/or the object of criticism in Cowhig's play is no more stable. Are we to
understand "the people" as the eponymous source of power in the People's Republic of
China (PRC), as "the people" of U.S.-style constitutional democracy, the people in the
audience, or the specific people onstage in front of us? Perhaps more important is the
question of what or who is the source of the "shit" that the people happily digest?

Cowhig's play follows Sunny, Li Han's daughter, after she is born into rural poverty
in 1992. Sunny is discarded and left to die in a garbage can when her gender is revealed
as female at birth. Surviving against the odds, she grows up and leaves her home for the

---

1 Ai Weiwei, *Ai Weiwei's Blog: Writings, Interviews, and Digita Rants, 2006-2009*, ed. Lee Ambrozy
(Cambridge, MA: MIT Press, 2009).

bustling urban center in Shenzhen to find work in a factory. There, Sunny is caught up in a web of corporate and political intrigue. Due in part to her aspirations to climb the corporate ladder and become a self-made success, Sunny becomes a pawn in a transnational company's cynical public relations campaign, resulting in her utter destruction.

The play is set between 1992 and 2012, an era of extraordinary transformation that arguably began with the brutal government and military crackdown on the 1989 Democracy Movement. Popular Western conceptions of June 4, 1989, often frame it as a pro-Western democratic uprising against the staunch authoritarianism of the Chinese Communist state. But the 1989 protests were a complex constellation of grievances that were partially responding to the state's use of anti-democratic measures to forward anti-socialist reforms in pursuit of then President Deng Xiaoping's newly articulated "socialist market economy." As many cultural critics have since observed, many of the students were motivated by criticism of the rampant corruption fostered by capitalist reforms as well as opposition to the increased privatization of formerly worker-controlled and state-owned industry. In other words, students were not only protesting for democratic reform but in some cases simultaneously protesting against the state's increasingly capitalist policies.[2]

The specter of the June 4 massacre in Tiananmen Square hangs heavily over *The World of Extreme Happiness*, most notably in the form of Li Han's brother who we learn was killed while protesting in Beijing. But it is not the past that most compels Cowhig's characters so much as the promise of the future. That Sunny is born in 1992 is important. After a few years of internal instability following the events of 1989, the PRC shifted to governance by what cultural critic Xudong Zhang describes as the pro-market reform, "bureaucratic and technocratic elite, itself the biggest beneficiary of Reform policies."[3] In 1990 and 1991, stock exchanges were opened in Shanghai and Shenzhen, respectively. Deng Xiaoping, who handed the Presidency over to Jiang Zemin in 1989, publicly re-emerged in 1992 (the year of Sunny's birth) to promote his vision of pro-market reform. By 1997, with the support of the Fifteenth Congress of the Chinese Communist Party, President Jiang publicly endorsed a shareholding system that would further facilitate the privatization of state-owned enterprises in an increasing shift towards capitalist reforms. Named Sunny, our heroine thus embodies the dawn of this new era in Chinese politics. She is literally rescued from the garbage bin of the past and her story signifies a new kind of ideal Chinese subject, with a self-sacrificing, entrepreneurial, pro-market spirit. Her journey from rural China to the bustling urban center of Shenzhen might then be understood as reflective of the shift from the peasant proletarianism of the Maoist era to the pro-market ideology of the new one. In this sense, the play is much more than a simple critique of the PRC. Rather, it is a nuanced meditation on labor and life in the post-Tiananmen period whereby, as Zhang remarks, "the central political tension in Chinese society today is not so much the discrepancy

---

2   For more, see: Xudong Zhang, ed. *Whither China: Intellectual Politics in Contemporary China* (Durham: Duke University Press, 2001).

3   Xudong Zhang, "The Making of the Post-Tiananmen Intellectual Field: A Critical Overview," in *Whither China: Intellectual Politics in Contemporary China*, ed. Xudong Zhang (Durham: Duke University Press, 2001), 7.

between a Communist government and a market environment—since the two have already effected a corporate-style merger—but rather an intensifying conflict between this interest group's rational self-interest and its unchecked power and corruption, which put it in direct confrontation with society at large."[4]

To this end, the setting of the play, in Shenzhen, is significant. As the owner of the factory where Sunny finds employment explains, Shenzhen is one of China's Special Economic Zones (SEZs). Located largely along China's eastern border, SEZs were established as spaces that are exempt from a range of the PRC's laws and regulations in order to, in the words of the Fifth Congress, "encourage foreign citizens . . . to set up factories and establish enterprises and other undertakings."[5] SEZs are largely reliant upon migrant labor from rural areas and, as anthropologist Aiwha Ong observes, "zone workers are considered peasants unprotected by China's labor laws and are not entitled to social benefits due workers elsewhere in the country."[6] What makes SEZs unique is thus the fact that they are effectively outside of what many in the West refer to as the administrative state of "Communist China." They are instead capitalist zones that function under direct control of the central Chinese government. The result is that, as in similarly constituted free-trade zones in places such as Indonesia, "workers are denied the most basic of social protections and are generally unshielded from the onslaught of capital while remaining vulnerable to the state's repressive apparatus."[7] These are precisely the conditions that result in Sunny's destruction.

That the exploitative conditions inside the SEZs were established with the explicit goal of attracting foreign capital undermines any attempt to read *The World of Extreme Happiness* as a strict critique of the PRC's governing policies, insofar as global circuits of production and consumption are equally culpable. Here we encounter the "source" of the abject filth that "the people" are willing to swallow, save that it is plural. There is the repressive apparatuses of the central Chinese state *and* the economic conditions produced by transnational neoliberal capitalism. The regime of capitalist exploitation that structures labor conditions within factories in Shenzhen is present throughout the play and Cowhig is careful to remind us that Western economic ideology, investment, *and* consumption are prime structuring factors in this model of development. For example, factory owner James Lin and business executive Artemis Chang are literal embodiments of the New Era's marriage to Western market reforms. They have taken recognizably Western names and, indeed, Artemis (the daughter of alleged counter-revolutionaries) is neatly representative of the new economic elite in China. Educated at Harvard and a shining example of global cosmopolitanism, Artemis wants nothing more than to place the past under erasure, embracing a vulgar capitalist ideology of selfishness and the pursuit of wealth: "There are only two roads to walk down . . . You can see the truth—and always be in pain. Or we can look away and be rich. And safe. And happy." But look away from what?

4   Ibid.
5   Fifth National People's Congress, "Regulations on Special Economic Zones in Guangdong Province." Available at: http://www.novexcn.com/guangdong_regs_on_sez.html
6   Aihwa Ong, *Neoliberalism as Exception: Mutations in Citizenship and Sovereignty* (Durham, NC: Duke University Press, 2006), 106.
7   Aihwa Ong, *Flexible Citizenship: The Cultural Logics of Transnationality* (Durham, NC: Duke University Press, 1999), 224.

Early in the play, as James and Artemis discuss a "spate of worker suicides" at Lin's factory, Chang suggests that Lin "follow the example of Foxconn and ask them to sign a no-suicide pledge." Foxconn is a multi-national Taiwanese-owned corporation responsible for the manufacturing of many popular commodities including Apple's iPhone and iPad. Foxconn became notorious for its exploitation and abuse of laborers in its Shenzhen factory. Drawing a subtle connection between the horrors and abuses that structure the world of the fictional factory in the play and the very real Foxconn, Cowhig is gently asking the audience to look towards and at the exploitative labor conditions that are rendered invisible in the final commodity form of the popular electronics that line our pockets. And if we are quick to indict the Chinese government for using brutal tactics to maintain this system of production, the play is unwilling to allow consumers to shirk responsibility for our role in these practices. This is most apparent when Artemis complains about the "violent tactics" of the Chinese government to policewoman Qing Shu Min. To this, Qing wryly quips, "Why would we change when everyone wants to sleep with us just the way we are?" Having made the link between Foxconn, the Western media, and Western consumers earlier in the play, this exchange is a subtle indictment of the audience's own complicity with and relationship to the violence that we see carried out on stage. Qing deploys a sexual metaphor, which also invites us to think back to Li Han's dream and question what it is that we've been willing to "look away" from in order to continue "sleeping" with a regime that allows us to consume and digest the sweet and salty "shit" that surges forth from Shenzhen's factories.

If both capitalism and state repression are targeted by Cowhig's narrative, part of what makes *The World of Extreme Happiness* so compelling is the author's unwillingness to relinquish Sunny's own agency in her story. Although she is crafted to be sympathetic and even likeable, she's hardly uncompromised. Perhaps more than any other character in the play, Sunny embraces the ideology of self-promotion and corporate ambition. With resonances of Artemis's personal history, it is not difficult to imagine Sunny as a younger version of Chang. Throughout the play Sunny literally speaks in the catchphrases of capitalist opportunism, becoming an enthusiastic protégé of Mr. Destiny's smoke-and-mirrors self-help classes. At one point, she defines her desire for class mobility in relatively petty terms: once she makes her fortune she wants to "go back to the countryside and laugh at everyone who's still poor . . . and living in dirt." Her ambition leads her to betray her best friend and her pettiness results in an act of cruelty against her father that, though matched by his own callous treatment of his children, is no less horrifying to watch. In fact, Sunny only truly becomes a heroine in the final instance, when she performs a public account of the horrible conditions experienced by the working masses in the New Era.

If Sunny's birth reflected the dawning hope of the New Era in China, her death might be understood as the loss of a hope that was little more than a lie. The mode of hope that we watch Sunny consume—a mode of hoping that ultimately comes to destroy her—seems resonant with what critical theorist Lauren Berlant describes as "cruel optimism." This is a mode of social, political, and affective relation in which hope for the "good life" becomes an impediment to its attainment, if it does not in fact become a force that keeps one trapped in relations of subordination and unfulfillment.[8]

8   Lauren Berlant, *Cruel Optimism* (Durham, NC: Duke University Press, 2011).

It was Sunny's evangelical belief in the promise of a better life, sold and peddled by hucksters like Mr. Destiny (or Donald Trump) that delivered her to ruin. In the final sequence, she is destroyed, mentally and physically, by the state's violent response to her revolutionary action. But in this last scene Pete, Sunny's brother, offers us yet another glimpse of hope in the form of a utopian vision of a changed and better world.

The world of happiness that we imagine as the "Sunshine Revolution" is not one of unrestrained free-market entrepreneurialism or state-based repression. Rather, Sunny's brother Pete tells the story of a world in which the people collectively and spontaneously reject the filth that they have been digesting in order to rise up against the forces that have appropriated the people's name and their constituent power. Against capitalism's false assurances of individual enrichment, and against the authoritarianism of the Chinese central government, Pete allows Sunny (and by extension, the audience) to imagine a "perfect society" built on the empowerment of the masses, true democracy, liberty, and the promise of the collective struggle for justice. By allowing us to imagine this promise, we are assured that such a world is possible. In what he does next, Pete underscores the painful gap between that world and the one we live in. We are reminded, once more, of the difficulty we are all faced with when attempting to discern the forms of galvanizing, transformative hope that we need to survive, from those that keep us trapped in a world that peddles hope on the collective path towards annihilation.

The King of Hell's Palace

The King of Hell's Palace was first staged at the Goodman Theatre's Owen Theatre (Robert Falls, Artistic Director; Roche Schulfer, Executive Director), Chicago Illinois, on September 25, 2016. The cast for this workshop production was as follows:

Yin-Yin / Pei-Pei	Jo Mei
Lili / Pearl	Celeste Den
Shen / Kuan	C.S. Lee
Wen / Minister Li	Wai Yim
Luo Na / Dr. Gao	Mia Park
Old Yang / Wang Wei	James Saito
Little Yi	Rammel Chan
Jasmine / Han-Han	Michelle Krusiec

Director	Tea Alagić
Scenic Design	Kevin Depinet
Costume Design	Rachel Lambert
Lighting Design	Jesse Klug
Sound Design	Richard Woodbury
Dramaturg	Rebecca Adelsheim
Stage Manager	Jonathan Nook

The King of Hell's Palace was originally commissioned and developed by the Goodman Theatre and the Royal National Theatre.

The King of Hell's Palace was first staged in the United Kingdom at the Hampstead Theatre (Roxana Silbert, Artistic Director; Greg Ripley-Duggan, Executive Producer), London, on September 5, 2019. The cast for this world premiere production was as follows:

Yin-Yin / Luo Na	Celeste Den
Lili / An Mei / Ruzhen	Tuyen Do
Shen / Han-Han	Christopher Goh
Wen / Johnny	Vincent Lai
Kuan / Wang Wei	Kok-Hwa Lie
Old Yang / Minister Li	Togo Igawa
Jasmine / Pei-Pei	Millicent Wong
Little Yi / Peter	Aiden Cheng

Director	Michael Boyd
Designer	Tom Piper
Lighting Design	Colin Grenfell
Composer & Sound Design	Nicola Chang
Movement	Liz Ranken
Fight Directors	Rachel Bown-Williams & Ruth Cooper-Brown

Cast, with Possible Doubling

Kuan, *38. Migrant worker.*
Also plays: **Wang Wei**, *39. Ministry of Health employee.*
　　　　Police Officer 4.

Wen, *35. Migrant worker. Kuan's brother.*
Also plays: **Johnny**, *31. Executive at Phoenix Pharmaceutical.*
　　　　Xiao Kang, *27. Public Security Officer.*

Shen, *32. Ministry of Health employee. Yin-Yin's husband. Wang Wei's brother.*
Also plays: **Han-Han**, *19. Luo Na's son.*
　　　　Postman Zhou, *45. Rural mailman.*
　　　　Police Officer 2.

Yin-Yin, *31. Infectious disease specialist.*
Also plays: **Luo Na**, *37. Rural blood seller.*

Jasmine, *24. Ministry of Health employee.*
Also plays: **Pei-Pei**, *14. Kuan's daughter.*

Little Yi, *16. Wen and Lili's son.*
Also plays: **Peter**, *25. Executive at Phoenix Pharmaceutical.*
　　　　Police Officer 3.
　　　　Public Security Officer.

Lili, *34. Potato farmer. Wen's wife. Luo Na's sister.*
Also plays: **An Mei**, *29. Public Security Officer.*
　　　　Ruzhen, *30. Lab Technician.*

Old Yang, *65. Potato farmer. Kuan & Wen's father.*
Also plays: **Minister Li**, *59. Minister of Health.*
　　　　Police Officer 1.

Place and Time

Rural and urban Henan province. 1992 and 1998.

Act One

Scene One

A rural highway in Henan. Early February, 1992. Sunset on the eve of Chinese New Year. **Kuan** *and* **Wen**, *brothers and migrant workers, move briskly along the side of the road, weighed down by overstuffed canvas bags.*

Wen   Deng Xiaoping says, "It doesn't matter if the cat is white or black. As long as it catches mice, it is a very good cat."

Kuan   Black cats are bad luck.

Wen   That's called "backwards thinking." We survived the biggest tragedy of the twentieth century—

Kuan   That German killed more.

Wen   Mao caused five times as many deaths. His ghost must be pissed the German's getting more credit. We're survivors. Can we agree on that?

Kuan   I agree we're not dead.

Wen   Which means: it's time to have bigger dreams!

Kuan   Things are better now.

Wen   Compared to disaster.

Kuan   Our fields are fertile. They produce high yields—

Wen   Of a crop worth less than paper. Half our potatoes feed pigs. The famine is over! Why grow a plant that yields so little profit we spend fifty weeks a year in the mines and go home for two weeks?

Kuan   Potatoes are practical.

Wen   Deng Xiaoping wants to help us get rich. He won't succeed if we cling to ancient ideas and reject modern thinking. Let's switch to a cash crop, stay home and live with our family.

The sound of firecrackers from a nearby courtyard.

Kuan   Move faster. This highway's not safe after dark.

Wen *huffs his armpits, smells his breath, then rummages through his bag.*

Wen   Lili's waited eleven months for this moment. I should smell fresh.

Kuan   Corpse flowers are fresh.

Wen   What's a corpse flower?

Kuan   They bloom once a year and smell like rotting flesh.

Wen   You have no idea how much better my girl fries my rice when she's into me. (*Points to surrounding fields.*) I could just roll through these fields if we grew something fragrant—like jasmine or peonies.

Kuan   And end up smelling like shit. What flower blooms in the middle of winter?

Wen   Ma's under those fields! Let's grow something good with soil made from her—

Kuan (*cutting him off*)   It's good to have food in your belly.

Wen (*as he continues to search bag*)   Peonies are practical. They symbolize good fortune, riches and prosperity. City folks need them for New Year's, weddings and Grand Openings.

The sound of a large truck approaching.

Kuan   Get off the road.

Wen   The money's not just in the blooms. A woman who eats white peony root becomes as beautiful as the flower itself.

Kuan   Are you trying to die?

The truck grows closer. **Wen** *crows triumphantly, pulls out a can of spray deodorant and sprays it liberally all over himself.*

Wen   Peonies are good medicine. They cure all kinds of dis—

LOUD, LONG HONK. **Kuan** *pulls* **Wen** *off the road. The sound of the truck whooshing past.*

Wen (*to truck driver*)   Fuck your ancestors!

More firecrackers. **Kuan** *walks faster.*

Wen   I mean it about switching crops. I've had enough gold mines for six lifetimes.

Kuan   With peonies it's three years to first harvest.

Wen   Let's put roots in the ground soon.

Kuan   How will we buy root stock? How will we live while they're growing?

Wen   Better than we would breathing dust in the mines. Gold lung is a hard way to die. Even on dry land you feel like you're drowning.

Kuan   We're home for two weeks. Enjoy it. Don't talk to me about illegal petitions.

Wen   Miners are dropping like flies. Families should be compensated for their deaths.

Kuan   We won't sign it.

Wen   What if I already did?

Kuan   Idiot! What were you thinking? If management finds out—

Wen Management did. Happy New Year! We won't be breathing gold dust anymore!

Kuan We?!

Wen They think like Red Guards.

Kuan *punches* **Wen**. *He falls to the ground.*

Wen You should thank me! (*Off the sound of more firecrackers.*) See? The King of Heaven is celebrating! We endured the chaos, the famine and the mines! It's time for peaceful family life.

Kuan How will we live?

Kuan *kicks* **Wen** *again, then exits towards the village.* **Wen** *calls after him.*

Wen By switching to a cash crop. Good-bye ugly potatoes, hello pretty peonies! Deng Xiaoping says: "Be bold in reforms and have the courage to experiment. Don't act like women with bound feet, stuck in the past and never advancing."

Wen *brushes himself off, sniffs his armpits, then hurries to catch up.*

Wen Peonies are a good investment, brother. A single plant can live for a century!

Scene Two

The living room of a modest, work-unit assigned apartment in Zhoukou township, the second largest city in Henan province. Late afternoon. **Shen,** *a middle-class public health official, selects a tune on a karaoke machine. It's the tune to the Indonesian folk song "Dayung Sampan," popularized by Teresa Teng.* **Shen** *sings lyrics into a potato.*

Wang Wei (*from kitchen*)   Excellent choice!

Shen (*singing*)   "Sweet honey"

Wang Wei, **Shen**'s *older brother, emerges from the kitchen. He's dressed in more formal attire.*

Shen *and* **Wang Wei** (*singing*)   "Your smile is sweet honey. . . ."

Yin-Yin, **Shen**'s *wife, another public health official, enters through the front door, weighed down with groceries. She's three months pregnant.*

Wang Wei Yin-Yin! Welcome home!

Shen *and* **Wang Wei** (*singing*)   "Like a flower blooming in the breeze"

Jasmine, *an attractive woman in her early twenties, follows carrying a box of individually wrapped Asian pears.*

Jasmine Sorry to trouble you.

Yin-Yin   Don't be polite.

Shen *and* **Wang Wei** (*singing*)   "Blooming in the breeze"

Yin-Yin *peels off her heavy winter coat and motions for* **Jasmine** *to do the same.*

Yin-Yin   This is my brother-in-law. He lives in a bigger apartment upstairs. That's my husband, serenading a potato.

Wang Wei   I forgot the microphone.

Shen *and* **Wang Wei** (*singing*)

"Where have we?
Where did our eyes meet?"

Jasmine   Sweet potatoes have better shapes.

Wang Wei *makes a face.*

Wang Wei   Sweet potatoes?

Yin-Yin *pauses the karaoke song.*

Yin-Yin   This is Jasmine, the pear-seller's daughter. She's too young to remember the famine.

Jasmine   Sorry!

Wang Wei   Don't be!

(*Sings a capella into potato.*)

We all wish we had your memory
Her young memory

Wang Wei *restarts the karaoke song, tosses the potato at* **Shen** *and looks at him pointedly.* **Shen** *tries to sit down, but assumes a presentational karaoke stance when* **Wang Wei** *shoots him a look.*

Wang Wei (*over intro music*)   Do you work at the fruit stand?

Jasmine   When I can. I just finished nursing school.

Shen (*singing*)   "Sweet honey"

Wang Wei   Congratulations!

Shen (*singing*)   "Your smile is sweet honey"

Jasmine   Thank you.

Shen (*singing*)

"Like a flower blooming in the breeze
Blooming in the breeze"

Wang Wei *shuts off the karaoke machine mid-song and applauds sarcastically.*

Wang Wei (*sarcastic*)   I pronounce you ready for our big business meeting.

Shen *mock-hurls the potato at his older brother.* **Wang Wei** *easily catches it.*

Yin-Yin   Did you have fun in the United States?

Wang Wei   It was spectacular!

Shen   Don't encourage him.

Wang Wei   Executives from every pharmaceutical company wanted to meet us. Everyone wants to do business with Henan Province. It's a new gold rush. Now that Deng's opened the door to market reform, we can all leap into the sea of commerce!

Jasmine   I better learn how to swim.

Wang Wei *playfully steps towards* **Jasmine**.

Wang Wei   No problem maiden. I'll show you some moves.

He starts miming a breast stroke. **Shen** *and* **Yin-Yin** *snuggle on the couch as* **Jasmine** *imitates* **Wang Wei**'*s movements.*

Jasmine   Where are we swimming to?

Wang Wei   Our first stop is the countryside. Let's go to your village and start searching for capital. What do you see?

Jasmine   My grandmother climbing our pear trees.

Wang Wei *switches to a forward crawl.* **Jasmine** *follows.*

Wang Wei   Pear trees are your family's capital. What does the Ministry of Health need?

Jasmine   Patients?

Wang Wei   How about farmers, like your grandmother?

Jasmine   How can farmers be capital? We have capital. Orchards and tools and fertile soil—

Wang Wei   There's something more valuable here—something you're already looking at. What moves through your grandmother's heart at the average rate of five kilometers per hour?

Jasmine   Her spirit?

Wang Wei *bursts out laughing. He walks away from* **Jasmine**.

Wang Wei   I give up. I give up. This maiden's too pure.

Jasmine *stands awkwardly, embarrassed.*

Jasmine   Sorry. I'm too stupid.

Yin-Yin (*nudging* **Shen**)   Put her out of her misery.

Shen   My brother's the director of Zhoukou's first Plasma Collection station.

Jasmine   Blood!

Wang Wei   Plasma. We only pay for the yellow stuff. Yin-Yin will be Vice Director, second only to me!

Yin-Yin   Thanks, but I'm happy in Infectious Disease.

Yin-Yin *heads to the kitchen.* **Wang Wei** *blocks her path.*

Yin-Yin   I'm hungry.

Wang Wei   We need you, Yin-Yin. Don't do this to me.

Yin-Yin   Don't get between a pregnant woman and her snacks.

Wang Wei   Name your price.

Yin-Yin   I'm not interested in business.

Wang Wei   All healthcare is business. The Central Government doesn't fund us. Every public health program we run is paid for with income we generate.

Shen   One day profits from Wang Wei's station will support your Hepatitis research.

Wang Wei   When it does you will thank me.

Yin-Yin   And you'll thank my lab for monitoring the blood supply and keeping your "capital" clean. Move!

Wang Wei   What do I have to do, take off my shoes and threaten to jump in a river?

Shen *wraps his arms around* **Yin-Yin** *and turns to* **Jasmine**, *attempting to defuse the situation.*

Shen   Yin-Yin doesn't pay attention unless she thinks she can save you.

Wang Wei   Do you want to hear a good love story?

Jasmine   Please. They're my favorite kind!

Wang Wei *steps aside.* **Yin-Yin** *glares at him and exits into the kitchen.*

Shen   We were in a long-distance relationship. I was here, starting my career at the Ministry of Health, and Yin-Yin was in Wuhan, taking a course in Epidemiology –

Wang Wei   And one day my brother gets a letter informing him he's been dumped.

Jasmine   Oh no!

Shen   She'd met a guy in her Epidemiology course who was more boring than me.

Yin-Yin *returns with a bag of prawn crackers.*

Yin-Yin (*mouth full*)   The words I used were "even-tempered."

Shen   I took a pedicab to the bus station, a bus to Wuhan, and waited outside her classroom. When class got out, Yin-Yin unlocked her bike and walked right past me.

Yin-Yin   I hadn't seen you in months!

Shen   I walked her home, over a bridge—

Wang Wei   And said: "Marry me!"

Jasmine   How romantic! What did you say?

Yin-Yin   "No, I won't marry you. I don't like your temper."

Wang Wei   My little brother takes off his shoes, walks to the railing and tells Yin-Yin he's going to drown himself in the Yangtze river if she doesn't change her mind.

Yin-Yin   I said "Do it! Jump! I don't want you."

Shen   I walk to the railing, stare at the river, look back and say three words.

Jasmine   "I love you?"

Wang Wei   "Can he cook?"

Yin-Yin   My future flashes before my eyes—

Shen   And it tastes like cardboard.

Yin-Yin   It's true. My classmate was great at mapping how infectious disease spreads to rural areas across long distance bus lines—

Shen   But the only thing he'd ever done in the kitchen was crack an egg into a bowl of instant noodles.

Jasmine (*applauding*)   That is a very good story.

Wang Wei   Yin-Yin, my shoes are off and your apartment's far from the ground.

Yin-Yin   I'm flattered, but I'm happy in Infectious Disease. But I know from Jasmine's mother that she loves karaoke. Maybe my husband would appreciate a nice nursing school graduate singing in his place.

Shen   That's a genius idea!

Yin-Yin   I know. (*To* **Jasmine**.) What do you think?

Jasmine   I'd be honored to help the Henan Ministry of Health.

Wang Wei   Then it's settled! (*To* **Shen**.) Keep working on her. (*To all.*) Wish me luck at the banquet!

Yin-Yin *and* **Shen**   Good luck!

Wang Wei   All the big shots will be there. The Henan Governor, the Party Secretary, the Minister of Agriculture—

Shen   Agriculture?

Wang Wei   If he'll classify Henan Blood an agricultural product, we can export it tax-free.

Jasmine   I should go too. Sorry to trouble you!

Yin-Yin   Good night Jasmine. Thanks for your help.

Shen *and* **Yin-Yin** *stand to see their guests off. Once they exit* **Yin-Yin** *collapses onto the couch.* **Shen** *picks up the potato and sings into it, using the same melody as before.*

Shen (*singing*)
  They are things
  You do in your sleep

Yin-Yin   Stop!

Shen (*singing*)
  Liver panels, blood types
  Tests for iron deficiency

Yin-Yin   I'm an infectious disease specialist.

Shen (*still singing*)
  Just six months
  Then maternity leave

Yin-Yin   Go die in the street.

Shen (*still singing*)
  Then back to Infectious Disease
  Infectious Disease

Yin-Yin   I'm in the middle of a major Hepatitis C study.

Shen   You must have colleagues who can continue that research.

Yin-Yin   I'm the principal investigator.

Shen   I'll do all the diapers for a whole year.

Yin-Yin   That's your job already.

Shen   He helped us get our first positions. We owe him our careers.

Yin-Yin   Says who? I was first in my class!

Shen   He's never asked for anything like this before. Who can you count on, if not your own family?

Yin-Yin   Yourself.

Shen   I'll love you extra, for the rest of your life.

Yin-Yin   Even when I have an old lady beard?

Shen   Especially when you have an old lady beard.

Yin-Yin   And my boobs drag on the floor and my toenails turn yellow.

Shen   And every month you have moles in new places.

Yin-Yin   Apologize to your child.

Shen   For?

Yin-Yin   Making the next six months a bore.

Shen *gets on his knees and bows three times towards* **Yin-Yin**'*s stomach.*

Shen   Forgive me.

Yin-Yin (*to stomach*)   He'll make it up to you when you're born. (*To* **Shen**.) Never interfere with my career again.

Shen   I won't. I promise.

Scene Three

Rural Henan. A traditional courtyard on the first day of the new lunar year. Sun bleached doorways are flanked with bright red New Year's couplets. A cracked plastic stool and bundles of spindly firewood lie by the door. Red confetti—debris from early morning firecrackers—is strewn across the ground.

Little Yi, *a teenager in a worn track suit, Chicago Bulls cap and fake Adidas-looking sandals has a pile of red envelopes on his lap and counts the contents—dozens of small denomination fen, jiao and yuan notes. His younger cousin,* **Pei-Pei**, *preps dirt-caked potatoes for sale. She wears hand-me-down clothes. There are holes in her shoes.*

Little Yi   It's not enough.

Pei-Pei   Be glad you got anything. Your whole family's lazy. Especially your mom.

Little Yi   At least I have one.

Pei-Pei   She's not really a mom. More like a cow that plays mahjong.

Kuan *enters from the fields, dressed in mud-caked farming attire. He carries buckets of freshly harvested potatoes. He sits on a stool and cleans dirt off potatoes with a stiff brush.*

Pei-Pei   Ba. I only have enough lucky money for one month of school. It's not enough to enroll.

Little Yi   He can't help you, rice bucket. He doesn't have a job.

Pei-Pei   Whose fault is that?

Lili *emerges from the house in a festive sweater dress and red velvet leggings. She has permed hair and wears gold jelly shoes.*

Lili   Happy New Year everyone! May your money and treasures be plentiful.

Pei-Pei   Thank you Auntie! May you continue to eat enough food.

Wen *bursts out of the house in pajama pants and flip-flops, wraps his arms around* **Lili** *and tries to lure her inside.*

Wen   You forgot to finish your bed exercises . . . .

Lili (*smacking him off her*)   Don't eat my tofu!

Wen   How about some "fried rice"?

Lili (*pointing to his hickies*)   You have strawberries all over your neck!

Wen   These babies are from the Year of the Sheep. I'm hunting for peach blossoms in the Year of the Monkey!

Wen *throws* **Lili** *over his shoulder and starts to carry her towards the bedroom.* **Old Yang** *enters the courtyard in his best clothes.*

Old Yang   May your house be filled with jade and gold!

Little Yi   Happy New Year Gong-Gong! I wish you good health and long life!

Old Yang   Little Yi! When did you get so polite?

Pei-Pei   He's not polite. He just wants your money.

Lili   Aiyah, Pei-Pei—your shoes are full of holes! You can't wear them on New Year's—your luck will run out!

Little Yi (*to* **Old Yang**)   Thank you for everything you've given me. May the Year of the Monkey bring you mountains of fortune and oceans of money.

Pei-Pei (*meaning "suck up"*)   Horse fart spirit.

Old Yang   Who wants lucky money?

Little Yi *and* **Pei-Pei** *raise their hands.* **Old Yang** *hands each a red envelope.*

Pei-Pei / Little Yi   Thank you Gong-Gong!

Old Yang   May it bring health, wealth, peace and prosperity!

Little Yi (*off contents of envelope*)   It's not enough.

Lili (*instantly enraged*)   Don't make me slap you!

Little Yi   Last year I got more.

Lili (*advancing towards* **Little Yi**)   Son of a rabbit!

Wen   No fighting on New Year's!

Little Yi   Yeah, ma! You'll beat away your good luck!

Lili   It's not good luck I'll beat—it's my insolent son!

Luo Na *and her teenage son* **Han-Han** *enter the courtyard, carrying gift bags.* **Han-Han** *wears a bright red tracksuit and red high-top sneakers. Bulky headphones hug his neck.* **Luo Na** *wears a new dress, heeled sandals and carries a fake Prada purse.*

Luo Na   The country flourishes and people live in peace.

Han-Han   May you have a stinking rich New Year, filled with expensive things!

Lili   Luo Na! Han-Han! We were expecting you tomorrow.

Luo Na   Tomorrow we're busy. Today we have time.

Wen   The two of you look like city people!

Han-Han (*handing* **Lili** *gifts*)   May you have money all year round.

Lili   This fruit must have cost a fortune! And—where did you get that purse?

Luo Na   This old thing?

Little Yi   It's not possible—it can't be possible. (*Off* **Han-Han**'*s shoes.*) Are those . . . Air Jordans?

Han-Han   The newest kind.

Little Yi   I can't look. It hurts. I'm blinded by beauty.

Han-Han   Hands off. I just conditioned them.

Luo Na   Aiyah, Lili! Old clothes on New Year's?

Lili   My stockings are new. And I've only worn these shoes once.

Wen   Happy New Year, Luo Na. You look very nice.

Luo Na   You're welcome to look. Maybe you picked the wrong wife.

Lili   Are you gambling again?

Han-Han   Ma kicked that nasty habit years ago.

Wen   What crops are you growing?

Luo Na   No one in our village wastes time on crops.

Pei-Pei   You're not farming?

Luo Na   Times have changed.

Han-Han   Why put yourself at the mercy of sunshine and rain?

Luo Na   Last year we became self-reliant. Even my lazy son turned a new leaf.

Han-Han   Everything I'm wearing I bought with my own money.

Little Yi   You have a job?

Pei-Pei   Must be black market.

Han-Han   Our business is one-hundred percent legal.

Luo Na   Let's make a deal.

Lili   A deal?

Han-Han   Ma will tell you everything she knows.

Luo Na   In exchange, anyone who uses our knowledge gives me fifty percent of their first profit.

Lili   Ten.

Luo Na   Forty.

Lili   Fifteen.

Luo Na   Thirty.

Lili   Twenty, for one-hundred percent crystal clear information. Don't waste our time with your tricks.

Luo Na   Why would I play tricks on my favorite fox spirit?

Old Yang   This woman is spicy!

Han-Han   We need to be in Lin village by lunch.

Luo Na   We have time to go over this once.

Han-Han (*dropping into their fast-paced recruitment routine*)   Our village has become a blood-selling squad.

Lili   You're selling blood?

Han-Han   It's the perfect economy.

Luo Na   A renewable resource we make with our bodies!

Lili   It's bad luck to sell your family essence.

Luo Na   When did my own sister become so old fashioned?

Han-Han   Every two weeks twenty of us take one of those motorized pedicabs to Zhengzhou.

Luo Na   We spend a night in a motel—

Han-Han   Rise at the crack of dawn—

Luo Na   And line up outside the blood station.

Han-Han   They're run by the Ministry of Health, so they're very modern and efficient.

Luo Na   You go to the registration desk—

Han-Han   Show your ID—

Luo Na   Give a few drops of blood—

Han-Han   Then wait while they test to make sure you don't have iron deficiency.

Luo Na   They call your name, you give blood—which gets split into red and yellow parts.

Han-Han   The yellow gold's what they're buying.

Wen   Yellow gold?

Luo Na   It's called "plasma."

Han-Han   The red stuff's put back, so you can sell again sooner.

Wen   Hear that, brother? There's gold in these arms.

Luo Na   When it's over, you go to the cashier, they give you fifty-three kuai—

Pei-Pei   Fifty-three kuai?!?!?!

Luo Na   —and stamp your arm with a red seal.

Little Yi   Aren't you afraid of depleting your chi?

Luo Na   You're such a bumpkin! The blood in our arms is a bottomless spring.

Han-Han   Pound rice liquor and eat a plate of fried liver.

Luo Na   You'll be good as new in a week.

Han-Han   My body has gotten so used to selling blood that if I miss a trip my arms feel heavy, like they're going to burst.

Luo Na   Our village has seventy percent participation. A year ago we were as dirty and backwards as you.

Han-Han   Now we have new houses, a movie theater and a dance hall.

Little Yi   I want to dance!

Pei-Pei   I want to watch movies!

Han-Han   Show me some moves!

Little Yi and **Han-Han** *have a mini dance off. All but* **Kuan** *clap along.*

Luo Na   Last week I became the first person in my village to own a blender.

Lili   A what?

Luo Na   You'd have to see it to believe it. We even pooled funds to build a new school!

Wen   Why waste time in gold mines if there's gold in this body? This is our opportunity to switch our crop from potatoes to peonies!

Old Yang   Peonies?

Wen   If we invest our family essence in this plan we could become the greatest flower farmers in the province, growing yellow, pink, red and white blossoms that win every ribbon at the Luoyang Peony Festival!

Pei-Pei   I could have a year's tuition in six trips!

Kuan   You shouldn't sell your life force.

Lili   Look at your daughter. Look at her clothes! Your wife must be rolling over in her grave.

Kuan   If you mention her again you'll regret it.

Pei-Pei *and* **Kuan** *exit towards the fields.*

Luo Na   Wasn't Mao's revolution supposed to wipe out old thinking?

Lili   Let's make him write a self-criticism.

Little Yi   Ma, can I sell blood?

Lili   Let's go as a family.

Little Yi   Yeah!!!!

Luo Na   The Ministry's opening a new station in Zhoukou. It cuts travel time by five hours.

Han-Han   Ma's heading to the new station next week.

Luo Na   If we take the six pm bus on Sunday we can be outside Zhoukou Blood Station by dawn Monday morning.

Old Yang   Let's spread the word.

Wen   If we recruit enough blood sellers, we can improve every life in Yang village by the Year of the Rooster!

Old Yang, **Little Yi**, **Wen**, *and* **Han-Han** *exit towards the rest of the village.*

Lili   When did my big sister turn into a pimp?

Luo Na   Think of me as a real estate agent, connecting sellers and buyers.

Lili   Are you recruiting sellers from every village?

Luo Na   We believe family should help family.

Lili   As long as you profit.

Luo Na   As long as we find situations where both sides receive benefit.

Lili   Come in. Don't be polite.

Luo Na   Let's try the apples I bought. They were flown in from Japan last week. You have never tasted anything so crisp and so sweet.

They disappear into the house.

Scene Four

A private room in a karaoke club. **Peter**, *a pharmaceutical executive in a fancy suit, serenades* **Jasmine** *with the classic Chinese song "Jasmine Flower."* **Jasmine** *wears a simple cotton dress that shows off her youthful beauty.*

Johnny, Peter*'s older brother, stands near* **Shen** *and* **Wang Wei,** *who are also in their best suits. The men are red-faced and sweaty, ties loosened, collars unbuttoned.*

Wang Wei (*toasting*)   To Chinese and American cousins enjoying Zhoukou's finest private club!

All but **Jasmine** *raise their glasses, down their drinks, then turn their glasses upside down to indicate they've been drained, a gesture of respect.*

Peter (*singing*)   "What a beautiful jasmine flower . . . ."

Wang Wei   Wah! Our mother's nephew can sing!

Peter   "What a beautiful jasmine flower. . ."

Johnny   Our father loves this song.

Peter *and* **Johnny** (*singing*)

"Fragrant blossoms kiss the air
Perfect petals everywhere. . ."

Wang Wei *stumbles over to* **Peter** *and* **Johnny,** *throws his arms around then and sings along drunkenly.* **Shen** *joins reluctantly.*

Peter *and* **Johnny** *and* **Wang Wei** *and* **Shen** (*singing*)

"Pluck one that is white and pure
Give it to one you adore. . . ."

Wang Wei (*giving microphone to* **Jasmine**)   Your turn, pretty maiden. Sing for our guests.

Jasmine (*singing*)   "What a beautiful jasmine flower. . ."

Wang Wei   A nightingale!

Jasmine (*singing*)   "What a beautiful jasmine flower. . ."

Shen (*to* **Peter**)   Are you enjoying your time in our country?

Jasmine (*singing*)   "Fragrant blossoms kiss the air. . ."

Peter   If I'm not watching folks hack loogies on the sidewalk, it's kids with split bottom pants doing "Number Two" on the street.

Johnny   Peter!

Jasmine (*singing*)   "Perfect petals everywhere. . . ."

Peter (*barreling on*)   If China's such an old civilization, why haven't you, in your thousands of years of history, wrapped your brains around basic sanitation?

Jasmine (*singing*)   "Pluck one that is white and pure. . ."

Wang Wei   The PRC is young.

Shen   We turned forty-three this year.

Jasmine (*singing*)   "Give it to one you adore."

The men applaud as **Jasmine** *finishes the song. She curtsies, beaming.*

Wang Wei (*to* **Johnny** *and* **Peter**)   You don't have women like this in your country. Next time, stay longer, and sample our "regional flavor." Bring your father too!

Peter   Ba won't come. He has nightmares about this place still.

Shen (*pointed*)   So do we.

Wang Wei   Jasmine—ask the hostess for another bottle of Scotch.

Jasmine *exits.*

Johnny   Ba's still, um—devastated about what happened to your . . .

Shen   All your father did was behave like the American he was about to become.

Wang Wei   My brother doesn't believe in abandoning his country.

Peter   Not even when the country abandons its people?

Johnny   Look . . . . it's hard for anyone to get their head around. That was the Summer of Love in California. Peace, love, understanding, all that stuff. And back here—Ba's swimming to Hong Kong and—

Shen   Our mother's wearing a sign that says "traitor's sister" and is being stoned to death by angry villagers.

Wang Wei   Family blood is thicker than the salt water that separates us.

Johnny   I'm sorry, man—for all of it. Us being here must. . .bring up a lot.

Peter   He didn't know.

Shen   Didn't know what?

Peter   Didn't know that she would—

Shen   I don't know how things work in your new country but here—the family always pays for the actions of the individual. Your father knew. He had to.

Jasmine *returns with two bottles of Scotch.*

Jasmine   Are two bottles better than one?

Wang Wei   Perfect timing!

Jasmine   They trained me well at the nursing academy.

Peter   Do you work at the Ministry?

Jasmine   I'm just helping out at my family's fruit stand. I graduated very recently.

Peter   I hear there's a new plasma station opening up under this guy's supervision. (*To* **Wang Wei**.) She'd be the prettiest nurse those farmers have ever seen.

Wang Wei (*to* **Shen**)   Have we staffed the nursing positions?

Shen   I'm about to make offers—

Wang Wei   Then it's settled!

Peter (*raising his glass in a toast*)   To Jasmine!

The Men   Jasmine!

Jasmine   To your family, in business together.

Wang Wei (*raising his glass*)   An excellent toast! And to the emerging partnership between the Henan Ministry of Health and Phoenix Pharmaceutical.

Minister Li, *the Henan Minister of Health, enters.*

Minister Li   Here, here!

Wang Wei   Minister Li!

Everyone rises to their feet. **Minister Li** *shakes hands with all the men. He ignores* **Jasmine**, *thinking she's an employee of the KTV lounge.*

Minister Li   I've been down the hall entertaining the Minister of Agriculture and want to share some good news. (*Clearing throat.*) Effective tomorrow, Henan Blood is officially an agricultural product—

Wang Wei   Which means we can export it to our friends at Phoenix Pharmaceutical. . . . .TAX FREE! Congratulations, Minister! That's just what we need!

Minister Li   It's a very good thing!

Peter   Well, Minister—Johnny and I have an early flight. Since you're here, why don't we talk business?

Minister Li   My favorite topic. (*He sits on the couch, then pats his lap and motions to* **Jasmine**.) Come here, little bird. Sit on daddy's knee.

A tense beat. No one dares contradict the most powerful man in the room. **Jasmine** *lowers herself onto* **Minister Li**'s *lap.*

Jasmine   Congratulations, Minister. You have done a remarkable thing for your country.

Minister Li (*resting a hand on her thigh*)   How are things on the American side?

Johnny   Our finance guys at Phoenix are impressed with the infrastructure you're developing and have authorized us to offer the Henan Ministry our preferred partner contract for raw plasma.

Minister Li   What an honor!

Shen   What does that entail?

Peter   That we buy from you and only you—

Minister Li   Like a good husband! You'll be faithful to us, and buy only from Henan.

Peter   And no other province.

Johnny   If you can triple your present plasma volume.

Beat.

Shen   Triple?

Minister Li   No problem. Henan has millions of farmers. All of them want to get rich.

Shen   Starting when?

Minister Li's *hands continue to subtly explore* **Jasmine**'s *body. She shifts positions so he can't get between her legs.*

Peter   In three months.

Shen   Impossible. It's too fast.

Minister Li   Wang Wei, this is your call. Can we do it?

Shen   Brother—

Minister Li   What do you think, Director? Can you carry the Ministry of Health into the future?

Wang Wei   Absolutely.

Peter   We're in business!

Johnny   We'll have our lawyers send over a contract next week.

Minister Li *rises, pushing* **Jasmine** *aside. As the men shake hands,* **Jasmine** *stands nearby, face burning, in shock and hurt by how she's been treated.*

Minister Li   Congratulations, Director. You have your work cut out for you.

Wang Wei   It will be an honor to serve the Ministry.

Minister Li *turns to* **Peter** *and* **Johnny**.

Minister Li   Shall I introduce you to Henan's finest flavors?

Johnny   I'm starving.

Shen (*to* **Johnny** *and* **Peter**)   Have a safe flight home. Give our best to your father.

Peter, **Johnny** *and* **Minister Li** *exit.* **Wang Wei** *waves until they are out of sight, then collapses onto the couch.* **Shen** *and* **Wang Wei** *are so drunk* **Jasmine** *barely registers.*

Shen   You're insane.

Wang Wei   We don't have a choice.

Shen   You could have said "no"!

Wang Wei   And end my career?

Shen   There is absolutely no way we can triple our output in three months!

Wang Wei   Don't yell, Shen-Shen. A big headache's coming.

Shen   Get up.

Wang Wei   I can't walk.

Shen   Try harder.

Wang Wei (*as* **Shen** *tries to help him up*)   I dreamed about Ma last night.

Shen   We'll take a cab.

Wang Wei   We were on a train. Sitting beside her. Holding hands. The train moved fast. We couldn't see where we were going.

Shen   Keep walking.

Wang Wei   It had one destination. King Yama's Station. I got scared. I didn't want us to go to the King of Hell's House. But the train stopped. We had to get off. (*As they exit.*) You and I saw what hell is. We lived through it. We must do whatever it takes to keep from falling back into it.

Jasmine *stands back, watching the brothers exit, then slowly exits in the same direction.*

Scene Five

Zhoukou Blood Station, morning. **Little Yi, Lili, Old Yang, Wen,** *and* **Luo Na** *squat outside a bustling urban waiting room. They all have plastic bracelets around their wrists, containing their name and blood type.*

Luo Na   If I was at a Blood Station with men from my village, they'd be in handstands against that wall.

Little Yi   To hide how ugly they are.

Luo Na   When you're upside-down blood rushes to your arms. It puts you in peak condition.

Lili   My sister thinks she has a PhD from Bloodseller's University.

Little Yi *approaches the wall, plants his hands onto the ground, attempts to kick up into a handstand, then crashes to the ground.*

Luo Na   My nephew's more ambitious than his father.

Lili   My man's an ox. He's always in peak condition.

Old Yang (*to* **Little Yi**)   One more time.

Little Yi *tries again.* **Old Yang** *catches him and holds him against the wall.*

Little Yi   Are my arms filling up?

Luo Na   Be patient. It takes the stuff in your feet a few minutes to flow to your fingers.

Jasmine, *dressed in a nurse's uniform, enters holding a clipboard.* **Little Yi** *comes out of his handstand.*

Jasmine   The Ministry of Health is ready to buy blood from Han Lili, Yang Wen, Yang Guo and Yang Yi.

Lili   You forgot my sister. Han Luo Na.

Jasmine (*checking* **Luo Na**'s *bracelet*)   Come back tomorrow. We only buy two blood types a day.

Luo Na   Other stations don't have this policy.

Jasmine   They will soon. It's more efficient.

Little Yi   Hurry up, nurse! My arms are overflowing!

Luo Na   Fine. I'll wait outside. You owe me my cut.

They start to exit, following **Jasmine**.

Little Yi   Ma, whatever I make with my blood is mine, right?

Lili   You think I'd steal from my son?

Little Yi   I think you might take a cut.

Lights come up on **Wang Wei** *sitting at a table in the employee lounge area of the blood station. He drinks a jar of tea.* **Shen** *enters.*

Shen   It's not too late to back out.

Wang Wei   There are dozens of health officials ready to replace me.

Shen   It's an impossible target.

Wang Wei   Not if we don't limit ourselves to the physical constraints of this building.

Shen   I need to get back to Human Resources. Tell Phoenix we need more time to expand.

Wang Wei   Think outside the box. Outside this building. Could we convert a line of buses and manage overflow on the street?

Shen   It'd take a year to get the right permits.

Shen *exits.*

Wang Wei (*calling after* **Shen**)   If we wait the military will monopolize the plasma business and we'll be cut out of this funding stream completely.

Yin-Yin *enters wearing a lab coat. She hands a sheet of paper to* **Wang Wei**.

Yin-Yin   Here's the purchasing request.

Wang Wei (*off paper*)   Five thousand blood bags?

Yin-Yin   We're almost out.

Wang Wei   It's a shame you can't sterilize them. (*Off another item.*) What's this?

Yin-Yin   Incineration costs for medical waste.

Wang Wei   I'll burn it myself at that price.

Jasmine *enters with a jar of tea.*

Yin-Yin   Not sanitary.

Wang Wei (*as he exits*)   Nurse Meng.

Jasmine   Nice to see you!

Wang Wei *exits.*

Yin-Yin   That uniform looks great on you.

Jasmine (*twirling playfully*)   Thank you Yin-Yin—and thank you for introducing me to your brother-in-law.

Yin-Yin   He's cute, right?

Jasmine   Doctor Zhou. Are you trying to make me a wife?

Yin-Yin   His career ambitions have kept him too busy. As soon as he's climbed one ladder, he's looking for the next. I think he'd be happier if he slowed down and made time for a family. I like how close you are to your parents. I think you'd be a good influence.

Jasmine   I'm going home in July to help with the cherry harvest. You should come visit.

Yin-Yin   How fun! I haven't climbed a tree since I was pushed out of one as a kid.

Jasmine   Poor thing! Who pushed you out of a tree?

Yin-Yin   A Red Guard.

Jasmine   For what reason?

Yin-Yin   Trying to "steal" an education.

Jasmine   From a tree?

Yin-Yin   I'd been kicked out of school because my father had been accused of being a Kuomingtang spy—which made me a "spy daughter." There was a dead oak tree behind the school. I borrowed my brother's binoculars and tried to follow lessons through the window.

Jasmine   You *were* a "spy daughter"!

Yin-Yin   They made me one. I used rope to bind the binoculars to my face, so my hands could be free to copy the characters my teacher was writing.

Jasmine (*noticing time*)   Oops! Time to get blood out of the centrifuge. Thank you again, Yin-Yin.

Yin-Yin   I had help when I was a medical student. Someday you'll help someone too.

Jasmine *exits. Lights come up on* **Little Yi**, **Lili**, **Old Yang**, *and* **Wen** *reclining in plastic lounge chairs. There is an empty IV-rack beside each of them, connected to plastic tubing taped to the inside forearm of each person.*

Wen   They should keep the red blood and pay us double.

Lili   It's only the yellow part that's worth anything.

Little Yi   Nurse Jasmine says getting our red blood back helps recovery.

Old Yang   Little Yi has a big crush.

Lili   Next time drink more wine. It'll thin your blood and make it flow faster.

Little Yi   Why would I do that if slow moving blood gives my future wife a reason to massage and caress me?

Wen   You're hopeless.

Little Yi   Next time I'm bringing her peonies. White, to match her uniform.

Lili   Stupid egg. White's the color of death. She'll think you're planning her funeral.

Little Yi   Red then, to symbolize the blood she stroked out of my body.

Jasmine *enters, pushing a medical cart filled with blood bags containing red blood cells.*

Jasmine   Did you travel a long way to get here?

Little Yi   Nine hours.

Jasmine   You poor things. That's such a long trip.

Lili   We're lucky the bus station's an easy walk from our village.

Jasmine *methodically connects blood bags to the IV-racks, and checks to make sure the blood is flowing back into their arms.*

Little Yi   What is it for?

Jasmine   Plasma has many uses.

Little Yi   Like?

Jasmine   Medicine, and makeup.

Little Yi   Makeup?

Jasmine   Things that need a creamy base, like lipstick and foundation.

Little Yi   Are you wearing blood makeup?

Jasmine   Lie back and relax while your red blood cells return to your arm.

Little Yi   Don't you need to massage it?

Jasmine   Are you in a rush?

Little Yi   Nurse Jasmine, my red blood cells look scared. They're not used to being out of me. You have special training. If you encouraged them they'd stop being afraid and start running back to my body.

Jasmine   You're cute.

Jasmine *exits.*

Little Yi   SHE THINKS I'M CUTE!

Lili   I didn't know my son was such a sweet talker.

Old Yang   He takes after his grandfather.

Little Yi   I'm going to marry that nurse and live with her in the mountains and violate the one-child policy thirty times! We'll have thirty-one kids who each have thirty-one pairs of Air Jordans and—(*He pauses to catch his breath and rub his eyes.*) Live in a mansion with—

Wen   Don't make yourself dizzy.

Little Yi   Are the lights off?

Old Yang   When your blood is back in we'll eat more liver and drink rice liquor and you'll be good as new.

Little Yi   I can't see.

Wen   What?

Little Yi   Are my eyes closed?

Wen   No—

Little Yi   Why can't I see

Wen   Your eyes are open you're looking at me—

Little Yi   Why can't I see you why is it black?

Wen   Why can't he see me?

Little Yi *passes out.*

Lili   Nurse! NURSE!

Wen   Little Yi—Little Yi, wake up!

Yin-Yin *and* **Jasmine** *hurry in.* **Yin-Yin** *checks* **Little Yi***'s vital signs.*

Lili   What's wrong with my son?

Yin-Yin   His pulse is weak.

Jasmine   He was fine a minute ago.

Lili   Save my son. Please. Save my son!

Yin-Yin *checks* **Little Yi***'s hospital bracelet and blood bag, then immediately disconnects it from the IV drip running into his arm.*

Yin-Yin   Get five bags of B plasma. Run!

Jasmine *exits.* **Yin-Yin** *checks bracelets and blood bags.* **Wang Wei** *enters.*

Wen   What's happening to him?

Lili   What did she do?

Yin-Yin   Get the family out.

Jasmine *returns with the plasma bags.*

Lili   What did you do to my boy?

Yin-Yin *(demonstrating, to* **Jasmine***)*   You check the blood-type on the bag, you check the blood-type on the bracelet, you make sure they match—

Wang Wei   He got the wrong blood?

Jasmine   I'm so sorry.

Lili   Witch! Evil Fox Spirit!

Wang Wei   Let's give the doctor some room.

Wang Wei *ushers* **Wen***,* **Old Yang***, and* **Lili** *into the next room.*

Jasmine   I'm so sorry.

Yin-Yin   How could you be so careless?

Jasmine   After I divided the AB blood back into the blood bags I forgot there was B blood in the other machine.

Yin-Yin   Divided the AB blood?

Jasmine   After it was combined for the centrifuge.

Yin-Yin   Why was it mixed in the centrifuge?

Jasmine   We only have two.

Yin-Yin   When we put red blood cells back into the seller it is crucial that person only gets their own blood back—only their own blood! *(A beat, as she realizes.)* We have to shut down this station.

Jasmine   I'm sorry, Yin-Yin. I was following the protocol.

Yin-Yin   Who told you to mix blood?

Wang Wei *enters.* **Jasmine** *motions meaningfully towards him, answering* **Yin-Yin***'s question.*

Wang Wei   That auntie of his is quite the negotiator. I had to offer the family five thousand before she'd stop screaming.

Yin-Yin (*handing* **Jasmine** *blood bag she disconnected*)   Bring this to the incinerator.

Jasmine *exits.*

Wang Wei   We'll fire that farm girl and get somebody who knows what she's doing.

Yin-Yin (*after a beat*)   Why are you mixing blood in the centrifuge?

Wang Wei   It's more efficient.

Yin-Yin   If one person has a blood disease, you will infect the other sellers when you combine their whole blood in the centrifuge, then put the red blood cells of multiple sellers back into each person's body.

Wang Wei   We don't need to worry about those things. Henan blood is farmer's blood and farmer's blood is clean.

Yin-Yin   I came from a Hepatitis Lab. It's not clean.

Wang Wei   Ministry of Health stations across the province follow the same protocol.

Yin-Yin   That's terrifying. They're doing it wrong. Shut down the plasma stations.

Wang Wei   Shut them down?

Yin-Yin   Until you fix the centrifuge protocols and add Hepatitis screening to the blood tests.

Wang Wei   That's out of my control.

Yin-Yin   This is serious. If you need me to report it directly to the Director of Infectious Disease I can—

Wang Wei   I'll take care of it. Right away. Thank you, Yin-Yin. You did good work today.

Yin-Yin *exits.* **Wang Wei** *gently checks* **Little Yi***'s vital signs, then sits beside him, lost in thought.* **Jasmine** *enters.*

Jasmine   Director?

Wang Wei   (–)

Jasmine   Sorry to trouble you.

Wang Wei   What do you want?

Jasmine   How's Little Yi?

Wang Wei   Stabilized. No thanks to you.

Jasmine   Why don't you go home? It's so late. Let me monitor him.

Wang Wei   I wish I could. But I don't have a reliable nurse.

Jasmine   I will never make that mistake again.

Wang Wei   That's for sure.

Jasmine   You have my word.

Wang Wei   I don't need it. You're fired.

Jasmine   Please, let me explain—

Wang Wei   What if he died and there were riots outside the station? We can't have more chaos. We must develop peacefully, through business—it's the only way to stay out of the abyss. You're too young to know about it. You don't understand—

Jasmine slaps her cheek, punishing herself.

Wang Wei   What are you doing?

She slaps herself again, across the other cheek.

Jasmine   I'm so stupid.

She slaps herself again and again. **Wang Wei** *moves towards her, restraining her.* **Jasmine** *breaks away from him. A spark.*

Jasmine   I stayed up all night thinking about your problem. That's why I didn't sleep.

Wang Wei   My problem?

Jasmine   Tripling your output.

Wang Wei   That's not your concern.

Jasmine   I found a solution.

Wang Wei   You're dreaming.

Jasmine   I was so grateful for this opportunity. I wanted to distinguish myself. With good ideas. From the very beginning.

Wang Wei   What does a pretty farm thing know about the plasma economy?

Jasmine *hardens. She looks directly at* **Wang Wei** *. His dismissiveness emboldens her.*

Jasmine   My brother drives a refrigerated truck.

Wang Wei   Leave now.

Jasmine   It's a long distance route. He delivers ice to rural areas all over the province, and comes home once a month to rest, restock and visit our parents. When he arrives in Zhoukou, the truck is empty.

Wang Wei   Leave my—

Jasmine *puts a finger on his lips.*

Jasmine   It's a very big truck. Large enough to hold ten times your present volume.

Wang Wei   (–)

Jasmine   Maybe someone can help you set up rural blood stations along his existing route.

Wang Wei   We don't have the staff.

Jasmine   Maybe someone can help you train villagers.

Wang Wei   Peasants?

Jasmine   Most have experience giving injections to farm animals. Is human blood different?

Wang Wei   Can they run a business?

Jasmine   The accounting is simple math. I'm from the countryside. I know how they think.

Jasmine *moves even closer to* **Wang Wei**, *adding her own flesh and blood capital to the proposed collaboration.*

Jasmine   With your brains and my connections we could make a powerful team.

Wang Wei (*singing*)

"What a beautiful jasmine flower
What a beautiful jasmine flower. . . ."

Jasmine (*singing*)

"Fragrant blossoms kiss the air
Perfect petals everywhere
Pluck one that is white and pure
Give it to one you adore. . . . ."

Wang Wei *pulls* **Jasmine** *on top of him and fumbles with his pants.*

Scene Six

Urban apartment, afternoon. **Yin-Yin**, *eight months pregnant, is on the couch.* **Shen** *is beside her, massaging her feet.*

Yin-Yin (*off his foot massage*)   Ow ow ow that spot shot deep up my jaw!

Shen (*pushing it again*)   This spot?

Yin-Yin *yelps and smacks him.*

Shen   It's the tender spots that you're supposed to dig into hardest.

Yin-Yin *grabs* **Shen**'s *hand and digs her thumb into the pressure point between* **Shen**'s *thumb and index finger.*

Shen   OWWWW!

Yin-Yin   Tender? Hmmm. Shall I press harder?

Shen   Don't make me push a pregnant woman off our couch.

Yin-Yin   Like you'd brain damage your child.

Shen   Just a little. Smart kids are a pain.

Yin-Yin   That's sweet. You think it will take after me.

Shen *responds by digging harder into* **Yin-Yin**'*s foot. She shrieks and pulls her feet away.*

Yin-Yin   That's it. My feet are off limits.

Loud knock. **Shen** *answers the door.*

Shen   Wang Wei. Have you eaten?

Wang Wei *storms into the apartment.*

Wang Wei   True or false: Weasels don't mate outside their species. True or False?!

Shen   Biologically, that's true.

Wang Wei   If my brother's wife is a weasel, and weasels don't mate outside their species, by the law of nature should I conclude my own brother is a weasel too?

Shen   Why are we weasels?

Wang Wei *thrusts a report into* **Shen**'*s hands.*

Shen   What's this?

Wang Wei   A report written by your own weasel wife! A report she wrote without my permission! Going over my head!

Yin-Yin   When I reported the contamination to you nothing happened.

Shen   Contamination?

Yin-Yin   The plasma stations are vectors for Hepatitis C.

Wang Wei   When you have a hammer everything looks like a nail.

Yin-Yin   Your position has corrupted you.

Shen   Who received this report?

Yin-Yin   The Director of Infectious Disease, the Director of Epidemic Prevention, the Vice Minister—

Wang Wei   Are you trying to destroy me?

Yin-Yin   Has sitting behind a desk made you forget your medical training?

Wang Wei   Officials from the main office did an end-to-end inspection of the building. Every plasma collection station in the province has been ordered to add a Hepatitis test to the blood screening—

Yin-Yin   Finally.

Wang Wei   Starting in one year.

Yin-Yin   A year? Do they know how many people they can infect in that time? This doesn't stop at Hepatitis. If you don't fix this, AIDS will come.

Wang Wei   AIDS? (*To* Shen.) Your wife is hysterical.

Yin-Yin   AIDS will come.

Wang Wei (*to* Shen)   Please let her know her assistance is no longer needed.

Yin-Yin   At a job I didn't even want in the first place. A job I only took because both of you guilt tripped me into it. I'm glad I took it. I am exactly what you needed.

Shen   Slow down.

Wang Wei   We need progress! We need social stability.

Shen   Yin-Yin set up the lab. Give her time to train someone else.

Wang Wei   That won't be necessary. The position has been filled internally.

Shen   Internally?

Wang Wei   I'm sure Infectious Disease will be glad to have her back.

Shen   Filled internally? By who?

Wang Wei *goes to the front door and opens it.* **Jasmine** *enters the department.*

Wang Wei   Meet Vice Director Meng. Our new rural outreach specialist.

Jasmine   Sorry to trouble you.

Yin-Yin   You're an enemy of the people.

Shen   Let me handle this.

Yin-Yin   They're committing crimes against humanity! Jasmine, be reasonable. You can't be Vice Director, you don't have the right training!

Jasmine   My boss disagrees.

Shen   Let's do a county-wide search. Of course Jasmine can apply, but—

Wang Wei   I've made my decision. Be careful, little brother. We both know the dangers of being related to traitors.

Wang Wei *and* **Jasmine** *exit.*

Yin-Yin   We have to report this. He's cracked, it's too much pressure. You have to do something.

Shen   Why do you care more about strangers than your own family?

Yin-Yin   Did you hear what I said?

Shen   Do you recall what happened to you—and your mother—and your poor brothers—because your father fought for the wrong army?

Yin-Yin   The Kuomingtang army also taught my mother medicine she used to save lives.

Shen   Why were you kicked out of elementary school? Why can't your second brother walk? Why did your first brother die in a labor camp? Why did Red Guards put your parents in dunce caps on stage in front of thousands of villagers and try to make their nine-year-old daughter denounce them?

Yin-Yin   Because people forgot how to think for themselves.

Shen   If you don't stop we will suffer.

Yin-Yin   This will affect urban residents too. If the blood supply is contaminated, you could contract a blood disease during a routine transfusion.

Shen   There's a right and wrong way to raise questions. There's a right and wrong way to take action.

Yin-Yin   Do you want our child to have access to clean blood?

Shen   I want our child to have a mother.

Yin-Yin *gets ready to leave the house.*

Shen   Where are you going?

Yin-Yin   Back to Infectious Disease.

Shen   You're about to give birth.

Yin-Yin   I didn't choose this path. I wanted to be an eye doctor. But the government said no. There's a Hepatitis epidemic. You will be an infectious disease specialist. The Ministry of Health chose my career. The Ministry of Health wants me to prevent epidemics. To do that right, I need to monitor the blood supply.

Shen   Yin-Yin, I'm begging you—

Yin-Yin   If they're not looking for AIDS, they won't find it.

Shen   It's not just about you.

Yin-Yin   That's exactly right. It isn't.

Yin-Yin *storms out of the apartment. The front door slams shut.*

Scene Seven

Rural courtyard. Sunset. **Wen** *and* **Old Yang** *carry a table covered with gold sequined cloth into the center of the courtyard.*

The table is decorated with gold-hued bobble-head Buddhas. In pride of place are a brand new blender and karaoke machine. Both have price tags and store labels on them.

Strands of unlit string lights surround the new machines. The power cords for the blender, string lights and karaoke machine all connect to a power-strip whose extension cord snakes into the house.

Lili *follows carrying a tray of smoothie ingredients—ripe bananas, white sesame seeds, powdered milk, and bottled water.*

Old Yang   Where's the guest of honor?

Wen   In the house getting dressed.

Lili   That boy is too vain.

Wen   He bought a lot of new clothes in the city.

Lili   He bought too many choices! You men make the music work. I'll whip up something tasty in my new BLENDER!

As **Old Yang** *and* **Wen** *scrutinize the user manuals for the karaoke machine,* **Lili** *peels bananas and puts them into the blender.* **Luo Na** *and* **Han-Han** *approach from the road.*

Luo Na   Sorry we're late!

Old Yang   You're not late. Little Yi hasn't even shown his face.

Luo Na *pushes* **Han-Han** *towards the men puzzling over the manual. She hovers over* **Lili** *and the blender.*

Luo Na   Add the powdered milk.

Lili   How?

Luo Na (*sarcastic*)   With your foot.

Lili   I don't want it to clump.

Luo Na   That's the beauty of a blender.

Lili   I'll sprinkle it just in case. What about the sesame seeds—should I grind them first?

Luo Na   Why buy a machine if you're doing the work?

Lili *adds sesame seeds to the blender.* **Old Yang** *examines the karaoke system manual.* **Pei-Pei** *and* **Kuan** *enter with buckets of dirt-caked potatoes balanced over their shoulders on a central bamboo pole. They sit and start cleaning them.*

Wen   We hooked everything together.

Han-Han (*off karaoke machine*)   Try again.

Old Yang (*trying karaoke switch*)   It's broken.

Han-Han   It works in my village.

Luo Na   Cover it with water.

Lili   Who wants a smoothie? It's good for your blood!

Luo Na   Idiot! You have to blend it!

Lili (*flicks switch, nothing happens*)   Piece of shit.

Little Yi (*offstage, inside house*)   Are you ready?

Wen   Hold on!

Lili   Give me my money back.

Luo Na   I didn't sell you this junk.

Lili   It wasn't "junk" when you told me to buy it.

Pei-Pei *crawls under the table.*

Lili   Pei-Pei! Get out of there!

Pei-Pei *flicks the power strip under the table "ON." The string lights, karaoke machine, and blender start working.* **Lili** *squeals with delight. The song on the karaoke machine is the tune to the 1930s ballad "Kangding Love Song."*

Luo Na (*to* **Han-Han**)   Your skinny cousin is smarter than you.

Han-Han   Technically we're not related.

Luo Na   Good thinking. Make your move.

Wen (*singing into microphone, to* **Lili**)

"High above on the mountain side
Floats a cloud so white
There lies peaceful Kangding town
Bathed in silver moonlight"

All But Kuan (*singing*)   "Moonlight shines bright over Kangding town, oh. . . ."

Old Yang *grabs the microphone from* **Wen** *and croons the next section to* **Luo Na.**

Old Yang (*singing*)

"Lovely maid with a smile so sweet
Li the woodcutter's daughter
Geng the blacksmith's eldest son
Came through moonlight to court her. . ."

All But Kuan (*singing*)   "Moonlight shines bright over Kangdingtown, oh..."

Han-Han *grabs the microphone and improvises a verse for* **Pei-Pei.**

Han-Han (*singing*)

"Dirty girl from the Yang clan
I can't help but love you
You'd be better off with me
Cleaning and cooking me good food. . . ."

Pei-Pei   Go die in the street.

Lili (*to* **Old Yang**)   Drink this, it's good for your blood. (*To* **Wen**.) Try my first smoothie. Not bad, right?

Wen (*after he tries it*)   I'm not sure. I better sample some more.

Little Yi (*offstage, inside house*)   Ba!

Wen *makes a karaoke selection. Music shifts to a karaoke version of an American song from the Eighties—something upbeat, like Paula Abdul's "Straight Up" or Michael Jackson's "Bad."*

Wen (*into microphone*)   Hello everyone. Thank you for supporting Little Yi. This has been a challenging season. A weaker guy might have died. But he persevered— because that's what the Yang family does. We fight together—for a better life. For all of us.

Little Yi (*offstage, inside house*)   HURRY UP!

Wen   We fight for our ancestors. We fight for the great-great-great-great-great—

Little Yi   Han-Han!

Wen   —grandchildren we'll never—

Han-Han   I got you!

Han-Han *turns the music up, drowning out the microphone.* **Little Yi** *bursts out of the house, dressed to the nines in a brand new tracksuit, gel-spiked hair and—the piece de resistance, revealed when he rips off his baggy, breakaway pants in one flourish—bright red AIR JORDANS!*

All But **Kuan** *clap along as* **Little Yi** *executes a celebratory breakdance designed to showcase his new shoes.*

Wen *changes the music to a soft, brooding love song and hands* **Little Yi** *the microphone.* **Little Yi** *bows, then speaks into the microphone.*

Little Yi   Last season I was a kid. All I cared about was making sure Ma cooked enough noodles. Now that life's made me a man, I'm going to be less selfish and take care of my family. Ma, Ba, Gong-Gong—no matter how old and boring you get, you will have a home with me. Even when you smell like piss and need to wear diapers, I will find a responsible maid to take care of you.

Luo Na   Such a good boy.

Little Yi (*into microphone*)   Han-Han, you taught me to be self-sufficient and not compromise my taste in quality footwear.

Han-Han   Don't forget to condition them.

Little Yi (*into microphone*)   Auntie, I thought I was going to make 53 kuai, but because you wouldn't let city people take advantage of me, I have one-hundred times that much. If either of you ever need a loan, I promise to give you a low rate.

Lili   Change the music! I want to dance!

Little Yi (*into microphone*)   Finally, I want to say something to my cousin Pei-Pei.

Luo Na   Isn't he thoughtful?

Little Yi (*into microphone*)   You lost your mom, you're weak, flat-chested, and you won't inherit any property. Your only hope is education. Until you look old enough to sell blood, I'll help you get it.

Little Yi *takes 300 kuai in ten-yuan notes out of his pocket and fans it out to reveal the huge-to-them wad of cash he's holding.*

Little Yi (*into microphone*)   Study hard and make sure I get good value for my money.

Pei-Pei (*as she reaches for the money*)   Thank you—!

Kuan (*stopping her*)   We're not beggars.

Pei-Pei   I'll pay him back.

Kuan   A father should provide for his child.

Pei-Pei   Then why don't you?

Pei-Pei *stalks off, upset.*

Old Yang   Pei-Pei! Come back!

Kuan   You shouldn't sell your life force.

Old Yang   During the famine, when you and your brother were so weak you couldn't get out of bed, I disappeared for a week and returned with food. I told your mother I'd borrowed the cash from a distant uncle. I didn't. I sold blood. Every month for two years. It's why you didn't starve. Whether you lose it to work in dark mines, assembly lines or endless years in the fields, selling life force is what a parent does for his children.

Kuan   Blood is sacred. It's different than work.

Han-Han   It's easier than work.

Luo Na   All you have to do is rest and your body will make more while you sleep.

Wen   Deng Xiaoping is helping the whole country get rich. Pei-Pei is a bright girl. Shouldn't we help her have a shot at something better?

Luo Na   I think your brother-in-law's scared of needles.

Lili   Your wife would want you to do it. Be a man. Take care of your family.

Wen   Lili.

Lili   She'd be ashamed of what he's become. Doesn't her ghost deserve to be happy?

Little Yi   NURSE JASMINE?!?!

Jasmine, *dressed elegantly, enters from the road, pulling a red suitcase.*

Jasmine   Little Yi. I'm so happy to see you.

Little Yi   Ma! The pretty nurse came to see me!

Lili   The nurse who almost killed you!

Jasmine   That's why I'm here.

Luo Na   To finish him off?

Lili   How dare you show your face here!

Jasmine   I made a terrible mistake.

Luo Na   You're lucky you live today. In the old days you'd be executed.

Jasmine *starts to cry.*

Jasmine   You're right. I deserve to be executed.

Lili   We'll settle for you getting the fuck out of our village.

Little Yi   Ma, stop! Don't make the pretty nurse cry. I got paid, didn't I? More than everyone makes in a year.

Lili   She's an educated person. Isn't that why we sold blood in the city? Who can we trust if educated people don't know what they're doing?

Jasmine (*still crying*)   I'm so sorry.

Lili   She should be crying! She made me so scared my soul jumped out of my body.

Jasmine *drops to her knees.*

Jasmine   No parent should experience what you did. All you wanted to do was improve your life. Instead I almost destroyed it. Forgive me.

Jasmine *bows deeply. The family is stunned.*

Wen   Get up. Don't get your nice city clothes dirty.

Old Yang   Little Yi. Get a chair for the nurse.

*As **Little Yi** gets a chair **Wen** and **Old Yang** help **Jasmine** to her feet. **Lili** hangs back and watches them sullenly.*

Jasmine   I'm sorry. I shouldn't have come.

Wen   Stay. You've travelled a long way.

Old Yang   Sit. Join us for dinner.

Jasmine   I really can't. I need to reach Wong Village before nightfall.

Luo Na   Wong Village is dirty and backwards. What are you doing there?

Jasmine   They're tired of making the long trip to the city and want to set up a plasma station in one of their grain houses.

Luo Na   A local blood station?

Jasmine   My brother drives a long-distance truck route through this area. He's going to stop at Wong Village once a month to collect plasma, and deliver it to me in the city.

Lili   What's their cut?

Jasmine   Villagers buy plasma for forty kuai, then sell it to me for forty-five.

Han-Han   Five kuai profit per customer?!

Jasmine   Wong Villagers are smart. They saved enough funds to make a capital investment in our partnership.

Little Yi   A capital investment?

Jasmine   Start-up money, to buy a freezer to store the plasma and pay the first rounds of blood-sellers.

Little Yi   How much do they have?

Jasmine   A few thousand. It's more than enough.

Han-Han   What about the equipment?

Jasmine (*motions to the red suitcase*)   The tubing, needles, blood bags and gauze are in here. All they need now is the centrifuge.

Luo Na (*to* **Kuan**)   That separates the red and yellow blood.

Jasmine   My brother's delivering one to Wong Village in the morning. (*Moving to leave.*) I wish you all good health and a long life.

Luo Na (*to* **Jasmine**)   Wong villagers are idiots.

Lili   They can't make rice without burning it.

Little Yi   Forget those Wong Villagers.

Han-Han   Forget them.

Little Yi   Do business with us.

Wen   My Ba's good with numbers. He can keep track of money very easily.

Jasmine   Little Yi. This is a big investment. Are you sure?

Little Yi   I am a man who means what he says—and I say yes.

Jasmine   I'll give my brother a new address for tomorrow's delivery.

Kuan   When will the station be ready?

Jasmine   You can be up and running in two weeks.

Kuan (*to* **Little Yi**)   Don't give Pei-Pei your money. I'll send her to school in eight weeks.

Little Yi   Uncle, you can have the honor of being my first customer.

Han-Han   I'll be your second!

Kuan *downs a cup of blood-building smoothie and exits towards the fields.* **Wen** *puts "Kangding Love Song" back on the karaoke machine.*

Wen (*to* **Lili**)   May I have this dance?

Lili   If you think you can keep up.

Jasmine *offers* **Little Yi** *her hand.*

Little Yi   You're so pretty!

Luo Na *grabs* **Old Yang**. **Han-Han** *dances around them.*

All (*singing*)

> "He fell in love with her smile so sweet
> And her pleasing ways, oh
> She could cook, sew and care for him
> For the rest of his days, oh. . . .
> Moonlight shines bright
> Over Kangding Town oh. . . ."

They dance and sing, illuminated by blinking string lights as the sky turns red.

End of Act One.

Intermission.

Act Two

Scene One

Rural Highway. April 1998. Six years later. **Lili, Wen, Little Yi, Kuan,** *and* **Old Yang** *walk along the side of the road. Each has a basket strapped to their back that overflows with bunches of red, white and yellow peonies. The family walks as a single unit, boisterous and upbeat, faces rosy from crisp spring air.*

Lili (*singing*)

"I fell in love with his smile so sweet
And his pleasing ways oh
So I cook, sew and care for him
For the rest of his days oh"

Wen   I'm a lucky man.

Whole Family (*singing*)

"Moonlight shines bright
Over Kangding town ohh"

Wen   More like sunlight and good fortune!

Kuan   Don't get your hopes up.

Old Yang   This is our first peony festival. We've been waiting six years for this moment. Just making it there's an achievement.

Wen   Speak for yourself. These beauties deserve the blue ribbon!

Little Yi   I'm tired.

Lili   We're almost there. We'll get a breadbox van at the bus station that will take us straight to the fair.

Kuan   Maybe in a few seasons our yellow maidens will have a shot at a ribbon.

Lili   My money's on our red girls. Nothing in the world's more perfect than their petals.

Little Yi   Last week I caught Ma with her face buried in them.

Old Yang (*ribbing* **Wen**)   You have competition!

Lili   He knows I won't fry his rice unless he surrounds our mattress with peonies.

Wen   She saw a picture in one of those lady-magazines of pink blossoms floating in bowls of fresh water.

Lili   And I thought, fuck those city bitches, a country woman should enjoy her crop and not just pack them up for rich people's enjoyment.

Wen   Every night Little Yi puts a peony blossom in each sneaker before going to sleep.

Little Yi   It keeps shoes from smelling like feet.

Lili   Now figure out how to store one under each armpit.

The sound of a large truck approaching.

Wen   Stay off the road. No one's allowed to get hit.

Old Yang   There was a report in the paper about a guy in Zhou Village. A few months ago he got hit by one of those gravel trucks.

Lili   His poor family.

Old Yang   They sued the gravel company for his death and got ninety thousand in compensation.

Wen   Wah. Ninety thousand?

Little Yi   How much could I make if I got hit a little bit but not killed?

Lili   Don't get hit, baby. Your ma's having a good year.

A very sick woman enters from the opposite direction. She uses two canes to walk and is wrapped in many layers.

Little Yi   That beggar looks sick.

Old Yang   She must have the Fever that's going around other villages.

Lili   Let's cross. She might be contagious.

Wen   I think that's your sister.

Lili   Don't be stupid. Luo Na thinks we're all hicks. There's no way she'd come by—blood pimping made her head big.

Wen   It's your job to visit. You're the younger sister.

Lili   Why would I visit when all she does is judge us and criticize? She thinks we're idiots to quit blood buying and do flowers full time.

*The very sick woman approaches. It is **Luo Na**, afflicted with untreated full blown AIDS. Her face and neck have lesions on them.*

Little Yi   Auntie?

Lili   Stay back. The Fever wiped out half a village last winter.

Little Yi   Her face is covered in spots.

Wen   Luo Na—is that you?

Luo Na *wobbles a bit, steadies herself on her cane, then takes in* **Little Yi.**

Luo Na   Han-Han. Give your ma a kiss.

Lili   Stay away from my son.

Luo Na   The road to the King of Hell's house is forty-nine days long. It's easy to get lost.

Little Yi   Is Han-Han dead?

Old Yang   The fever must have got him.

Luo Na   Your ma will join you very soon. Remember this face. I'll look for you.

Luo Na *falls to her knees and coughs blood onto her hands and face. She lies on her back and stares at the sky.* **Little Yi**, **Lili**, *and* **Old Yang** *keep their distance.*

Luo Na   Soon we will be in a room made of salt. King Song, who rules the third court, will give us the tortures meant for those who injure people and practice medicine without the right training.

Little Yi   A room made of salt?

Luo Na   Our ribs will be pierced with rusted nails, our faces cut with copper knives. He'll pull out our eyes and scrape fat from our bodies. His demons will carry us to the Home Gazing Terrace to see all the family we have left in this world, but there will only be empty rooms.

Little Yi   Why?

Lili   She's talking nonsense.

Little Yi   Why are the rooms empty?

Luo Na   Blood sellers get erased from the Book of the Living.

Lili   Blood sellers?

Old Yang   Is the Fever divine punishment for selling family essence?

Little Yi   Look, Ma. Gong-Gong has those same spots on his arms.

Lili   Those are moles.

Little Yi   What about the spot on my neck?

Lili   You've had that since the day you came out of this body.

Luo Na   Wait for me, Han-Han. Your Mama is coming.

Luo Na *is still.* **Old Yang** *pulls a white peony blossom out of a basket and lays it on* **Luo Na***'s chest.*

Scene Two

Urban apartment. The living room is set up for a birthday party for a six year old girl. There are streamers and balloons with a festive "6" on them. **Shen** *is tidying and sweeping the floor.*

Shen   Yin-Yin?

Yin-Yin, *offstage, hums tune to Happy Birthday song.*

Shen   What are you doing in the kitchen

Yin-Yin (*offstage; muffled, mouth full*)   I'm not doing anything. (*Continues to hum song.*)

Shen   I hope that includes not eating the lamb meatballs I spent all morning preparing.

Yin-Yin (*muffled, mouth full*)   How dare you accuse me of taking food from our guests.

Shen   Bring out the cake.

Yin-Yin *enters from the kitchen, still chewing. She holds a plate containing a birthday cake.*

Shen (*sarcastic*)   Such a good hostess.

Yin-Yin   This morning Lan-Lan asked what the significance of a birthday was. I told her it meant she's a year closer to taking care of me.

Shen   A daughter is not a retirement strategy.

Yin-Yin   That's what a husband's for.

Shen   What would you do without a lab to escape to?

Yin-Yin   That reminds me—the Ministry approved my conference request! I got the visa! And they paid for the plane ticket!

Shen   Only you could get this excited about a Center for Disease Control conference.

Yin-Yin   Do you think it will be in the White House?!

Shen   That would be like having a Hepatitis conference in the Summer Palace.

Yin-Yin   It's a pressing public issue.

Shen   How long will I be a single parent?

Yin-Yin   One week. Can you handle it?

Shen   If you can you handle being kind to my brother and his wife for a few hours.

Yin-Yin   I won't hit them. How's that?

Shen   Better than you treat me.

Yin-Yin   Their kid's boring. He can't even talk.

Shen   He's six months old. You can't hold that against him.

Yin-Yin   Our daughter was never so dull.

Shen They might be here before I'm back with Lan-Lan—if they are, just—read some kid stories and sing songs to their son.

Yin-Yin It'll be fine. I'll pretend I've been lobotomized.

Shen Brilliant plan.

Shen *exits through the front door.* **Yin-Yin** *continues setting up for the party. After a moment, there's a knock on the door.*

Yin-Yin Come in! Don't be polite!

Yin-Yin *exits to the kitchen.* **Ruzhen**, *a Ministry of Health lab technician, enters the apartment. She's in a white lab coat, and carries a styrofoam cooler.* **Yin-Yin** *enters.*

Yin-Yin Ruzhen?

Ruzhen I ran here straight from the lab.

Yin-Yin Is something wrong?

Ruzhen Is anyone else here?

Yin-Yin Just me.

Ruzhen I finished your study.

Yin-Yin We're running dozens.

Ruzhen The one the Director of Infectious Disease doesn't know that you're doing. Sixty-two.

Yin-Yin Sixty-two—?

Ruzhen Of the 408 samples you collected last month from area blood stations and hospitals tested positive for HIV.

Yin-Yin Are you sure?

Ruzhen *hands* **Yin-Yin** *the cooler.*

Yin-Yin What's this?

Ruzhen They can't be in the lab.

Yin-Yin Are these—

Ruzhen The sixty-two positive samples.

Yin-Yin We're about to sing songs and eat cake!

Ruzhen They'll be fine through the night. I used extra dry ice.

Yin-Yin This is—a bomb. This is a bomb. You brought a bomb to my house.

Ruzhen This is evidence.

Yin-Yin It's not a good time for my family. It took so long for everyone to start talking again—

Ruzhen   What do you think will happen if business-types learn of your study? Your brother-in-law's about to launch the Ministry's new blood products company.

Yin-Yin   You're right. Of course. We don't have a choice.

Ruzhen   What's the right course of action?

Yin-Yin   Let's see. . . .officially there's no AIDS in the country. Test-kits we use only confirm results to ninety-eight percent accuracy. We need to confirm our results to one-hundred percent accuracy before we write about our findings.

Ruzhen   We don't have that technology.

Yin-Yin   Not locally. Our options are test centers in Shanghai and Beijing.

Ruzhen   Can we ship them our samples?

Yin-Yin   We can't risk them disappearing. I'll refund your train ticket. (*Tries to return the cooler.*) Take these to the Virology Institute in Beijing. If you leave now you can be back tomorrow evening

Ruzhen *backs away.*

Ruzhen   I'm sorry Dr. Zhou. My family's suffered too much already.

Yin-Yin   I understand.

Yin-Yin *stares at the cooler.*

Yin-Yin   It's not a bomb.

Ruzhen   Just the blood of sixty-two farmers.

Yin-Yin   Sleeping in glass. Inside a styrofoam house.

Ruzhen *exits.* **Yin-Yin** *picks up the cooler, considers it, then takes it to the kitchen.*

Scene Three

A private room in a karaoke lounge, day. **Shen, Wang Wei,** *and* **Jasmine** *are seated on a couch.* **Peter** *and* **Johnny** *enter.* **Shen, Jasmine,** *and* **Wang Wei** *rise to greet them.*

Wang Wei   Johnny. Peter. Welcome back to Henan!

Peter   Good to see you. Our father sends his best.

Wang Wei   Give him our regards.

Johnny   He would have loved to sing karaoke with his nephews. He has a big set-up in his living room back home.

Jasmine   We'll just have to visit him in Orange County and sing with him there—

Wang Wei   After a lot of drinking.

They laugh.

Peter   I'm sorry we had to meet so early. The ambiance isn't the same.

Johnny   Too much light. No place to hide.

Wang Wei   Before we begin, some happy news: Jasmine's taking over my position as Director of our Plasma Collection Station.

Peter   Congratulations! What's next for you?

Wang Wei   I'll let our new Director give you the update. Jasmine?

Jasmine (*as they are seated*)   Let's start with some context. Henan's plasma collection volume increased exponentially over the last six years, driven by the accelerated establishment of new plasma stations in rural areas.

Peter   Your growth rate is astonishing.

Jasmine   If Henan was a country we'd be fourteenth largest in terms of population. On the basis of volume potential alone we are positioned to become a leader in the global blood industry marketplace.

Johnny   The price of blood products keeps rising. The peak retail price of fibrinogen and human coagulation factor eight rose fifty percent last year.

Jasmine   The Henan Ministry of Health intends to take full advantage of this fact. Because of continued national policy support and current high market prosperity, we plan to open thirty new plasma stations next year.

Johnny   You just keep growing.

Jasmine   This year, we plan to launch an in-house blood products company.

Peter (*to* **Wang Wei**)   Your new gig! Ambitious play.

Wang Wei   We are confident it will become one of Henan's top grossing companies if we focus on the sale of human coagulation factor eight, which is projected to continue its dominance as the top valued asset in the global blood product market.

Jasmine   Which brings us to our first question.

Johnny   Shoot.

Jasmine   Would Phoenix Pharmaceutical be willing to purchase manufactured blood products from us instead of raw plasma units?

Wang Wei   We are confident we can manufacture these items domestically at a much lower price.

Johnny   I don't doubt that. It's quality control I'm worried about.

Wang Wei   What if you sent your technicians over to set up the facility—to your specifications?

Johnny   That wouldn't address my concerns.

Wang Wei   Tell us what the issues are. We'll come up with a solution together.

Johnny   We better cut to the chase. Peter?

Peter   We received notice that there's AIDS in the Henan blood supply.

Wang Wei (*laughing it off*)   That's impossible.

Peter   Impossible?

Wang Wei   AIDS is a Western disease.

Peter   It seems to have arrived in your country.

Wang Wei (*still laughing*)   "Received notice." Sounds like officials from another province are trying to slander us.

Peter   After we were alerted we took it upon ourselves to test your most recent shipment.

Johnny   Three units tested positive for HIV.

Wang Wei   Three units out of thousands is statistically insignificant. We'll send you the next batch free of charge. You have my word—our product will be clean.

Johnny   We're suspending our contract.

Wang Wei   Suspending—?

Jasmine   That sounds different than cancelling.

Johnny   Totally different! We're not cancelling anything.

Jasmine   What do you propose?

Peter   Family to family—once you fix this, we'll be back.

Johnny   We'll consider it a supply-chain issue. Come back when it's fixed.

Jasmine   We understand. We'll be back soon.

Wang Wei   If farmer blood is dirty, we'll buy from students instead.

Peter   As long as it's clean.

Wang Wei   Can I count on your discretion while we address the situation?

Johnny   If news gets out, it won't be from our end.

Everyone shakes hands. **Johnny** *and* **Peter** *start to leave.*

Jasmine   You said you "received notice."

Peter   That's right.

Jasmine   From?

Peter   Someone inside your Ministry.

Jasmine   Which department?

Peter   Infectious Disease.

Johnny   You have a researcher doing quality control studies on the Henan blood supply.

Jasmine   We understand everything. Have a safe flight.

Johnny *and* **Peter** *exit. A long pause.* **Wang Wei** *is stunned.* **Jasmine** *pours herself a glass of water.*

Wang Wei   Why can't you control your wife?

Shen   Yin-Yin is doing her job.

Wang Wei   It's not her job to go over my head.

Shen   What would you have done if Yin-Yin reported the problem to you?

Wang Wei   The Henan Governor's on an inside track to become a major player in the Central Government. What do you think he'll do if someone tries to smear his reputation?

Shen   What would you have done?

Wang Wei   Protected her.

Shen   Would she be in this position if an idiot man-child who can't say no to the Minister of Health hadn't betrayed us by agreeing to triple the output of our stations / when he knew—

Wang Wei (*interrupting at /*)   What choice did I have?

Shen   When he knew there was no way to do it safely without cutting corners?

Wang Wei   You've put your wife in grave danger.

Shen   You want too much for one lifetime.

Wang Wei   The only way to be safe from the government is to be inside it. We learned this before we learned to ride bikes!

Shen   Those days are over!

Wang Wei   Do you know who threw the rock that hit her in the middle of the forehead? Do you remember that sound?

Shen   This is different.

Wang Wei   You don't. I do. How can that be? We were both there. Maybe you were sobbing into my stomach and my hands were over your ears. It must be nice to be safe and protected in Human Resources, while someone else sticks his neck out and makes the decisions that put meat on your table and a roof over your head.

Shen   You could have said no! We could have grown slowly and safely!

Wang Wei   The minute I say that word I'm gone and someone else is here saying "yes" and the train is moving forward at exactly the same speed.

Jasmine *rises to her feet, collects* **Wang Wei** *and exits with him.*

Wang Wei   Get your house in order, brother. Fix it before someone fixes it for you.

Scene Four

Apartment, night. **Shen** *is still standing on stage.* **Yin-Yin** *enters holding a basket of dry laundry. She and* **Shen** *fold bedsheets and little girl's clothing together.*

Yin-Yin   It took six stories, thirty minutes of back rubbing and two cups of water, but I think she's fallen asleep.

Shen   Do you know what I enjoyed most about Rabbit's birthday last week? My family, relaxed. Laughing together.

Yin-Yin   Good performance, right? I should get a trophy.

Shen   For doing your job?

Yin-Yin   Last time I checked, I wasn't a hostess.

Shen   Last time I checked, we'd agreed to keep politics out of our house.

Yin-Yin   We all work for the same Ministry of Health.

Shen   And yet somehow my wife—who is supposed to be on the same side—

Yin-Yin   I'm on the public's side—

Shen   —has contacted our buyer and said our product's dirty.

Yin-Yin   I didn't contact Phoenix.

Shen   Are you calling my cousins liars?

Yin-Yin   No. But I didn't talk to them.

Shen   Then—

Yin-Yin   I talked to their father.

Shen   You called my uncle?

Yin-Yin   He's a very nice man. He invited us to visit him—

Shen   Never talk to that traitor again! You had no right—

Yin-Yin   I was a scientist first. Before I became your wife. Before I had a daughter.

Shen   Priorities should change.

Yin-Yin   Says who?

Shen   Are there two children living in this apartment?

Yin-Yin   I'm not a child just because I don't share your values—

Shen   Sometimes I think you got stuck in your nine year-old way of seeing—

Yin-Yin   Maybe it's a more honest way to see.

Shen   It's a stupid, idiotic way that will get you killed if you're not careful.

Yin-Yin   My priorities haven't changed.

Shen   They should. You should.

Yin-Yin   I never said I would change.

Shen   Am I crazy for thinking that in a marriage you should consider the happiness of the other person?

Yin-Yin   You're crazy for thinking your happiness matters more than the welfare of ninety million peasants.

Yin-Yin *exits to the bedroom and returns with a red overnight bag and the Styrofoam cooler.*

Shen   Are those the—?

Yin-Yin *nods.*

Shen   Where are you going?

Yin-Yin   The Virology Institute. In Beijing.

Shen.   Right now?

Yin-Yin   A train leaves in two hours. I need to confirm my results to one-hundred percent accuracy.

Shen   It's not a good time.

Yin-Yin   It's the perfect time.

Shen   Phoenix Pharmaceutical just suspended their contract.

Yin-Yin   Really?

Shen   Stop smiling.

Yin-Yin   It's good news.

Shen   It's terrible news. Once again, the Ministry of Health knows the traitor is you!

A soft knock on the front door. **Shen** *approaches, but doesn't open it.*

Jasmine (*offstage*)   Sorry to trouble you!

Yin-Yin *covers the cooler and overnight bag with laundry.* **Shen** *opens the door.* **Jasmine** *enters, nursing an infant that is concealed by a blanket. She focuses on* **Shen**, *and largely ignores* **Yin-Yin**.

Shen   Have you eaten?

Jasmine   I'll be direct. Senior health officials are very upset. The contract with Phoenix was a significant income source.

Shen   We are aware of that.

Jasmine   This funding is lost due to Yin-Yin's actions.

Shen   What can be done about this situation?

Jasmine   Yin-Yin, I'm afraid your career at the Ministry of Health is over.

Yin-Yin   You mean I've been fired from Infectious Disease?

Jasmine   Not only that. You will not work in a medical capacity in Henan Province again.

Yin-Yin   I prevented our 'product' from infecting overseas buyers.

Jasmine   I need you to tell me where the samples are.

Yin-Yin   What samples?

Jasmine   The so-called HIV-positive blood you say exists in our county.

Yin-Yin   Why do you need my samples? All you need to do is collect more local blood and run your own tests.

Shen   They're in cold storage.

Jasmine   Where?

Shen   At the Ministry.

Jasmine   You didn't hide them somewhere else? Perhaps in this house?

Yin-Yin   Am I such a terrible mother that you'd think I'd hide HIV-positive blood under the roof where my own daughter sleeps?

Shen   Why don't you meet there tomorrow morning?

Jasmine   I can be outside Infectious Disease at nine-thirty.

Shen   She'll be there.

Jasmine   Have a good night.

Jasmine *exits.* **Shen** *turns to* **Yin-Yin**.

Shen   You do this then you're done. Understand?

Yin-Yin   If I confirm my results I have to report it.

Shen   The Virology Institute is part of the Chinese Academy of Science. They have fifty thousand researchers—it's the largest think tank in the world. Find one scientist who can make this their problem. Deal?

Yin-Yin *picks up her cooler and overnight bag.*

Yin-Yin   Deal.

Shen *and* **Yin-Yin** *move in to kiss. Before their lips touch, the scene shifts.* **Shen** *and* **Yin-Yin** *move away from each other as sound, light and movement suggest that* **Yin-Yin** *is boarding a train.*

Scene Five

Rural courtyard, late morning. Three bamboo clotheslines lined with wire hangers are full of dry clothes, most of which are obviously **Little Yi's** *apparel.* **Kuan** *and* **Old Yang** *sit on a stool, prepping bundles of peony buds for sale. Buckets full of long-stemmed peony buds surround them. Spent yellow and red blossoms wither on the pavement.*

Lili *emerges from the house with a basket of damp laundry, which she sets down, exasperated, when she sees there's no place to hang them.*

Lili   Little Yi! (*To others.*) Pei-Pei left at the crack of dawn. Is that son of a rabbit still sleeping?

Old Yang   Let him rest. He's a growing boy.

Lili   If that lazy turtle won't take down his own clothes he should marry a woman who will. (*Yelling into house.*) Little Yi!

Little Yi (*offstage, muffled*)   I'm having a good dream!

Lili *storms into the house.*

Lili (*offstage*)   Get the fuck up and take care of your clothes.

Little Yi (*offstage*)   Stop—I'm dreaming—ow! Ma!

Lili *storms out of the house holding* **Little Yi** *by the ear. She drags him to the bamboo clothesline filled with his clothes.* **Little Yi** *is naked except for his underwear.*

Little Yi   You stretched my earlobe!

Lili   You should thank me. Giant ears symbolize future prosperity.

As **Lili** *sweeps the floor furiously,* **Little Yi** *surveys his clothesline options, and takes down two socks, pants, a shirt and a jacket, clearing half the line, putting on each item of clothing as he takes it down.*

Little Yi   There.

Lili   Sit the fuck down and let your ma fix your hair.

He does, but not before reaching for a prize pair of high-top sneakers, which he details as **Lili** *yanks a comb through* **Little Yi's** *snarls.*

Little Yi Ow! Go easy!

Wen *enters from the fields, shirtless, carrying two baskets of peony buds on a bamboo pole that he balances over his shoulders. Another basket is strapped to his back. There are a constellation of lesions on his torso.* **Wen** *sets the baskets down and joins* **Kuan** *and* **Old Yang** *in the work of processing peonies.*

Little Yi Ba has new spots.

Lili Don't make me slap you.

Little Yi I can see them from here.

Kuan (*sharply, to* **Wen**) Pei-Pei will be home for lunch soon.

Wen *puts on a shirt, hiding the lesions.*

Little Yi Uncle has one on his neck.

Lili Get the makeup stick from my purse.

Wen *extracts a concealer stick from* **Lili**'s *gaudy, faux Prada purse, and offers it to* **Kuan**.

Kuan You do it.

Wen *gently dabs the foundation stick on* **Kuan**'s *neck, covering the lesion.*

Lili Now do me.

Wen There's no need. You're perfect already.

Little Yi The spot on your chin's showing.

Lili Erase it. What kind of man are you?

Wen (*about to break*) Lili—

Lili If you can't be a rock go cry in the fields!

Wen *doesn't move.*

Lili If Pei-Pei sees tears she won't ace her test and all of this is for nothing.

Wen *pulls his shirt over his eyes, turns towards the family altar and rocks back and forth.*

Lili Be a man, or go water the flowers.

Wen *turns back to* **Lili**, *completely composed, and covers her lesion with makeup.*

Old Yang Pass me that when you're through.

He does. **Old Yang** *covers some lesions on his arms, then covers one on* **Little Yi**'s *neck.*

Little Yi Maybe my blood's in that stick.

Lili I bought that piece of shit in an alley. That low price paint doesn't hold my son's essence.

The sound of a scooter approaching, then **Postman Zhou***, 58, enters wearing a scooter helmet and a mailman's uniform. A mailbag is slung over his shoulder.*

Old Yang   Postman Zhou!

Postman Zhou   Good morning!

Wen   Have you eaten?

Postman Zhou   Don't be polite. I remember when your Ma wiped that ass with corn husks and old paper.

Lili   Was my husband a cute kid?

Little Yi (*off comb*)   Ow!

Postman Zhou   He would have been if he wasn't so damn skinny. Back then we were all walking skeletons.

Postman Zhou *hands* **Old Yang** *a newspaper.*

Little Yi   Do you deliver mail to my aunt's village?

Postman Zhou   I wouldn't dare. In that place babies are born with the Fever.

Old Yang   The poor things.

Postman Zhou   Those crazy ex-farmers haven't worked land for years. Their fields are so thick with old weeds they can barely plant their new crop.

Little Yi   What new crop?

Kuan   Corpse flowers.

Postman Zhou   It's like the old days, when there'd be fresh mounds of dirt to burn incense by each time the sun woke you up in the morning.

Old Yang   Has the Fever taken so many?

Postman Zhou   My elementary school classmate builds coffins in a warehouse not far from there. Business is better than it's been in forty years.

Postman Zhou *exits.* **Pei-Pei** *approaches on a beat-up bicycle. She wears a tracksuit with her high school's name embroidered on it. The family brightens, dropping into a high octane performance of wellness and vitality.*

Pei-Pei   I'm home!

Old Yang   How's our scholar?

Lili   Obviously acing the big test.

Pei-Pei   It's not easy.

Wen   Burn oil, Pei-Pei. We're fighting for you.

Lili   When you're famous and rich, don't forget our blood helped you get there.

Pei-Pei   Thank you, everyone, for your support.

Old Yang   That's what family essence is for.

Kuan   It was worth every drop.

Wen   Soon, you will be the first generation in our family to go to a university.

Old Yang   The first in our village too!

Pei-Pei   I haven't even finished the test.

Lili   Have faith, Pei-Pei. You're a once in a blue moon type.

Pei-Pei   If I get in, I'll use my education to benefit everyone.

Wen   Thank you, Pei-Pei. You honor us all.

Pei-Pei   Uncle, your face is pale. Do you need to lie down?

Lili   I fried his rice hard last night. He hasn't recovered.

Wen   Your auntie has a blue ribbon in draining men's chi.

Pei-Pei (*to* **Lili**)   You must be getting really strong.

Lili   I could carry you back to your test.

Kuan   Sit down, Pei-Pei. I'll get you some food.

Pei-Pei   I'll do it.

Old Yang   It's exam week. Let your Ba spoil you.

Kuan *exits the house.*

Pei-Pei   You should all rest more. You're working too hard.

Lili   We're slaves to these flowers, Pei-Pei. They keep our men home.

This comment breaks **Wen**. *He turns away before his face crumples.* **Little Yi** *notices, and tries to distract* **Pei-Pei**.

Little Yi   Yo nerd queen, listen up!

Pei-Pei   What?

Old Yang *stands over* **Wen** *and begins a tai-chi form, successfully shielding him from* **Pei-Pei**'s *line of sight.*

Little Yi   If—uh—hypothetically—you were a crazy boring bookworm who did nothing with her life expect study for the entrance exam, and LITTLE YI'S WONDER TRUCK pulled up and parked in front of you, what kind of music would it take to make you look up from your flashcards and check out my wares?

Lili   The kind full of hidden messages to every test question.

Pei-Pei   That wouldn't make me go in your creepy truck.

Little Yi   What if I had a high-top sneaker with side pockets where you could store paperclips and a calculator?

Pei-Pei   Maybe if you line the inside of the shoe with chemicals that keep you awake and give you prehistoric energy.

Little Yi   If I'm going to market a caffeine delivery system, I should do it through disposable socks, so my customers can buy a seven-pack every week and never do laundry.

Lili   Add a chemical that makes the wearer remember to wash her face and comb her hair.

Kuan *exits the house with a lunch tin, which he hands to* **Pei-Pei**.

Kuan   Study in the warehouse. I'll make sure these loud mouths don't bother you.

Pei-Pei   Bye, everyone!

Little Yi   Don't fuck up!

Lili   Good luck!

Old Yang   Burn oil!

Wen   We're fighting with you!

Pei-Pei *rides off with her lunch pail. Everyone waves brightly at her as she leaves, maintaining the illusion of normalcy and cheer until she disappears from sight. Long silence.* **Wen** *stands next to his father and flows through a taichi form with him.*

Old Yang   My parents did a full form here every morning. They weren't at war with famine, Nationalists, Japanese or the fever. Some years floods took our crops. Other years had drought and locusts. It was a cycle. The Yang family lived through it.

Kuan   Pei-Pei will carry us forward.

Lili   She just has to find one of those humble, submissive types who will take the Yang name.

Wen   The Ministry of Health set up our blood station—and the one we went to in the city. Shouldn't professional people know what they're doing?

Lili   It's been years since Nurse Jasmine came here. What if the Ministry doesn't know people are getting the Fever?

Little Yi   Maybe we should tell Nurse Jasmine.

Kuan   There's no point.

Little Yi   There is if she can help.

Kuan   Why would she?

Little Yi   We were her staff. Doing work for the Ministry.

Kuan   You're dreaming.

Lili   The Ministry compensated us when Little Yi got the wrong blood. We made them rich. It's only right to share profits if blood-selling makes people sick.

Old Yang *and* **Little Yi** *silently flow through a taichi form.* **Lili, Wen,** *and* **Kuan** *continue processing flowers.*

Scene Six

Sound, lights and movement suggest that **Yin-Yin** *is getting off a train and entering a busy train station. She is wearing a different outfit. She carries a stuffed rabbit and her red overnight bag. The cooler is gone. Uniformed* **Public Security Officers** *(Chinese secret police) approach.*

Public Security Officer 1   Doctor Zhou?

Yin-Yin   Yes?

Public Security Officer 2 *thrusts a black hood over* **Yin-Yin***'s head, then swiftly guides her out of the station.* **Officer 1** *follows, carrying* **Yin-Yin***'s bag and the stuffed rabbit.*

Scene Seven

A cheap hotel room. Early evening. The bed is still made. The stuffed rabbit and **Yin-Yin***'s overnight bag is on the floor.* **An Mei** *and* **Xiao Kang,** *two uniformed Public Security Officers, play a rapid-paced drinking game. There's a flirtatious edge to their interactions.*

An Mei   One, two, three—FIVE!

She puts out five (one open hand, palm down) and zero (a closed fist). **Xiao Kang** *puts out two closed fists. The total is five, like* **An Mei** *predicted. She wins!*

An Mei   Ha hah!

Xiao Kang   Still your turn.

An Mei   One, two, three—FIFTEEN! (*Off her correct guess.*) I win!

Xiao Kang   Shhhh!

An Mei (*loud whisper*)   One, two, three—TEN! (*Off her correct guess.*) So predictable.

Xiao Kang   Again.

An Mei   One, two, three—TWENTY! (*She loses.*) NOOOO!

Xiao Kang   Accept your punishment.

An Mei *reluctantly extends both of her hands, palms down.* **Xiao Kang** *slaps the tops of her hands, hard.*

An Mei   Ow!

Xiao Kang *knocks on the closed bathroom door.* **An Mei** *lights two cigarettes.*

Xiao Kang   Dr. Zhou. (*When there's no response.*) Dr. Zhou. Have you fallen into a hotel toilet?

An Mei   If she did the Henan Governor would be very relieved.

An Mei *hands* **Xiao Kang** *a cigarette. As he takes a long drag, the bathroom door opens and a disheveled* **Yin-Yin** *emerges. Her eyes are red. Her clothes and hair are rumpled. She moves, zombie like, to the chair and plops into it.*

An Mei *takes a long drag of her cigarette and exhales lustily.* **Xiao Kang** *collapses playfully onto the bed and sidles up to* **Yin-Yin**, *like they are two friends at a slumber party.*

Xiao Kang   You're so . . . plain. And . . . normal looking.

An Mei   I'm also disappointed.

Xiao Kang   How can *this* be the "bastard" who smuggled Henan blood to Beijing?

Yin-Yin   (–)

An Mei   Bastard or not, she's an overnight celebrity.

An Mei *perches the cigarette between her lips, pulls out a polaroid camera and points it at* **Xiao Kang** *and* **Yin-Yin**.

An Mei   Say "Eggplant!"

Xiao Kang (*pushing his cheek against* **Yin-Yin***'s*)   Eggplant!

A photograph slides out of the camera. There's a knock on the door. **Xiao Kang** *and* **An Mei** *immediately shift into their professional roles, putting out their cigarettes, straightening their uniforms as they approach the front door.*

Xiao Kang (*to* **Yin-Yin**)   Don't let me forget to get your autograph.

An Mei (*opening door*)   Director Meng. Director Lin.

Jasmine *and* **Wang Wei** *enter in business attire. They are immediately followed by a third* **Public Security Officer**, *who escorts a black-hooded* **Shen** *to the bed. Though his face is obscured,* **Yin-Yin** *immediately recognizes* **Shen**, *and begins to sob uncontrollably.*

Wang Wei   Stop.

Yin-Yin *tries to compose herself.*

Wang Wei   Stop crying.

Yin-Yin   Unhood your brother.

Wang Wei *nods. An officer removes the black hood.* **Shen** *blinks in his surroundings, avoiding eye contact with* **Yin-Yin**.

Yin-Yin   Where's our daughter?

Shen   School.

Jasmine   Our nanny will get her. She can play with her cousin as long as she needs to.

Yin-Yin   I didn't break any laws.

Wang Wei   You didn't yesterday. Today, the law changed.

Yin-Yin   For what reason?

Jasmine   After you left the Virology Institute, one of their scientists called the Central Government, who ordered the military to shut down every plasma station in the country.

Yin-Yin   That should have happened six years ago.

Wang Wei   The Henan Governor and the Henan Minister of Health just met with the state media board. Starting today, all matters related to the so-called issue of HIV or AIDS in Henan Province are classified. They are State Secrets.

Yin-Yin   Secrets?

Jasmine   Domestic media outlets have been alerted. No one is permitted to print, publish or air anything related to Henan State Secrets.

Wang Wei   Chinese citizens who share state secrets will be arrested and prosecuted to the fullest extent of the law.

Shen   Tell them you're done.

Yin-Yin   (–)

Shen   You said you'd be done, Yin-Yin. You are finished. We can't live like this. My brother is trying to protect you. Do you want to go to jail? Do you want to disappear? Do you want to orphan our daughter?

Yin-Yin *shakes her head.*

Shen   Are you done?

Yin-Yin (*long pause*)   Yes.

Shen   Will you keep your mouth shut?

Yin-Yin (*shorter pause*)   Yes.

Shen   Do you swear?

Yin-Yin   I did what I could. It's too big.

Shen (*to* **Wang Wei**)   Please, brother. Let us go home.

Wang Wei *motions to the* **Public Security Officers**. *One grabs* **Yin-Yin**'*s overnight bag, the others gather up* **Shen** *and* **Yin-Yin**. *They all exit the hotel room, leaving* **Wang Wei** *and* **Jasmine** *alone together.*

Wang Wei   How do we fix this?

Jasmine   How much raw plasma is stockpiled?

Wang Wei   Including the shipment we were going to send Phoenix—twenty thousand units.

Jasmine   Can we sell them?

Wang Wei   It's bad product.

Jasmine   That's not what I asked.

Wang Wei   The units are contaminated.

Jasmine   Thanks to the media blackout only Phoenix knows that.

Wang Wei   Do you hear what you're saying?

Jasmine   We need to convert our stockpile into useable capital immediately. The longer the product stays in our freezers the less it will be worth.

There's a knock on the door. **Wang Wei** *moves to answer it.* **Minister Li** *enters, formally dressed.*

Wang Wei   Minister Li. (*Off his silence.*) It's been handled. Everything's under control. My sister-in-law won't cause any more trouble.

Minister Li   We have to arrest one of you.

Wang Wei   Minister?

Minister Li   Not now! No one's around to take pictures. Next week. We'll book our best photographer. If every plasma station's being shut down, a head must roll.

Jasmine   And you prefer that head not be attached to your body.

Minister Li   Corruption has occurred! The people need answers!

Wang Wei   Respectfully, Minister, we executed your vision.

Minister Li   Don't overreact.

Wang Wei   Minister, you're asking us to—

Minister Li   This is insurance. If the media blackout fails, we can prove to the Central Government Henan Officials are furious and committed to justice. It's a photo op, with jail time. The stay will be brief. Afterwards, you'll still be rich, with a nice job at the Ministry.

Wang Wei   Our son's six months old. This isn't convenient.

Minister Li   Who said anything about convenient? I only have three months left in my term and the Henan Governor wants to be Party Secretary. If we stay on his good side we could follow him into the Central Government.

Jasmine   We'd be lucky to have you replace him as our Governor.

Minister Li   That will be difficult if blood scandal unfolds on my watch. I know you are parents. That's why I only need one of you.

Wang Wei   That's very thoughtful, Minister Li. But if the ban on AIDS-related news is not effective and my wife or I become the public face of blood disaster, I doubt even our excellent police force can protect us from a mob of angry peasants.

Minister Li   If that happens leave the country and join your rotten banana relatives in Orange County. (*Pressing on.*) This is a precaution. Don't take it too seriously. Just discuss it for a few days, then tell me who it will be.

Minister Li *exits.* **Wang Wei** *and* **Jasmine** *are alone in the hotel room.*

Scene Eight

Outside the Zhoukou Blood Station. Morning. **Lili** *and* **Wen** *approach the front entrance. They have baskets strapped to their backs, full of bundles of peonies.*

Wen   Here's the Blood Station. How much should we ask for?

Lili   Little Yi got five thousand when he got the wrong blood. Let's get five times that much since she hurt five people in our family.

Wen   What about the people we hurt by helping Nurse Jasmine buy blood?

Lili   Let's ask for extra money and medication to help all of our customers. She taught us how to run the station. We followed her methods exactly. Their lives are her responsibility.

Jasmine *enters from the street and approaches the blood station.*

Jasmine   Sorry, we're closed.

Lili   Nurse Jasmine. Do you remember us?

Wen   We ran your pilot rural blood station.

Jasmine   Of course. The Yang family. How are you doing?

Wen *lifts his shirt, revealing his lesions.* **Lili** *motions to hers on her chin, neck and arms.* **Jasmine** *recoils, stepping away from them.*

Lili   Every blood-seller in our family has the same spots and they're growing.

Wen   Did you know the Fever's a blood-selling disease?

Lili   We went to the Department of Complaints to file a report but they wouldn't accept it.

Wen   They called it a "state secret."

Lili   Why is what's happening to our bones and flesh a state secret?

Jasmine   I'm very sorry, but the blood stations are closed.

Lili   The Ministry compensated us when you gave my son the wrong blood.

Wen   We need five times that much for our family—

Jasmine   You want money.

Wen   And medicine. As much as you can spare.

Jasmine   Of course. I think we can do that. Wait here while I check if our cashier's around. And our pharmacist, for the medicine. It might take a while to count up all the cash we have in the building.

Lili   Take your time.

Wen   We're not in a rush.

Jasmine   Thank you. I'll see what I can do.

Jasmine *exits into the blood station.*

Lili   We shouldn't leave without half a million—

Wen   And enough medicine for one hundred blood sellers.

Yin-Yin *approaches with a small grocery cart filled with recent fruit and meat purchases. She walks up to the door of the blood station and tries to look in.*

Wen   The blood station's closed.

Yin-Yin   Just making sure.

Lili   I know your face. (*To* **Wen**.) Does she look familiar to you?

Wen   I'm not sure. Do you work at this station?

Yin-Yin   Not for six years.

Lili   That's it.

Wen   The good doctor!

Lili   You saved my son.

Wen   Right after the grand opening, when Nurse Jasmine gave him the wrong blood.

Yin-Yin   Of course. I remember him. How's your boy doing?

Lili   He has the Fever.

Yin-Yin   The Fever?

Wen (*revealing his stomach*)   The blood-selling disease.

Yin-Yin   What you have is full blown AIDS. The virus that causes it is called HIV.

Lili   We're from the countryside. We don't understand that stuff. Nurse Jasmine's helping us get medicine and compensation.

Yin-Yin   She said that?

Wen   She's with the cashier, counting the money.

Yin-Yin   There isn't any AIDS medication in the country.

Lili   Then why did she say—

Four **Police Officers** *enter. They might be in riot gear, or carrying machine guns. There should be a sense that this is a disproportionate response to the perceived threat.*

Police Officer 1   Go back to the countryside.

Wen   It's alright officers, we're doing business with health officials.

Police Officer 2   Move.

Lili   Nurse Jasmine is inside getting us money.

Police Officer 3   Stupid bumpkin.

Yin-Yin   Don't insult them.

Police Officer 3   Why would Director Meng give you anything?

Wen   Lili. Let's go home.

Lili   I won't.

Wen   They're not going to help us.

Lili   Nurse Jasmine said—

Police Officer 4   Are you deaf, woman? She's not coming.

Wen   I'm sorry officers—Lili, we need to leave.

Lili   She owes us.

Police Officer 3   You're dirt. She doesn't owe you anything.

Yin-Yin   Officers!

Lili   What did you call me?

Wen   Lili!

Lili   He just called your wife dirt. Are you going to defend me?

Wen   Lili, we need to go home. Nurse Jasmine lied to us.

Lili   You're wrong. She's going to help us.

Police Officer 1   Woman. Who the fuck do you think just called in a disturbance?

A beat, then **Lili** *lunges for the door to the station, finds it locked and pounds on it furiously.*

Lili   Bitch Jasmine! Fuck you to the Eighteenth Level of Hell!

The **Police Officers** *pull her back.*

Wen   Get your hands on my wife!

Yin-Yin   Officers, please—

Wen *tries to push away the* **Police Officers**. *They beat him with night sticks or the butts of their guns.*

Lili (*screaming, towards blood station*)   We are your mirror of retribution! Your sins live in our blood!

A **Police Officer** *pushes* **Lili** *to the ground. She falls, hard, hitting her head. Her forehead and nose start gushing blood.*

Police Officer 1   Arrest them all.

Wen   Please, no. I'm sorry. We'll go.

Police Officer 3   It's too late.

Yin-Yin   Officers, please. Leave them alone.

The **Police Officers** *pull out their handcuffs and prepare to arrest them.*

Lili   I have AIDS! HIV! If you touch me you'll get sick!

The **Police Officers** *back away from* **Lili**.

Police Officer 1   Arrest her.

Police Officer 2   You do it.

Police Officer 3   I'm not touching her.

The **Police Officers** *train their rifles on* **Wen** *and* **Lili**.

Yin-Yin   Officers, Director Meng is my sister-in-law. We live in the same building.

Lili   That bitch is related to you?

Police Officer 2   Let's get out of here.

Police Officer 3   Make sure that country trash goes straight to the bus station.

Police Officer 1   Stay out of our city. If any of you show your face around here again you'll get a one-way ticket to prison.

The **Police Officers** *exit.*

Lili   This isn't right. She needs to be punished.

Yin-Yin *rummages through her purse, pulls out a pack of wet wipes and hands them to* **Wen**.

Yin-Yin   Help her clean up.

He does. **Lili** *starts to sob.*

Lili   I don't want to die.

Wen   Let's go home.

Lili   You can't die before me. Promise you won't.

Yin-Yin   Don't lose hope.

Lili   You said it yourself! There's no medicine in the country! My sister's village has more ghosts than living people. If we don't get help we'll follow them out of this world.

Wen   Can you help us?

Yin-Yin   There's medicine for the pain. And nutritional supplements.

Lili   We don't want anything. Our bodies are worthless. Just save our son.

Wen   I can tell you're a very educated person. We don't understand this stuff.

Lili   We're stupid. We can't even tell when someone's lying to us.

Yin-Yin   I'm sorry. I have a daughter now, if it was just about me—

Lili *drops to her knees.*

Lili   I don't care about my life. My boy's grown. He doesn't need me. You saved my son once already. Your spirits are linked. Save him again.

Wen *prostrates himself beside* **Lili**.

Wen   He's not even twenty-five yet. His soul should stay in his body.

Lili   Save our son.

Wen   You have the face of a good person.

Lili   You must have been a monk in your last life. You're our Goddess of Mercy.

Wen   When we get to the underworld we'll tell the King of Hell what a good person you've been.

Lili   You'll get so much karma you'll be reborn a rich and powerful person.

Yin-Yin   Even if medicine arrives in the country, it will be very expensive.

Wen   We'll find a way to make money. Get us medicine. Bring it into our country.

Yin-Yin   I'll do what I can.

Lili *makes* **Yin-Yin** *a giant bouquet of peonies and presses it into her hands.*

Lili   Our flowers will give you strength.

Yin-Yin   I have to go home. My daughter's expecting me.

Wen   Goodbye, good doctor. We wish you peace with every step.

Lili   Don't forget us. We'll find a way to get money.

Yin-Yin *exits with the bouquet of peonies.* **Lili** *watches her leave, and keeps her eyes trained on the direction she's exiting.*

Wen   We should go to the bus station.

Lili   You go ahead. I'll finish selling these flowers.

Wen   It's not safe—

Lili   I'm a peasant. No one will see me.

Lili *ties a scarf around her hair and exits, following* **Yin-Yin**.

Scene Nine

Rural courtyard, dusk. **Kuan, Wen, Little Yi**, *and* **Old Yang** *work under florescent lights, bundling peonies.*

Wen   This is the last harvest of the season. After we sell this batch, it's going to be nine months before we can make income from flowers.

Kuan   In the fall we can subdivide rootstock and sell plants to the farmer's cooperative.

Wen   Or dry them out and sell the roots as traditional medicine.

Old Yang   If we harvest root crop they'll be fewer flowers next year.

Kuan   We could sell every plant and only have enough for one month of medicine.

Wen   We could transfer our land rights.

Old Yang   Our family has tended these fields for hundreds of years. If we don't care for land, we don't have a place here.

Little Yi   What do you want to come back as?

Old Yang   In some parts of the world there are trees as tall as skyscrapers that live for two thousand years.

Little Yi   I don't want to come back.

Wen   You don't have a choice. But if you're calm at the moment of death you can improve your chance at a good incarnation.

Pei-Pei *enters. The men brighten.*

Little Yi   What's up Pei-Pei?

Wen   Have a seat. Rest for a minute.

Pei-Pei *sits by them and helps process peonies.*

Kuan   What's wrong?

Pei-Pei   Nothing.

Wen   Tell us, Pei-Pei. You can be honest with family.

Old Yang   How's our bookworm?

Pei-Pei   Fine.

Wen   Our scholar's better than fine. She's a genius!

Little Yi   Pei-Pei just realized there's one book in our village she hasn't read—

Wen   The phone book.

Little Yi   And tomorrow's the National Phone Book Exam.

Old Yang   Start studying, quick!

Wen   How long will it take to memorize all those numbers?

Pei-Pei   I got in. (*Off their silence.*) I'm number ten in the county. I was accepted to a human sciences program at Zhengzhou University. I'm moving to the city in eight weeks.

Kuan *explodes out of his seat.*

Kuan   YESSSSS!!!!!!!!!!!!!!!!!

The others join in the fun and pelt **Pei-Pei** *with peony blossoms, singing and clapping and dancing.* **Kuan** *alternates between sobbing and laughing. This is the most joyful and sorrowful we've ever seen him.*

All (*singing*)

"High above on the mountain side
Floats a cloud so white
There lies peaceful Kangding town
Bathed in silver moonlight
Moonlight, shines bright
Over Kangding town oh. . . ."

Kuan (*to sky*)   Do you hear that, Little Flower? Our daughter's going to college!

Pei-Pei   Don't cry, Ba.

Kuan   You can rest now. Stop tormenting me. She's getting out. Our daughter will leave this land and never come back.

Pei-Pei   Of course I'll come back, Ba. Every New Year.

Kuan   Don't come back, Pei-Pei. Never return. Move forward. To the future. Forget us. Have a good life in the city.

Pei-Pei   Don't say that.

Old Yang   He's proud of you. Ignore his babbling.

Wen   He's never said so many words.

Kuan   We'll be inside you, Pei-Pei. In your blood, Just study, study, study. Don't think about anything else. You will be the first Yang from this village to live off the brain instead of the body.

Old Yang *hands* **Little Yi** *money.*

Old Yang   Buy your cousin red bean ice to celebrate.

Little Yi   Nerd Queen! Let's do this!

Pei-Pei   Let's go as a family.

Kuan   Gong-Gong will join you.

Pei-Pei   Where's Aunt Lili?

Wen   She's catching a later bus. She'll be back in the morning.

Pei-Pei   Don't be too long. Little Yi will eat all the good stuff.

Pei-Pei, **Little Yi**, *and* **Old Yang** *exit.* **Kuan** *and* **Wen** *remain.* **Kuan** *smiles, and takes a deep huff of a peony flower.*

Kuan   Thank you for helping my daughter.

Wen   I didn't help. I delivered a death sentence. I cancelled my son's future so I could live with my family.

Kuan   It's not cancelled. Little Yi is still living.

Wen   Fighting's useless. If medicine comes, we can't pay.

Kuan   Follow me. There's still a way we can fight for Little Yi.

Kuan *and* **Wen** *exit together.*

Scene Ten

Urban apartment, night. The peonies **Lili** *gave* **Yin-Yin** *are in full bloom on the table.* **Yin-Yin's** *purse and coat are by the door.* **Shen** *enters in formal attire. He looks very tired.*

Shen   I'm home.

Yin-Yin *enters from the bedroom.*

Yin-Yin   Why aren't you at the banquet?

Shen   I couldn't find a place to sit.

Yin-Yin   Isn't there a hostess who seats you?

Shen   It doesn't matter. I'd rather be here. Is Lan-Lan asleep yet?

Yin-Yin   She's spending the night at my aunt's.

Shen   In the middle of the school week?

Yin-Yin   I wanted to get some cleaning done without her pestering me constantly for a story. You know how annoying she gets. My aunt will take her to school. You can pick her up after work.

Shen   Since when do you clean?

Yin-Yin *punches him playfully, trying to inject levity.* **Shen** *smiles.*

Yin-Yin   What happened at the banquet?

Shen   Forget the banquet. It's boring people in suits. I'm happier having dinner with you. Have you eaten?

Yin-Yin   I have.

Shen   But you'll eat again if it's delicious, you always do. I bought ground lamb this morning, how about I make your favorite meatballs?

Yin-Yin   Do you remember the Virology Conference the Ministry of Health was sending me to?

Shen   In Washington?

Yin-Yin   At the Center for Disease Control. I still want to go. I'm still a scientist. Even if I don't have a job.

Shen   They didn't cancel your plane ticket?

Yin-Yin   I bought another. My visa's still good. There will be other people in my field. Maybe I can find another job.

Shen   That's not a bad idea. When's the conference?

Yin-Yin   My flight leaves in three hours.

Shen   Three hours. Were you just—were you just going to leave?

Yin-Yin *exits to the bedroom, and returns with a large suitcase.*

Shen   You were. You were going to leave without telling me.

Yin-Yin   I didn't want to worry you.

Shen   You didn't think I'd be worried when I arrived home expecting to see my family and instead found my apartment completely empty?

Yin-Yin   I was about to write you a note.

Shen   A note. How long will you be gone?

Yin-Yin   The conference lasts five days.

Shen   That's a very big suitcase for such a short trip.

Yin-Yin   I've never left the country. I didn't know what to pack.

Shen *pushes the suitcase onto its side, unzips it and begins to rummage through it.*

Yin-Yin   Stop that. Hey. What are you doing?

Shen   Heavy sweaters in the middle of summer?

Yin-Yin   The weather in Washington's unpredictable this time of year.

Shen   Family pictures?

Yin-Yin   Five days is the longest I've been away from our daughter.

Shen   Three—no—five jars of hot sauce?

Yin-Yin   I heard American food is lacking in flavor.

Shen *pulls everything out of the suitcase, tossing aside all of* **Yin-Yin***'s personal belongings. He reaches a thick parcel wrapped in brown paper and twine.*

Shen   What is this?

Yin-Yin *walks over to the peonies and quietly rearranges them in the vase.* **Shen** *rips open the package and pulls out reams of folders, lab notebooks, charts and graphs. He begins to cry.*

Shen   Why don't you want us?

Yin-Yin   I want you both. So much.

Shen   You can't want us and smuggle state secrets out of the country. You'll never be able to come back. They'll harass your relatives. They'll put us under house arrest.

Yin-Yin   I'll apply for asylum and find a new job. You could both join me once I'm settled.

Shen   I won't abandon my country. I'm a forty year-old man. I can't just start over! This is my life. This is our home. Don't do this to us.

Yin-Yin   Fewer people will die. Thousands, maybe tens of thousands fewer, once it is known publicly that there's a rural AIDS epidemic in our country. Once it is known, there can be education. Medicine will be brought in. None of that can happen if it stays a state secret. We're just three people. One family.

Shen *sinks to his knees, still holding the notebooks.*

Shen   It can't be you. It must not be you.

Yin-Yin   What would your mother do, do you think? Was her head bashed in with rocks just so her sons could spend their lives on their knees, always living in fear?

Shen   The world you want isn't real. It doesn't exist. It will never exist.

Yin-Yin   Why do you want me to act like I have bound feet, like I'm illiterate, like I don't understand exactly what's happening?

Shen   So you won't die.No one would talk to me at the banquet. All my colleagues, people I've known for years, wouldn't acknowledge me when I spoke to them. They looked right through me. Like I was already a ghost.

Yin-Yin   Do you know what your uncle told me when we spoke on the phone? It's not what he tells his sons. He wasn't going to leave your mother.

She made him. She forced him to run. Your mother wanted her brother to grow into the man she knew he could become. She wanted him to keep living.

Shen *starts crying again. He starts tearing pages out of the lab notebooks.* **Yin-Yin** *wrestles all the folders and notebooks away from him.* **Shen** *remains on his knees.*

Shen   I'm in hell. You made my life hell.

Yin-Yin   If we're in hell it's because you carried us here by not standing up to your brother—by not listening to me, when I told you what would happen if we didn't shut down the stations. I told you exactly how contamination was happening, exactly how the epidemic would spread. I showed you all of this, my data, my evidence, reports that I sent all over the Ministry.

Yin-Yin *slaps* **Shen** *across the face with a hardcover lab notebook. His head whips sideways.*

Yin-Yin   WHY WOULDN'T YOU LISTEN TO ME?

Shen *slowly turns his face forward. He stares ahead silently. He remains on his knees.*

Yin-Yin   You are a Department Head, you're a man, you had more power than me. People might have listened to you. They couldn't have dismissed you as a hysterical woman who should be home in the kitchen. If just one hundred people had stood up together and said NO with one voice—

Yin-Yin *slaps* **Shen** *again with the notebook, this time hitting his nose. His face whips sideways. He doesn't look back at her.*

Yin-Yin   I let you delay me, I let you slow me down, talk me out of things, make me weak. I thought you wanted what was right for me—for who I want to be, for how I want to be living—but I see you now. You are seen. You just wanted to be comfortable, and safe, at home, eating dumplings with your family. You'd spend your whole life on your knees, as long as you can play tennis with your brother every morning.

Yin-Yin *raises the notebook again, but stops herself.*

Yin-Yin   Why do you let me hit you? Why don't you stop me?

Shen *turns towards* **Yin-Yin** *and looks at her. Blood streams out of his nose and onto his chin and neck, staining his white shirt. They regard each other silently.* **Yin-Yin** *picks up the lab folders, lab notebooks and reports and stuffs the evidence in her purse. She puts on her shoes and exits the apartment with only her purse, leaving* **Shen** *and her exploded suitcase behind.*

Scene Eleven

City street, night. **Jasmine** *and* **Wang Wei** *are out walking.* **Wang Wei** *is in a suit,* **Jasmine** *in something more casual. She pushes a stroller containing their sleeping son, who is obscured by stuffed animals and sheets.*

Jasmine   We'll visit every week. Twice when we can. Minister Li doesn't think you'll have to be in there for more than a few months. It won't be a normal prison, it will be the nice kind bankers go to—more like a three star hotel.

Wang Wei   The rural blood stations were your idea. Why does it automatically have to be me, just because I was—

Jasmine   You were what?

Wang Wei   Born into a male body.

Jasmine   Do you have opinions on the fairness of the body I was born into?

Wang Wei   I think you received a very nice, very healthy body that was fortunate to arrive after the chaos and after the famine.

Jasmine   Can your male body breastfeed our son?

Wang Wei   We can hire a wet nurse for that. Or if it's really such a nice prison, maybe they'll let you bring a crib and an army of nannies.

Jasmine   You are still Director of the Plasma Collection Station. My promotion hasn't been announced. What symbolic justice can be had with my arrest when this happened under your leadership? Should three people lose their freedom instead of one?

Wang Wei   There will be a picture of me in the paper. In handcuffs. I'll become a public target. How can I show my face anywhere after that?

Jasmine   If everything goes as planned, you'll get out of prison and fly straight to Orange County.

Wang Wei   Orange County?

Jasmine   I spoke with your cousins. They agree that between my experience in rural outreach and their inside access to top secret Henan Ministry of Health information, we are ideally positioned to launch a subsidiary company under Phoenix Pharmaceutical that meets the demands of China's newest emerging market.

Wang Wei   What emerging market is that?

Jasmine   AIDS medication.

Wang Wei   AIDS medication?

Jasmine   It's called "Vertical Integration." It's a key growth strategy of successful corporations. With luck we'll make enough that by the time you're out of prison we'll have green cards, a house on Laguna Beach and enough investments in American business to become economic citizens.

Wang Wei   Are you really that shameless?

Jasmine   My love. Have you forgotten that it was you who taught me how to swim through the "Sea of Commerce"?

Jasmine *starts to straighten* **Wang Wei**'s *tie. He grabs her wrists, stopping her. She pulls away and moves towards the stroller.*

Wang Wei   I should get to the banquet.

Jasmine   Yes. You should. Thank you for the flowers.

Wang Wei   Flowers?

Jasmine   There's peonies on the table.

Wang Wei   The housekeeper must have brought them.

Jasmine   They make the apartment smell wonderful.

Wang Wei *exits. In the stroller, the baby stirs.* **Jasmine** *bends down to check on him.*

Jasmine (*singing*)

"Two tigers, two tigers
Running fast, running fast—"

Lili *appears from behind a bench. Her face is wrapped in scarves.*

Jasmine (*singing*)   "One has no ears, one has no tail—"

Lili *approaches* **Jasmine**. *She's holding a large rock.*

Jasmine (*singing*)   "How strange. How strange—"

Lili *slams the rock into the back of* **Jasmine**'s *head.* **Jasmine** *collapses to the floor, too stunned to make a sound.* **Jasmine** *puts her hands on the back of her broken skull. They come away bright red and wet with blood.*

Lili   Soon you will be in a room made of salt.

Jasmine   Please—

Lili   King Song, who rules the third court, will give you the tortures meant for people who practice medicine without the right training.

Jasmine   My baby.

Lili   Your ribs will be pierced with rusted nails. Your face cut with copper knives.

Jasmine   Don't hurt my baby.

Lili   He'll pull out your eyes and scrape fat from your body.

Jasmine *tries to get up, then falls down, weakened by the blood gushing out of her head.*

Jasmine   Don't hurt my baby.

Lili   Han Lili erases you from the Book of the Living.

Lili *slams the rock into* **Jasmine**'s *forehead, hard, then, using both hands, beats* **Jasmine**'s *head with the rock over and over until it's a bloody pulp. A prolonged* *stillness, as* **Lili** *catches her breath, surveys her work, spits on* **Jasmine**'s *body, then disappears into the shadows.* **Jasmine** *lies dead, illuminated by streetlights, near her sleeping son.*

Scene Twelve

Rural highway. Night. **Wen** *and* **Kuan** *walk along the shoulder, carrying flashlights and smoking cigarettes. The sound of frogs, crickets, night birds, passing cars and wind blowing through trees.*

Kuan   Don't forget to fertilize the peony fields next week. Use compost, crushed bones and rotted manure.

Wen   I'm not good with living things.

Kuan   You overdo it. They're carefree flowers. They do better with less attention.

Wen   Remember how quiet it was during the famine?

Kuan   (–)

Wen   No birds. No bugs. No leaves to be blown by the wind. Back then I thought hell was a place without sound. (*He listens to the night.*) It's going to be quiet like that again.

Kuan   When it's winter, don't smother them with mulch. If it's cold, cover our girls loosely with shredded bark or pine needles.

Wen   Pei-Pei put one parent in the ground already.

Kuan   You sold blood for my daughter. It's right I repay my debts to your family.

Wen   That's idiot math.

Kuan   If ants swarm the buds, don't spray them. They kill bud-eating pests, and don't hurt the plant.

A truck approaches. **Kuan** *puts out his cigarette.*

Wen   Brother—

Kuan   When fall comes, cut their stems down, level with the soil and—

Wen   Let me do it.

Kuan   Compost all remaining blossoms and petals.

Wen   Little Yi has two parents.

Kuan   When you get medicine, save it all for Little Yi. It's better to help one person live a long time than give everyone a few months.

The sound of the truck approaching. A bright light appears in the distance.

Wen   He's stubborn. He won't take more than his share.

Kuan   Put something else in your pill bottles. Take it when he gets the real thing.

Wen   Wait. Brother—

Kuan *turns off his flashlight. He motions for* **Wen** *to do the same.*

Kuan   I'll call out the license plate. Don't settle for less than ninety thousand.

Kuan *steps onto the highway—then is yanked back, as* **Wen** *lunges forward and pulls him to safety. The sound of the truck passing. Headlights fade. The brothers fight.*

Wen   I'd rather die a death of a thousand cuts than outlive my wife.
I thought I could face it but I can't.
She wants me to be the strong one, but I can't be. I can't watch her die.
Please don't make me shame myself. Let me be a hero.
If you go, I'll wait for the next truck and follow you out of this world.
Let her remember me as the man who fought for her until his last breath.
Alive I'm worth nothing. Let my death buy my son medicine.
Let my flesh feed our flowers.
Some people have meaningful lives. Let my death have a meaning.
Please, brother. Give this to me.

Kuan *steps aside.* **Wen** *stands on the edge of the highway and faces the approaching truck. He tries to step onto the road. His knees buckle. His body's frozen in fear.* **Wen** *pounds on his legs with his fists.*

Wen   MOVE!

Kuan   You have life in you still. This isn't your end.

Kuan *steps into the blinding headlights of an oncoming truck.*

LOUD, LONG HONK.

Kuan   In the next life we'll be a family again.

The WHOOSH of blood rushing through arteries, increasing to a DEAFENING OCEANIC VOLUME as—

Pei-Pei *pushes an oversize altar onstage.*

The altar contains framed portraits of **Old Yang**, **Wen**, **Kuan**, **Lili**, **Luo Na**, *and* **Han-Han**, *and is decorated with offerings for the dead—paper joss clothing, food, incense, beer and peonies.*

Little Yi *approaches, supported by a cane. His clothes hang off his body. Though pale and weak, he still has his familiar swagger. He lights a handful of incense, then hands half to* **Pei-Pei**.

Ocean sounds subside as **Little Yi** *and* **Pei-Pei** *kneel in front of the altar, and bow three times.*

The **Ghosts** *of* **Old Yang**, **Wen**, **Kuan**, **Lili**, **Luo Na**, *and* **Han-Han** *enter.*

They might approach the altar, surrounding the living, or they might appear on a different level, in another realm.

Ghosts (*singing*)

> "High above on the mountain side
> Floats a cloud so white
> There lies peaceful Kangding town
> Bathed in silver moonlight
> Moonlight shines bright
> Over Kangding Town oh."

End of Play.

Afterword

Joshua Chambers-Letson

It was 1987 when Ronald Reagan, the President of the United States, first publicly acknowledged the HIV/AIDS pandemic. The crisis had been underway for nearly a decade. There were already over twenty-five thousand AIDS deaths in the U.S., with many more people infected with HIV. In the years before this, and behind closed doors, the Reagan administration debated AIDS at length. It chose *not* to actively combat the disease, as evidenced by former Secretary of Treasury Donald T. Regan's admission that "The Reagan Administration realized that there was an AIDS crisis, but that it was being caused by immoral practices. And how far do you want to go to make the world safe for immoral practices? . . . How much of the taxpayer's money do you want to spend to make that a safe practice."[1] Notice the set of conflations at play in this statement. Here, AIDS is commensurate with "immoral practices," but Regan also implicitly conflates AIDS with people who are *wrong* because of their engagement in "immoral practices." People whom we can only assume to be—since these are the populations most vulnerable to the disease—queers, people who use drugs, sex workers, and people of color. These, he implies, are people who aren't *worth* saving: "How much of the taxpayers' money do you want to spend to make that a safe practice?" These, he suggests, are people who, by virtue of their immorality, are not quite people—and the difference in their infected blood proves it. They are not to be protected. They are to be protected against.

In a 1976 lecture at the Collège de France, the philosopher Michel Foucault described a shift in sovereign power that helps us to understand this dynamic. Foucault argued that in the modern era the feudal European sovereign's right to "take life or let live," was complemented by a new right to "make live and to let die."[2] Charged with the right to "make live," modern sovereignty (which often takes the form of the state) assumes the power to manage, promote, preserve, and protect the life of its population. If one of the state's central jobs is to keep the people alive, this obligation (to "make live") also becomes a source of its power. When "society must be defended" from threats both external and internal, the modern state assumes and asserts extraordinary powers, including the right to carry out war in order to protect the population from external threats. It similarly assumes and asserts the right to regulate, monitor, discipline and control its own population (to "make live," "let die," but also to kill or "take life"), this time to protect the population from threats within. Unwanted internal elements are identified and externalized as their difference comes to be defined as a threat to the body politic as much as figures of social difference (immigrants, Black, Latinx, Asian, and Indigenous folks, queers and trans people, and femmes) are figured as the abject

---

1 Deborah H. Strober and Gerald S. Strober, *Reagan: The Man and His Presidency* (Boston, MA: Houghton Mifflin Co., 1998), 138, 40.
2 Michel Foucault, *"Society Must Be Defended": Lectures at the Collège De France 1975–1976*, ed. Mauro Bertani and Alessandro Fontana, trans. David Macey (New York: Picador, 2003), 240.

limits against which the body of the ideal political subject is defined. In answer to a question he poses for himself ("What in fact is racism?"), Foucault suggests as much when he writes, "It [racism] is primarily a way of introducing a break into the domain of life that is under power's control: the break between what must live and what must die."[3] As we find in Frances Ya-Chu Cowhig's *The King of Hell's Palace,* by the end of the twentieth century, and for major powers like the People's Republic of China and the United States, AIDS (itself a disease highly inflected and impacted by questions of race, sexuality, and class) would provide another means for introducing and reinforcing "the break between what must live and what must die."

When power is consumed with the right to "make live and let die," life itself is transformed into a kind of currency for power to spend. Indeed, as it was during the transatlantic slave trade and as it is in the events depicted in *The King of Hell's Palace,* flesh, blood, and life can become actual commodities. In a 1993 essay, cultural theorist Rey Chow describes this dynamic in a description of power struggles over "human rights" during trade negotiations between China and various Western powers (including the U.S.):

> Like oil, "human rights" are what the West wants (to sustain its standard of life) and what the "third world" government refuses to release. In order to guarantee an unlimited supply of "human rights"—a demand that will perpetuate the present conflict between the West and China indefinitely—humans themselves are used to feed the speed machine that is "diplomatic exchange." . . . Such uses of humans (as bargaining chips, as hostages, as a means to an end) . . . [suggests that] humans are now on a par with the oil and speed that sustain the machines of global relations. Chinese authorities like Deng Xiaoping were being *economically precise* when they said, around June 4, 1989, that China had too many people to care about the loss of a few thousand at Tiananmen. Humans for China have always been the main economic resource as oil is for Middle Eastern nations.[4]

As Chow suggests, when the U.S. and China bargain with human life during trade negotiations, humans are reduced to being commodities: "humans are now on par with oil." Cowhig's play concerns itself with a similar and related effect, since these very negotiations helped to foster global market conditions that facilitate and expand the pursuit and conversion of human life, and Chinese flesh and blood, into an extractable, disposable, and exchangeable commodity.

The King of Hell's Palace is the third play to be produced in a suite of Cowhig's plays set in China. It was preceded by *The World of Extreme Happiness* (2013) and *Snow in Midsummer* (2017–18). Notably, the "China" of Cowhig's plays is not a fixed or stable entity so much as it is a set of practices and forces. The "China" on her stages is, to pilfer language from queer theorist Petrus Liu, "an overdetermined and heterogeneous effect, a complex construct that is irreducible to the People's Republic of China (PRC)."[5] In her

---

3   Ibid., 254.
4   Rey Chow, *Writing Diaspora: Tactics of Intervention in Contemporary Cultural Studies* (Bloomington, IN: Indiana University Press, 1993), 178–9.
5   Petrus Liu, "Why Does Queer Theory Need China?," *positions: east asia cultures critique* 18, no. 2 (2010): 291–332, 294.

dramatic interrogations of these effects, Cowhig keeps an audience's focus on the precarious and disposable forms of life that are routinely sacrificed on the altar of the Chinese economy and the global market's mutual development. In *The World of Extreme Happiness*, for example, Cowhig explores the commodification and callous disposal of rural laborers in the urban Chinese factories that service global supply chains. In *Snow in Midsummer*, the flesh of a rural woman is made into an extractable and disposal resource—a conceit that Cowhig continues to interrogate in *The King of Hell's Palace*.

Early in *The King of Hell's Palace*, one of the characters (Jasmine) asks "How can farmers be capital?" The answer that is supplied over the course of the play reflects something that capitalism, as a system, has always presupposed: there is gold buried in the flesh and its many labors. This is especially true for modern capitalism insofar as it was constituted in and through the trade in flesh, sometimes literally (as in the case of the transatlantic slave trade or the trade in "coolie" labor). *The King of Hell's Palace* depicts a similar scenario as it occurs in the Henan blood trade:

Luo Na   They call your name, you give blood—which gets split into red and yellow parts.

Han-Han   The yellow gold's what they're buying.

Wen   Yellow gold?

Luo Na   It's called "plasma."

Han-Han   The red stuff's put back, so you can sell again sooner.

Wen   Hear that brother? There's gold in these arms.

By Cowhig's account, the play was inspired by the story of the late Dr. Wang Shuping (1959–2019), a doctor who (alongside other activist doctors including Gao Yaojie and Wan Yanhai) helped to expose and fight the first waves of the AIDS crisis in China. In an account of the outbreak Cowhig depicts in *The King of Hell's Palace*, Gao suggests that the trade in Henan blood was one "root of AIDS in China": "From the late 1980s to early 1990s, the plasma market took off in several parts of Henan. Then Liu Quanxi became director of the Henan Health Department and strongly pushed the policy, which encouraged farmers to sell their blood. From 1992 to 1998, as a result of the administration of [the provincial party secretary] Li Changchun, blood-selling became an established 'industry.'"[6] In Chow's account, Chinese lives were used as "bargaining chips, as hostages, as a means to an end" during diplomatic exchanges between China and western powers. As Gao's statement makes clear, the global market also transformed Chinese flesh and blood into an industrially produced commodity. What Chow and Cowhig both illuminate, and offer a theory of, is the way contemporary state power in both China and the United States includes the power to "make live," "take life," and "let die," alongside the power to *sell life*.

Here, again, distinctions *within* the people serve a critical function insofar as they can help distinguish between those who must be protected and those who must be

6   Luo Siling, "Whistle-Blowing AIDS Doctor Reflects on the Roots of Epidemic in China," *The New York Times*. December 1, 2016. https://www.nytimes.com/2016/12/01/world/asia/world-aids-day-china-gao-yaojie.html

protected against: between those who are valued and those who are valuable only insofar as they can buy or, if not that, be bought and sold. Such a distinction involves a form of dehumanization and AIDS continues to be instrumentalized by dominant political and economic forces in China, the U.S., and beyond, to maintain this distinction. Writing about the persecution of sexually non-normative people in early twenty-first century Taiwan, for example, Liu has argued that within that context, "People living with AIDS, transgendered [sic] individuals, non-monogamous gay people, drag queens, transsexuals, drug users, prostitutes, and their clients are excluded from the definition of a human being."[7] By quoting this passage I do not mean to conflate Taiwan and the People's Republic of China. Instead, and as I have been suggesting, the dynamics Liu describes are also present in different ways in both the mainland Chinese context depicted in Cowhig's play and the portrait of Reagan's Cabinet that is supplied by Secretary Regan. In these three distinct examples (Taiwan, the PRC, and the U.S.) political forces instrumentalize AIDS to distinguish between who is worth protecting and who the state will "let die." Unworthy life is then "excluded from the definition of a human being" and may become valuable only insofar as it can become a consumer or, failing that, by being consumed (that is, converted into capital as flesh or blood becomes "gold").

In the early twenty-first century, years after the events of the play have concluded, the government in Henan province began to shift away from the dominant narrative summarized by Yin-Yin when she laments that, "officially there's no AIDS in the country." But care for the infected was often reliant upon the reproduction of an official narrative that AIDS was the effect of "practices" that the state still characterized as undesirable and morally tainted. As Gao observed, economic restitution for people who had been infected in Henan's blood banks was often dependent on the bureaucratic erasure of the blood bank's (and by extension, the state's) role in transmission. According to Gao, when infected people applied for restitution, officials "wouldn't let the victims say it was blood transmission, only homosexual activity or drug use or prostitution."[8] As in the U.S., AIDS was thus officially consigned to a delimited realm defined as "immoral practice." This, in turn, exposes the Henan AIDS patient to the forms of violence and disposability that are reserved for internal enemies: a reality that is fictionalized in the "disproportionate" police response to Lili's demands for justice from Jasmine.[9]

The King of Hell's Palace stages a critical inversion of dominant discourses that suggest AIDS is the product of "immoral practices" in order to emphasize instead, the often profoundly immoral political and economic practices through which HIV and AIDS are managed and responded to by various sites of power's exercise. In this way, Cowhig's work is resonant with the kinds of cultural practices that the late art historian, queer theorist, and AIDS activist Douglas Crimp called for in a seminal 1987 essay

7   Liu, *Queer Marxism in Two Chinas* (Durham, NC: Duke University Press, 2015), 163.
8   Siling.
9   For an account of the complicated terrain of social foreclosure that is navigated by people living with AIDS in the People's Republic of China, see Xiaopei He and Lisa Rofel, "'I Am AIDS': Living with HIV/AIDS in China," *positions: east asia cultures critique* 18, no. 2 (2010): 511–36.

where he also called upon the language of "practice" to describe the significance of AIDS. As with Cowhig, and in contradistinction to Regan or the Henan officials described by Gao, Crimp puts the onus for the "illness, suffering, and death" caused by AIDS on the "practices" through which the dominant culture theorizes, narrates, and responds to the disease:

> AIDS does not exist apart from the practices that conceptualize it, represent it, and respond to it. We know AIDS only in and through those practices. This assertion does not contest the existence of viruses, antibodies, infections, or transmission routes. Least of all does it contest the reality of illness, suffering, and death. What it *does* contest is the notion that there is an underlying reality of AIDS, on which are constructed the representation, or the culture, or the politics of AIDS. If we recognize that AIDS exists only in and through these constructions, the hope is that we can also recognize the imperative to know them, analyze them, and wrest control of them.[10]

Insisting that we understand AIDS to be an effect of the practices, power dynamics, and narratives that surround it, Crimp gives us a means for understanding AIDS as part of a broader social ordering with power effects that divide the wanted from the unwanted, marking the line that distinguishes those whom the state and the dominant culture must keep alive from those who must be protected against: the immoral, the sexual and racial deviant, the inhuman, the disposable, the impoverished, the infected.

Crimp's essay reinforces (and is reinforced by) Paula Treichler's argument that AIDS is an "epidemic of signification" as much as it is a medical epidemic.[11] To conceive of AIDS as an "epidemic of signification" is to gain a sense of the powers that cohered in the cultural and aesthetic practices that emerged in response to the AIDS crisis—a tradition in which *The King of Hell's Palace* is well situated. The long-documented use of art in the struggle against AIDS has repeatedly demonstrated the capacity of aesthetics to "re-signify" and "wrest control" of the meaning and significance of AIDS. It was for this very reason, Crimp insisted, that "we need cultural practices actively participating in the struggle against AIDS."[12]

Throughout *The King of Hell's Palace,* Cowhig employs a skillful knowledge of dramatic history and form to effect a dramaturgy that eschews the distinction between aesthetic and political labor.[13] *Snow in Midsummer* drew explicit inspiration from Yuan dramas of the thirteenth century and the revenge tragedies of the Elizabethan and Jacobean stage, and formal elements from both traditions appear in *The King of Hell's Palace*. In both Yuan and Elizabethan drama, theatrical conventions were commonly deployed to smuggle political critique into the work and blur the space between "artist" and "activist." Continuing this tradition, Cowhig deploys the power of the theater to

---

10 Douglas Crimp, "AIDS: Cultural Analysis/Cultural Activism," in *Melancholia and Moralism: Essays on AIDS and Queer Politics*, 27–41 (Cambridge, MA/London: MIT Press, 2002), 28.

11 Paula A. Treichler, "AIDS, Homophobia, and Biomedical Discourse: An Epidemic of Signification," in *AIDS: Cultural Analysis/Cultural Activism*, ed. Douglas Crimp, 31–70 (Cambridge: MIT Press, 1987).

12 Crimp, "AIDS: Cultural Analysis/Cultural Activism," 33.

13 This distinction between "art" and "politics" is a false binary anyway, since the aesthetic is always already political and aesthetic categories (such as "quality," "good," and "bad") have always been determined by political consideration.

interrogate and indict the dynamics through which "AIDS" comes to signify within a global context, documenting and depicting the process through which the lives of people living with AIDS are transformed into "bargaining chips" and "liquid gold."

Since the origins of the AIDS crisis in both the U.S. and the People's Republic of China, AIDS has been instrumentalized to reproduce an ongoing caesura within the biological population of both states. In both contexts, AIDS has been used to distinguish the wanted from the unwanted, and those forms of life that are worthy of protection against forms of life that are worthy only insofar as they can be converted into profit: a point that is callously underlined as the very operatives who cause the crisis in *The King of Hell's Palace* (Wang Wei, Jasmine, and Phoenix Pharmaceutical) begin scheming to make money from the "emerging market" of "AIDS medication." I have been suggesting that the continued struggle against these circumstances happens in the realm of activist interventions embodied by Drs. Gao and Wang, but also in the terrain of cultural production that is exemplified by *The King of Hell's Palace.*

Cowhig's narrative offers an insistent reminder that the struggle to transform the horizon from a state of foreclosure to a condition of possibility will require great personal cost from those who carry it out. Near the conclusion of the play, Yin-Yin, the doctor modeled on figures like Wang and Gao, leaves her family in China to enter into exile abroad. Her fate mirrors the biographies of both Wang and Gao: Wang struggled against government suppression of knowledge about the outbreak before she relocated to the United States in 2001, while Gao was subject to harassment and multiple arrests before she left China for the U.S. in 2009. In 2016, the *New York Times* reported that Gao, at 88, was living alone and on public assistance in New York City—planning her funeral from exile.[14] Then, in 2019, as Cowhig was preparing the play for a production at London's Hampstead Theatre, Chinese state security officials began to exert pressure on Wang to shut down the play. Wang was afraid for her own daughter and increasingly isolated from friends and family in Henan and Beijing who received visits from security officials and were afraid to maintain contact with her. Nonetheless, she didn't relinquish her support for the production, writing in a statement, "With bullying and censorship, the government has covered up the HCV and HIV epidemics in China very successfully. Why, in 2019, do they worry so much about a play being produced in London, 24 years after the events it depicts?"[15]

State authority did not halt the London Production, but the U.S. premiere was delayed and then canceled in response to the COVID-19 pandemic. We are living through that long winter now and in that time, we have witnessed retrenched forms of authoritarianism and securitization across the world, with catastrophic consequences in places like Hong Kong, Xinjiang province, Ferguson, MO, Minneapolis, MN, and Washington D.C. This new pandemic rages as AIDS continues to burn, and in it we find once more the state's decision between what forms of life are made to live and which are exposed to death. The melancholic ambivalence with which *The King of*

14 Siling.
15 Vanessa Thorpe, "From Beijing to Hampstead: How Tale of HIV Whistleblower Rattled Chinese State," *Guardian*, September 8, 2019. https://www.theguardian.com/stage/2019/sep/08/the-king-of-hells-palace-hampstead-theatre-shuping-wang-hiv-whistleblower-china

Hell's Palace concludes seems significant of the ongoing exigencies and uncertainties characterizing life in the present moment. Indeed, the play's final sequence illustrate the stakes of the ongoing battle against AIDS, and now COVID-19, where the horizon of the future is marked by the simultaneity of foreclosure (exile, the approaching spectre of the dead, and the advance of the disease in Little Yi's body) and hope (Yin-Yin's fugitive flight, new access to medications, or the Yang's family's desire for Pei-Pei to "be the first Yang from this village to live off the brain instead of the body"). As the play concludes with the emergence of "another realm," we are left with the question of what is to be done to bring better and other worlds into being. One possible answer, Cowhig's play suggests, can be found in the story of Dr. Wang's struggle in the service of more life.

Snow in Midsummer

Based on
The Injustice to Dou Yi that Moved Heaven and Earth
By Guan Hanqing

Snow in Midsummer was first performed by the Royal Shakespeare Company (Greg Doran, Artistic Director; Catherine Mallyon, Executive Director) at the Swan Theatre, Stratford-upon-Avon, on February 23, 2017.

Dou Yi	Katie Leung
Tianyun	Wendy Kweh
Fei-Fei	Emily Dao / Zoe Lim / Sophie Wang
Mother Cai	Jacqueline Chan
Nurse Wong	Sarah Lam
Handsome Zhang	Colin Ryan
Rocket Wu	Andrew Leung
Doctor Lu / Master Zhang	Daniel York
Worker Huang / Officer 1 / Judge Wu	Richard Rees
Officer 2	Kevin Shen
Worker Zhou / Officer 3	Jonathan Raggett
Worker Fang	Andrew Koji
Worker Chen	Lucy Sheen

Director	Justin Audibert
Designer	Lily Arnold
Lighting Designer	Anna Watson
Composer	Ruth Chan
Sound Designer	Claire Windsor
Movement Director	Lucy Cullingford
Fight Director	Rachel Bown-Williams and Ruth Cooper-Brown

Snow in Midsummer was first performed in North America by the Oregon Shakespeare Festival (Bill Rauch, Artistic Director; Cynthia Rider, Executive Director) at the Angus Bowmer Theatre, Ashland, Oregon, on August 2, 2018.

Dou Yi	Jessica Ko
Tianyun	Amy Kim Waschke
Fei-Fei	Olivia Pham
Mother Cai / Nurse Wong	Natsuko Ohama
Handsome Zhang	Daisuke Tsuji
Rocket Wu	Will Dao
Doctor Lu / Judge Wu	Cristofer Jean
Master Zhang / Worker Huang / Officer 1	James Ryen
Worker Fang / Officer 2 / Horse-Face	Moses Villarama
Worker Zhou / Officer 3 / Ox-Head	Román Zaragoza
Worker Chen	Monique Holt

Director	Justin Audibert
Scenic Designer	Laura Jellinek
Costume Designer	Helen Q. Huang
Lighting Designer	Jane Cox
Composer & Sound Designer	Paul James Prendergast
Dramaturgs	Christine Mok and Amrita Ramanan
Voice and Text Director	David Carey
Fight Director	U. Jonathan Toppo
Choreographer	Maija García
Production Stage Manager	Jeremy Eisen
Repertory Producer	Mica Cole

Characters

(With maximum possible doubling)

Dou Yi, *a widowed craftswoman.*

Tianyun, *a wealthy businesswoman.*

Fei-Fei, *Tianyun's nine-year-old daughter.*

Handsome Zhang, *owner of New Harmony Factories.*

Rocket Wu, *Handsome Zhang's fiancé.*

Nurse Wong, *bar hostess. Formerly Handsome Zhang's wet nurse.*
Also plays: **Mother Cai**, *a blind masseur. Dou Yi's Mother-In-Law.*

Master Zhang, *Handsome Zhang's father. Famed singer working for the People's Liberation Army. Founder of New Harmony.*
Also plays: **Doctor Lu**, *a surgeon in New Harmony.*
         Worker Chen, *a factory worker.*

Worker Huang
Also plays: **Officer 1**, *People's Liberation Army Police Officer.*
         Judge Wu, *New Harmony Magistrate.*

Worker Fang
Also plays: **Officer 2**, *People's Liberation Army Police Officer.*
         Ox-Head, *Guardian of the Underworld.*

Worker Zhou
Also plays: **Officer 3**, *People's Liberation Army Police Officer.*
         Horse-Face, *Guardian of the Underworld.*

Place and Time

New Harmony, a remote factory town in Jiangsu Providence. Present day and three years earlier.

Prologue

Three years before present day. A sultry night in midsummer, on New Harmony's busiest bar street. **Dou Yi** *enters with a basket filled with winged handicrafts woven from lush green palm fronds.*

Dou Yi

> Buy the fresh green palm weavings of the widow Dou Yi!
> Locusts, dragons, phoenixes and grasshoppers!
> Blue jays, unicorns, dragon flies and moths!
> Bumble bees, swans, ducks and cicadas!
> Support the widow Dou Yi and her green flying things!
> Weavings, fresh palm weavings!
> The universe is made of ten thousand things,
> With enough fronds I can weave all of them!
> Buy the fresh green palm weavings of the widow Dou Yi!
> Sir, would you care for a sparrow?
> I learned birds at seven, before I was sold to Mother Cai,
> Who I live with here in New Harmony.
> Every moon for ten years I wove a new bird and prayed for my birth mother's return.
> When I was seventeen and had a flock of more than one-hundred sparrows
> I married Mother Cai's son and wove dragons and phoenixes for our wedding.
> Miss, would you like a pair?
> Together they symbolize the blessings of marriage
> Like my necklace
> (*Pulls it out.*)
> Two single characters, each meaning "joy"
> Combine to create a new word
> A new future
> A new story—
> Double Happiness.
> I'll be weaving by lamplight beside the town bar—
> I take commissions!
> Do you have a daughter?
> Does she need wings?

Master Zhang, *an army official wearing his dress uniform, staggers on, drunk. He hums the tune to "The Bright Moon Represents My Heart."*

Dou Yi

> Weavings, fresh palm weavings!
> Sparrows, dragons, phoenixes and grasshoppers!
> Blue jays, unicorns, dragon flies and locusts!
> Bumble bees, swans, ducks and cicadas!
> Support the widow Dou Yi and her green flying things!

Dou Yi *sees* **Master Zhang** *and hurries offstage. He follows her off.*

Act One

Scene One

Three years later.

Sunset at a town bar in New Harmony, which has been decimated by a devastating drought. Trees and shrubs have long since crumbled into dust. Lakes and streams have dried up. The birds have fled. The only non-human life left is audible through the deafening hum of insects and the desperate squeaks of rats searching for water.

Nurse Wong, a boisterous bar hostess, reads a newspaper and tends to a rectangular grill covered with skewered locust kebabs. Plastic bean shoot barrettes emerge from the crown of her head, like sprouts coming out of a pot.

Worker Fang, an off-duty factory worker, sips a beer.

Nurse Wong (*off newspaper*)   It's official. Lake Tai is bone dry.

Worker Fang   This morning ten cars slid off the road! Ten cars, slipping over a mass grave of crushed crickets!

Nurse Wong   The poor things must have been trying to evacuate.

Worker Fang (*suddenly noticing a dead animal*)   A dead rat!

Nurse Wong   Get that nasty thing out of my bar!

Worker Fang (*picks it up by the tail, examines it closely*)   Must have been searching for water.

Worker Fang *chucks the rat out the window.*

Nurse Wong   No messy mishaps tonight. The new boss is coming.

Worker Chen and **Worker Zhou**, *more off-duty factory workers, enter carrying the pieces for a dragon dance, which are obscured by a plastic tarp.*

Worker Fang (*sharing news*)   Did you hear? Lake Tai is bone dry.

Worker Chen   My family has worked this land for twenty generations. That dry lake is unprecedented. There must be ten centuries of forgotten things suddenly seeing the light.

Worker Fang   It's leaves my family's missing. My poor ma weeps watching television when she sees a living tree.

Nurse Wong   What about those giant palms Handsome "planted"?

Worker Fang   You can't mark time with a plastic tree that doesn't change with the seasons.

Worker Huang, *another off-duty factory worker, enters the bar.*

Worker Huang   The new boss is single!

Worker Fang *spits into his hand, styles his hair, sniffs his pits and bares his teeth.*

Worker Fang   Do I have locust in my teeth?

Nurse Wong   She's out of your league.

Worker Fang   She could have a weakness for sexy salt of the earth types.

Worker Huang   If you want a chance with that bird, invest in a bottle of sesame oil—A.S.A.P.

Worker Fang   Comrade, your concern warms my heart, but hard liquor's the only lubricant I need.

Worker Zhou   Fucking rice bucket! It's for your bone dry desert skin.

Worker Huang (*pulling up shirt*)   Feel my chest. Sample my supple, succulent skin.

Worker Fang   Wah! He's soft as a baby!

Worker Huang   Because I oil myself head to toe every morning and evening. Heaven helps those who help themselves.

Worker Fang   If my parents weren't so old I'd help myself by becoming a migrant and getting the fuck out of this town.

Nurse Wong   This is the new normal. Adapt or be extinguished. Do what you will with your lives. Nurse Wong intends to survive.

Handsome Zhang, *a flashily dressed local entrepreneur in his mid-twenties, leads* **Tianyun Lin** *into the bar.* **Tianyun** *'s in her mid-forties, and carries herself like a woman used to getting her way.*

Handsome   Welcome to "Nurse Wong's," the official bar of New Harmony.

Nurse Wong   We're not for sale.

Tianyun   Where did you find such a feisty bartender?

Nurse Wong   Long before this flower prince knew Nurse Wong, he knew her right and left tits.

Handsome   You make me sound like a "customer."

Nurse Wong   Don't act like I couldn't have mastered that line of work. When I was young as a bamboo shoot I wasn't offering these sad little bean sacks. I had big hunks of tofu for sale! Even without teeth, Handsome Zhang was one hungry bastard. I've seen this lazy worm crawl, shit and say his first word!

Worker Fang   What was it?

Handsome   Money!

Tianyun   Were you his wet nurse?

Nurse Wong   Who says he's stopped nursing?

They laugh.

Nurse Wong   Handsome acts like a hard man, but he has a marshmallow heart, and tears that could fill Lake Tai.

Worker Fang   Start crying, quick!

Handsome   Comrade, I've cried enough for six lifetimes. Let someone else fill our lake.

Worker Zhou   We cried for months when we heard about your father.

Worker Fang   I grew up singing his songs.

Handsome   No more sad stuff. This is a joyful day for New Harmony. Please welcome Boss Lin—who's just a few signatures away from buying the factories—to our wonderful town.

Everyone claps.

Handsome   I trust you will show Boss Lin the same work ethic you honored the Zhang family with during the decade we built, then ran, all the New Harmony factories.

Everyone claps.

Tianyun   I can't tell you how excited I am to purchase a factory in my home province. I was born in a remote village several hours from here, became a migrant in my teens, found work in a factory and worked my way up from assembly line worker to unit manager. Today I own the largest synthetic flower company in the country.

Handsome   To New Harmony!

All   New Harmony!

Handsome   Boss Lin's peonies are available globally through every major bridal catalog.

Nurse Wong   They are more peony-like than natural peonies.

Worker Huang   How will you end the drought?

Worker Fang   She's not the Goddess of Mercy.

Worker Zhou   She could seed the clouds.

Worker Fang   When was the last time you saw a cloud in the sky?

Worker Zhou   It must have been during that freak summer snow.

Tianyun   While your water problems are a challenge, developments in transport technologies allow us to use drones to move product and avoid road issues completely.

Worker Zhou   Drones?

Worker Fang   This woman's a pro!

Fei-Fei *enters, wearing a white kung-fu uniform. She's holding a locust.*

Fei-Fei   Ma, I found a locust on my pillow.

Nurse Wong   Who's this fierce warrior?

Tianyun   This is my daughter, Fei-Fei.

Nurse Wong   How does a woman running so many factories find time to date and get married?

Fei-Fei   I'm adopted. She's single. End of story.

Tianyun   Fei-Fei turns seven in four days.

Nurse Wong   Then I must make you candied locusts!

Fei-Fei   Ew!

Worker Fang *takes the locust from* **Fei-Fei**.

Worker Fang (*to locust*)   Goodbye, friend. This is for the best. Hurry up and reincarnate into something more than a pest.

Worker Fang *impales the locust onto a wooden skewer and tosses it into a marinade bowl.*

Fei-Fei   You're mean!

Nurse Wong   Give those sticks on the grill a twist while you're at it.

Fei-Fei (*to her mother*)   You forgot to read me a story.

Tianyun   Go back upstairs. I'll read to you soon.

Fei-Fei   What if I fall asleep?

Tianyun   I'll wake you up.

Fei-Fei   Swear?

Fei-Fei *spits into her hand and extends it.* **Tianyun** *does the same. They shake.*

Tianyun   She's big on oaths.

Nurse Wong   What are you reading?

Fei-Fei   Records of the Grand Historian.

Worker Huang   Sounds scholarly.

Tianyun   It's an abridged version of the ancient dynastic stories.

Fei-Fei   With big pictures that show what everyone's wearing.

Rocket Wu, *a fashionably dressed man in his late twenties, saunters in.*

Rocket   Did anyone order a Rain Dance?

Handsome *crosses over to* **Rocket** *and kisses him on the lips.* **Worker Chen** *and* **Worker Huang** *pick up the dragon puppet and prepare for the Rain Dance.*

Fei-Fei   Is it for Ghost Month?

Worker Fang   Ghost month? It's for every month!

Worker Zhou   Every week.

Worker Huang   Wu Shamans performed sacrificial rain dances in times of drought.

Worker Chen   They danced all night inside a circle of fire!

Fei-Fei   Cool!

Worker Fang   Sweat dripping from the shaman's body made the skies open up.

Worker Zhou   I'd have more faith in the government rain dance of shooting missiles into the clouds.

Rocket   Dragon Dancers, are you ready?

Handsome   Wait. I have something to say. Something that's been trapped in my heart for a very long time.

Nurse Wong   I told you he was marshmallow fluff.

Handsome   Five years ago, you would have thought I had everything. In truth, my days and nights were lonely. One night in Shanghai, I stepped into Club Angel and saw a man dancing on a column, offering his soul to the heavens with each move. Our eyes met and I knew I'd move heaven and earth and stop at nothing to have a shot at spending my life with him.

Handsome *drops to one knee, and removes a gold band from his pocket.*

Fei-Fei   NO!

Tianyun   Fei-Fei!

Fei-Fei   You shouldn't!

Tianyun (*grabbing* **Fei-Fei**'*s hand*)   Forgive us.

Worker Zhou   This child is spicy!

Tianyun (*to* **Fei-Fei**)   Move your legs!

Fei-Fei   Don't propose during Ghost Month! It's an invitation for spirits to visit!

Nurse Wong   Wasn't the Cultural Revolution supposed to wipe out rural superstition?

Tianyun   Our housekeeper, a devout Buddhist, has brainwashed my daughter.

Tianyun *tries to lead* **Fei-Fei** *out of the bar.*

Rocket   Uncle Handsome has been waiting five years for this moment.

Fei-Fei   Do it next month. It's safer.

Nurse Wong   Not everyone shares your religious belief.

Fei-Fei   It's real!

Rocket   It may be bad timing, but I believe in this man. It will be an honor to grow old with him.

Handsome *puts the ring on* **Rocket***'s finger.*

Nurse Wong   Something's wrong—what's coming out of my eyes?

Worker Fang   They're called "tears."

Nurse Wong   Quick—take me to Lake Tai!

Rocket / Handsome   Master of Rain, water this land, we send you this dance—

Workers / Nurse Wong   OPEN THE SKY!

Rocket *puts on a techno track that pulses with sounds of thunder and pouring rain. The four workers perform a rollicking contemporary take on the traditional Dragon Dance.* **Handsome** *flicks a switch, flooding the patio with blue light then dances around* **Rocket***.* **Tianyun** *and* **Fei-Fei** *watch from the corner.* **Nurse Wong** *turns skewered locusts over glowing coals.*

Scene Two

New Harmony Guest House. Later the same night. **Tianyun** *enters, carrying a sleeping* **Fei-Fei***.* **Handsome** *and* **Rocket** *follow her in. The room is furnished with an ornate antique desk being used as a dining table, and several dining chairs. Sounds of early evening locusts have transitioned to choruses of crickets.*

Handsome   Sorry about the stuffy furniture. My father was a collector.

Tianyun   He had impeccable taste. I love pieces with history.

Handsome   I'm glad someone appreciates his hoarding.

Rocket   This is a scholar's desk, from the Yuan dynasty.

Tianyun   Was this Master Zhang's apartment?

Handsome   Only in name. His touring schedule made it difficult for him to grace us with his presence.

Tianyun (*to* **Rocket**)   Did you know him?

Rocket   We never met. Frankly I'm not sure—

Handsome (*interrupting*)   He would have adored you.

Tianyun *lowers* **Fei-Fei** *into a chair and guides her forward, so her head and arms rest on the table.*

Tianyun   Wake up, Fei-Fei. Time for a story.

Fei-Fei *stirs, but doesn't wake up.*

Rocket   Why don't you enjoy a lazy morning. I'll pick you up around noon.

Tianyun   I could tour the factory on my own if you'd rather watch Handsome sign legal documents. You have a lot to celebrate.

Handsome   We'll celebrate after closing with an around the world trip.

Rocket   To decide what country we'll move to.

Tianyun   How thrilling! What's on your list?

Rocket   Honolulu, San Francisco, Auckland, Vancouver, Copenhagen, Stockholm, and Oslo.

Tianyun   Those are all very green cities.

Handsome   How much you want to bet he boxes our entire apartment before we're signed?

Rocket   I'm a Pisces. Desert conditions don't do it for me. I need clouds and rain and thunder and mist and—

Handsome   You're getting it.

Rocket   You've said that before.

Handsome   Trust me.

Rocket   If this deal falls through I'm leaving without you.

Handsome   My happiness is in your hands.

Tianyun   I'll make sure my lawyers behave.

Handsome   Thank you.

Tianyun   Safe travels.

As **Tianyun** *sees* **Rocket** *and* **Handsome** *to the door, a sleepwalking* **Fei-Fei** *climbs onto her chair and then onto the table. Her long black hair covers her face, obscuring her features.* **Fei-Fei** *walks to the edge of the table and stands there, gazing out at a distant horizon only she can see.*

Tianyun (*entering*)   Okay, sleepyhead. I'll get your—Fei-Fei! What are you doing!

Fei-Fei (*flat, detached monotone*)   Heart of Sorrow, Tears of Suffering. How will you redeem my three-year rotting bones?

Tianyun   You're asleep, poor thing. You must be—

Fei-Fei (*detached*)   No rain and not an inch of grass has grown. Injustice killed this girl of youth and spring.

Tianyun   Injustice? / We must get you new—

Fei-Fei (*detached*)   No one on earth has avenged me.

Tianyun   You're / having a night terror—

Fei-Fei (*detached*)   Earth—why have you only mourned but not fought for me?

Tianyun   Fei-Fei, wake up.

Fei-Fei *starts to cough. A necklace on a red cord emerges from* **Fei-Fei**'s *mouth. She grabs onto one end and tries to dislodge it from her throat.*

Tianyun   What did you swallow? Let it out. (*Rubs her back.*) I'm going to pull very gently . . . (*The necklace comes out.*) You've done it.

Fei-Fei (*detached*)   Double Happiness.

Tianyun   Where did you get this wedding necklace?

Fei-Fei   Justice.

Tianyun (*annoyed*)   Wake up, darling.

Fei-Fei *grabs the necklace and holds it over* **Tianyun**'s *head.*

Fei-Fei   Promise.

Tianyun   Promise what?

Fei-Fei   Justice.

Tianyun   I promise I'll help you get justice . . .

Fei-Fei *tries to put the necklace around* **Tianyun**'s *neck.*

Fei-Fei   Swear.

Tianyun *puts on the Double Happiness necklace. She's playing along. She doesn't believe a ghost is possessing her daughter.*

Tianyun   I swear I won't remove this necklace until I help you.

Fei-Fei (*detached*)   Wait until snow falls in June and drought lasts three years. Only then will my innocent soul be revealed.

Fei-Fei *collapses into her mother's arms.* **Tianyun** *carries her to the bedroom.*

Scene Three

The Spirit World.

The **Ghost of Dou Yi** *crawls in, weak from hunger.*

She's dressed in a prison uniform—the clothes she was executed in. There's no blood on her clothes.

Around her neck hangs a cardboard sign containing the characters "Dou Yi" written in black brush ink characters. A red X has been drawn over the characters.

Dou Yi

> Fog locked, cloud buried
> Treading in darkness, traveling with the wind
> When will I escape this boundless ocean of grief?
> Here I am, a single shadow, without kin or kith—
> Swallowing my voice, making empty laments
> A mute woman suffering silently.
> Earth—
> Why have you only mourned but not fought for Dou Yi?

Scene Four

New Harmony Guest House, next day. **Tianyun** *leads a sleepy* **Fei-Fei** *into the living room. She carries an illustrated children's version of* Records of the Grand Historian.

Fei-Fei   I want to go back to sleep.

Tianyun   It's already noon. You've slept the day away.

Fei-Fei   I was making a snow girl.

Tianyun   In your dream?

Fei-Fei   She's cold. She doesn't have winter clothes.

She flips through her book, scanning the illustrations.

I need to pick a warm outfit to send her. Please get me crayons and white paper.

Tianyun   We'll go shopping after Uncle Rocket gives us a tour of the factories.

Fei-Fei   Can we get food too?

Tianyun   Have a cereal bar. We'll get proper meals later.

Fei-Fei *reaches for the cereal bar* **Tianyun** *offers her. There are flecks of blood on her sleeve.*

Tianyun   Are you hurt?

Fei-Fei   Huh?

Tianyun   There's blood on your sleeve!

Tianyun *pushes up the sleeves of* **Fei-Fei**'s *uniform, revealing raw, raised red-lines of scratches on each of her inside forearms—forming the characters "DOU" and "YI."*

Tianyun What have you done?

Fei-Fei Nothing!

Tianyun You've scratched yourself very badly. Did something bite you?

Fei-Fei No.

Tianyun We're cutting your nails—

Fei-Fei You can't cut nails during Ghost Month. It's an invitation for spirits to—

Tianyun (*suddenly recognizing shapes*) Are these characters?

Fei-Fei She wanted me to remember her name.

Tianyun Who?

Fei-Fei (*reading characters*) "Dou Yi." That's the name of the girl who's stuck in the snow.

Tianyun No more games.

Fei-Fei She was helping me make a snow girl. She's hungry! She doesn't have winter clothes.

Tianyun (*pulling a handkerchief out of her purse*) Let's get you cleaned up.

Fei-Fei Food and clothes! Food and clothes! (*Pointing to Double Happiness necklace.*) You promised!

Tianyun *rolls her eyes and starts to take off the necklace*

Fei-Fei Don't!

Tianyun *relents, and leaves the necklace on.*

Tianyun Stop playing.

Fei-Fei When a ghost wants something, you have to help. Bad things happen if you don't.

A knock on the door. **Tianyun** *answers it. It's* **Nurse Wong**, *carrying a plate of food.*

Nurse Wong I made onion pancakes.

Fei-Fei Food!

Tianyun Thank you. Come in.

She does.

Nurse Wong I'm surprised a woman of your standing doesn't have an army of nannies.

Tianyun I swore when I adopted Fei-Fei not to become an absentee parent.

Nurse Wong She resembles you.

Tianyun   I was thinking the same about you and Handsome.

Nurse Wong   It warms my heart to hear you say that. How was your morning?

Tianyun   I'm afraid my daughter has an overactive imagination.

Nurse Wong   Let her be a child. She'll be grown before you know it.

Tianyun   It's her superstitions that are driving me mad. We've barely been here a day and she already has an imaginary friend.

Nurse Wong   Handsome had several of those.

Tianyun   First there was Ming Ming, the unicorn panda. Then it was La La, the giant dust bunny. Now it's Dou Yi, the magical snow girl.

Beat.

Nurse Wong   Dou Yi?

Tianyun   Ridiculous, isn't it?

Nurse Wong   Did someone say that name in my bar?

Tianyun   Is there a local girl with that name?

Nurse Wong   There was.

Tianyun   Was?

Nurse Wong   She was executed.

Tianyun   For what crime?

Another knock. **Fei-Fei** *answers. It's* **Rocket**, *with a vibrant dragon wind-sock style kite that is similar in coloration to the one from the dragon dance.*

Rocket   I hear it's someone's birthday in three days.

Fei-Fei   Uncle Rocket! Is that for me?

Rocket   Now you can do your own rain dance!

Fei-Fei   Nurse Wong, is there bamboo and string in your bar?

Nurse Wong   I'm fresh out of bamboo and string. And cumin, and rat poison as well, come to think of it. Why don't you come with me on my shopping trip?

Fei-Fei   Can I?

Tianyun   You wanted to go shopping.

Nurse Wong   I'll even let you carry my bag.

Fei-Fei   I'll guard it from pickpockets and drop-kick anyone who tries to touch it.

Nurse Wong   Step on it. I don't have all day.

Fei-Fei *and* **Nurse Wong** *exit.*

Rocket   Handsome just texted. He says your lawyers are being very cooperative.

Tianyun   That's easy to do when the sale price is so reasonable.

Rocket   You can thank me for that.

Tianyun   Are you packed?

Rocket   Overpacked.

Tianyun   The secret is layers. Of all the cities you're trying, is there a top contender?

Rocket   I would love to split my time between Hawaii and Vancouver.

Tianyun   Wouldn't we all?

Rocket   You've made enough for six lifetimes. You could retire anywhere.

Tianyun   And be left to my thoughts? I wouldn't dare.

Rocket   I thought we'd start with the unit managers. They're very eager to—

Rocket *gasps and clutches his chest.*

Tianyun   What is it?

Rocket   It's fine. I just need to catch my—

Rocket *doubles over, moaning in pain.*

Tianyun   We must get you help.

Tianyun *helps* **Rocket** *rise to his feet. They exit the Guest House.*

Scene Five

A private hospital room, several hours later. **Rocket** *reclines on a stretcher.* **Doctor Lu** *is beside him, listening to his heart through a stethoscope.* **Tianyun** *enters.*

Tianyun   Handsome's leaving Shenzhen right away. He'll be back later this evening.

Doctor Lu   You've had what's called an ischemic heart attack. It's a stress-related event.

Rocket   Is something wrong with the transplant?

Doctor Lu   Your new heart is in excellent condition if I do say so myself. I can hardly see the scar.

Rocket (*to* **Tianyun**)   My original was defective. Doctor Lu did the surgery.

Tianyun   I had no idea.

Rocket   Boss Lin is purchasing the New Harmony factories.

Doctor Lu   Is that right?

Tianyun   My lawyers are finalizing the sale as we speak.

Doctor Lu   Welcome to our humble town.

Tianyun   A heart transplant. What a massive surgery.

Rocket   I'm very lucky.

Doctor Lu   Despite the Cultural Revolution's valiant efforts, most Chinese are superstitious and refuse to be organ donors.

Rocket   Times are changing. I'm a registered donor.

Tianyun   That's very generous.

Rocket   A teenager gave me his heart. It's the right way to thank him.

Tianyun   How did he die?

Rocket   A car crash.

Tianyun   His parents must have been glad to see some good come from their loss.

Rocket   We exchange cards every year.

Doctor Lu   I'm sure you were a great comfort.

Rocket   Was the boy from a northern province?

Doctor Lu   I don't recall. Why do you ask?

Rocket   I keep dreaming of snow.

Tianyun   Snow?

Rocket   I'm on the ground and it's swirling around me. Covering me up. Burying me. I can't move. I feel . . . desperately cold. Then everything fades to white.

Doctor Lu   Memory is stored in the brain. You're simply longing for good old fashioned wet weather, like every man, woman and child in this town. I haven't felt like myself since my vegetables dried up.

Rocket   I've never seen snow in my life. Not even when it fell three summers ago.

Doctor Lu   You'll see some very soon on your around the world trip.

Tianyun   What month did the snow fall?

Doctor Lu   June. The first week, I recall.

Rocket   So much happened that week.

Doctor Lu   You were in surgery.

Rocket   And Master Zhang's killer received her sentencing.

Tianyun   Handsome must have been in pieces.

Doctor Lu   Like you said, he must be glad some good came from his loss.

Beat.

Tianyun   When I said that, I had been referring to the teenage boy's family.

Rocket   What good could have come from Master Zhang's murder?

Rocket *groans suddenly and reaches for his chest.* **Doctor Lu** *listens to his heartbeat.*

Doctor Lu   There's nothing wrong with your heart. This is psychosomatic.

Rocket   Then why am I dreaming of snow? I keep seeing a white flag dripping with blood.

Doctor Lu   We all have bad dreams. It's how the subconscious deals with stress. Be grateful you're not grinding your teeth.

Rocket   Thank you, Doctor Lu. For everything.

Doctor Lu   It has been a privilege to devote my life to the needs of New Harmony.

Doctor Lu *starts to leave.*

Tianyun   When someone is executed, what happens to the body?

Doctor Lu   Might I ask—has the sale gone through?

Tianyun (*checks her phone*)   It just has.

Rocket   Congratulations.

Tianyun   To us both.

Doctor Lu   I'm delighted to serve our new leadership.

Tianyun   I'm just a businesswoman.

Doctor Lu   In the past we would have determined the death row inmate's blood type during a prison physical, then let the will of the free market handle the rest—

Rocket   The will of the free market?

Doctor Lu   Throughout time the power to prolong human life has always been our most exquisite commodity.

Rocket   Did Handsome try to acquire—

Doctor Lu (*interrupting*)   I suggest you ask him.

Rocket   He wasn't successful. My heart belonged to a boy who died on a highway.

Doctor Lu   Boy, girl, highway, execution ground. Death comes in many forms.

Rocket   Lord of the Blue Sky.

Doctor Lu   If the tale of a teenager lost to a car wreck was the fable you needed to fuel your recovery / it was the—

Rocket (*interrupting at /*)   Is the heart of an executed woman pumping blood through my body?

Doctor Lu   There is nothing a Zhang won't do for the person he loves.

Rocket   He knew I would never accept something not given freely.

Doctor Lu   Would you rather he watch you die while that woman's heart was packed in dry ice and expressed overseas?

Rocket   What kind of doctor lies to his own patient?

Doctor Lu   It's not my business—

Rocket (*interrupting*)   It's your business to inform your patient of the risks associated with any surgery.

Rocket *starts to leave.*

Doctor Lu   Your heart is in excellent condition.

Rocket   My heart is medical waste. It was incinerated three years ago.

Rocket *exits.*

Scene Six

The Spirit World. The Ghost of **Dou Yi** *enters.*

Dou Yi

> This missing body's name was Duanyun.
> When I was seven I was sold to Mother Cai
> Who changed my name to Dou Yi.
> Who is like me? No ending, no rest.
> Mother, I once swam in your belly
> I was made of ten thousand things
> Why can't you tell I've left the world of the living?
> Mother
> Clear my name.
> Give me a burial.
> But how can you bury your daughter if you can't find her body?
> Where are the lungs that you gave her?
> Where are the hands that wove sparrows?

Scene Seven

Town courthouse and execution grounds, later the same day.

Three **People's Armed Police Officers** *smoke cigarettes and play blackjack beneath plastic palm trees. Each has a tiny plastic bean sprout clipped to his hat.*

Officer 3   You don't know how stupid I get. My brain forms genius sentences that communicate the perfect balance of "I'm into you" and "I'm out of your league." But the shit that spews from my fingers is shameful.

Officer 1   Luckily for you, brother, I was a poet in the last life. What's the last thing she sent you?

Officer 3   It's private.

Officer 1   Sounds spicy!

Officer 2 *grabs* **Officer 3**'*s cell.*

Officer 2 (*reading*)   "My cat vomited a hairball that reminds me of your face—X"

Officer 3   X means kiss!

Officer 2   You remind her of cat puke.

Officer 3   It's romantic. She's seeing me everywhere.

Officer 1   PRIVATE YANG!

Officer 3 (*standing at attention*)   SIR YES SIR!

Officer 1   DO NOT SET YOUR STANDARDS SO LOW! That is a direct order.

Officer 3'*s nose starts to bleed. He doesn't notice.*

Officer 3   Look at my right hand. Look at these calluses! Why hasn't someone with a PhD declared this chick shortage a public health emergency?

Officer 2   What maiden wants a man who bleeds more than she does?

Officer 3 (*noticing nose bleed*)   Fucking drought!

He grabs a handkerchief from his pocket and plugs his nose.

Officer 1   You'd be better off shoving a tampon up each nostril.

Officer 3   I'm young. I'm sensitive. In any other place girls would line up for a date.

Officer 2   I'm starting to think Private Yang's a man of yellow blossom.

Officer 3   Shut your voice.

Officer 1   The poor bastard's a pressure cooker full of yang essence.

Officer 3   Just tell me what to text her!

Tianyun *emerges from the courthouse.*

Tianyun   Excuse me. Do you happen to know where—

Officer 2 (*interrupting*)   "Noodles tonight. Question mark."

Officer 3   Why would I text that?

Tianyun   I've been trying to speak to a clerk.

Officer 2   I'm not talking about everyday noodles. I'm talking long-life, it's-my-birthday, slurp-don't-bite-it kind of noodles.

Tianyun   Why isn't anyone in the courthouse?

Officer 3   "Noodles Tonight?"

Officer 2   It's short, casual, low risk—

Officer 1 (*grabs phone and types into it*)   Eggplant. Peach. Donut - it's sent!

Officer 3   What the—?!

Officer 1   You can name your son after me.

Officer 3   I'll name my next seven-hundred shits after you!

Tianyun   Officers!

Officer 1   Woman, we're on our lunch break.

Tianyun (*reaching for wallet*)   Let me pay you for the overtime.

Officer 2   You can get in big trouble bribing officers of the law.

Tianyun   Two-hundred per person?

Officer 1   It's a risk to speak candidly about internal affairs.

Tianyun   Three-hundred.

Officer 2   A massive risk.

Tianyun   Three-fifty.

Officer 1   You have to run a cost-benefit analysis. At the right point the scales tip.

Tianyun   Five-hundred.

Officer 1   For three minutes of our time.

Tianyun (*as she hands them money*)   I'm trying to learn about a woman / who . . .

Officer 2 (*interrupts at /*)   Aren't we all?

Tianyun   . . . might have been executed the day it snowed.

Officer 1   That's specific.

Officer 2   It used to snow every winter.

Tianyun   In the middle of summer.

Officer 2   Never heard of her.

Officer 3   You've heard of the Snow Maiden.

Officer 2   Shut your voice.

Tianyun   Who's that?

Officer 1   Just a random raving-mad strumpet—

Officer 3   Who's ruined our town!

Tianyun   What do you mean?

Officer 3 *gets a text. He checks it and blushes.*

Officer 1   Out with it.

Officer 3   "FYI I'm a sloppy eater."

Officer 2   She gave double meaning to your double meaning. That takes serious skill.

Tianyun   Was she wearing a necklace?

Officer 1   By the time we see them in the fields they are zipped into their jumpsuits.

Officer 3   Only Doctor Lu sees underneath.

Tianyun   Doctor Lu?

Officer 2   He does the official time of death stuff.

Officer 1   The tart claimed that if she was innocent, snow would cover her body.

Tianyun   Did it?

Officer 3   Exactly as she said it would.

Officer 2   A freak coincidence—

Officer 3   She also said that if she was innocent there'd be a drought that lasted three years.

Tianyun   You think she caused this drought?

Officer 1   No woman's that powerful. Not even my *ma*.

Officer 3   Wake up and smell the fake fucking flowers. Snow Maiden ruined this town!

Officer 1   It's called carbon emissions, you congee-for-brains ninny.

Officer 2   Do you need to blame this drought on a dead whore so you don't feel like part of the problem?

Officer 3   How am I a part of the problem? I've never taken a plane in my life!

Officer 1   Are you not exhaling carbon dioxide with each breath?

Officer 3   I am, but—

Officer 2   And using an air conditioner that's smashing our ozone?

Tianyun   Officers—

Officer 3   What should I do, hang myself from a plastic tree?

Officer 1   You'd find your service weapon more reliable.

Tianyun   Was she guilty?

Officer 1   There were eyewitnesses. That murdering minx pled guilty in court.

Officer 3   Then why did it snow in the middle of the summer? Why was that snow the last water that's fallen on New Harmony in three years?

Officer 1   Stop falling in love with the women we execute.

Officer 3   She was innocent. Her prophecies happened!

Officer 3 *gets another text.*

Officer 2   Is she sexting?

Tianyun   Who were the witnesses?

Officer 1   Time's up.

Tianyun   That's my last question.

Officer 2 (*grabbing phone, reads text*)   "My boyfriend's in town—"

Officer 1   Cocktease.

Officer 2   ". . . And he loves beef noodles. Let's take him to the place by the high school. Smiley face. Heart. Thumbs-Up. Flower."

Tianyun   Who were the witnesses? Where can I find them?

Officer 1   Lunch break's over, boys. Back to the rounds.

Officer 2   There's always your left hand.

Officer 1   Nothing's more important than loving yourself.

The **Officers** *exit.* **Tianyun** *exits in the opposite direction.*

Officer 3   I repeat: Public Health Emergency.

Scene Eight

New Harmony Guest House, night. **Fei-Fei**, *now in pajamas, flies her dragon kite through the space.* **Tianyun**, *also in her pajamas, prepares for bed. The area under the Yuan dynasty table is filled with pillows and a sleeping bag.*

Tianyun   Get ready for bed.

Fei-Fei (*motioning to table*)   I'm ready.

Tianyun   What's this?

Fei-Fei   My sleep-fort. Will you cut my nails?

Tianyun   I thought cutting nails during Ghost Month was an invitation for spirits to visit.

Fei-Fei   I like Snow Girl. I want her to visit.

Tianyun   Darling—

Fei-Fei   Can we adopt her?

Tianyun   Stop playing.

Fei-Fei   She needs our help. Bad things happen when you don't keep your promise.

Fei-Fei *hands* **Tianyun** *a pair of nail clippers.* **Tianyun** *clips her nails.*

Fei-Fei   I wish the trees would come back.

Tianyun   I wish for that too.

Fei-Fei   Real flowers are better than fake ones.

Tianyun   When we go back home, I'll get you some real flowers and we'll look for good climbing trees.

Fei-Fei   I want to climb trees here.

Tianyun *tucks* **Fei-Fei** *into her sleeping bag then sits back at the table.*

Tianyun   Even if it starts raining tomorrow it will take a very long time for any tree we plant here to grow big enough to climb. You might be as old as me.

Fei-Fei (*falling asleep*)   Then I hope it rains soon so we can climb trees together.

Tianyun   I hope for that too.

Silence. **Fei-Fei**'*s asleep. A beat, then* **Tianyun** *dozes off as well.*

The crickets suddenly fall silent. **Fei-Fei** *rises from beneath the table and sleepwalks out of the room.*

Tianyun *wakes up suddenly, sees that* **Fei-Fei** *is missing and jumps to her feet, looking for her. She can't speak.*

As **Tianyun** *looks for her daughter* **Judge Wu**, *the town magistrate, and* **Dou Yi** *enter from opposite directions.* **Dou Yi** *wears a prison jumpsuit and is shackled at the hands and feet. She is escorted by* **Officers 2 and 3**. **Judge Wu** *sits at the Yuan dynasty table.* **Tianyun** *watches this from a distance.*

Judge Wu   Cai Dou Yi, you pled guilty in court, and have been convicted of the murder of Master Zhang.

Dou Yi   Your honor, I'd like to change my plea.

Judge Wu   You confessed to the murder at the crime scene.

Dou Yi   I'm not a killer.

Judge Wu   Seven eyewitnesses disagree.

Dou Yi   They're lying.

Judge Wu   Officers—I need a moment alone with the prisoner.

The **Officers** *salute and exit.*

Dou Yi   Let me tell you the truth, plain and white—

Judge Wu   Master Zhang was a pillar of this community. This whole town feels his loss—not just in their hearts, but in their pockets as well.

Dou Yi   I'm innocent. Let me tell you what happened.

Judge Wu   The trial is over. This is a sentencing hearing. The only question now is whether you'll be executed or sent to a labor camp.

Dou Yi   My mother-in-law is sick. I'd like to care for her as long as I can.

Judge Wu   You may be a widow, but you're still young, and very pretty. I'm an old man and my wife is hairy and fat. Why don't we come to an arrangement in which both sides receive benefit?

Dou Yi   I'd rather die.

Judge Wu   Officers!

The **Officers** *return.*

Judge Wu   Cai Dou Yi has been sentenced to death. Inform Doctor Lu of the execution date, which I am setting for one month from today.

Officer 2   Your honor—

Judge Wu   What is it?

Officer 2   This was just delivered.

Officer 2 *hands* **Judge Wu** *an envelope. He opens and reads it.*

Judge Wu   There's been a change of plans. The convict will be executed tomorrow.

Dou Yi   What—why?

Judge Wu   Because the will of the state and the people requires it.

Dou Yi   Make sure my mother-in-law stays away. Please. I don't want her to see—

Judge Wu   Those days are over. You won't be paraded through the streets.

Judge Wu *exits.*

The **Officers** *unshackle* **Dou Yi**'s *feet, give her a tablet of medicine to take, and hang a cardboard sign around her neck. On it is written the characters "Dou Yi" in black brush ink. A red X is drawn over her name, indicating that this woman has been sentenced to death.*

The **Police Officers** *guide* **Dou Yi** *away from* **Judge Wu**'s *table and out of his room.*

Lights shift, indicating they are in a different space. **Dou Yi** *steps onto a dining chair and then stands on the table, which is now the court execution grounds.*

It turns into a lush summer day. Birds sing. A brook bubbles nearby. A white flag flaps overhead.

Dou Yi

I didn't think I'd draw such a crowd.
Why have so many come to watch one woman die?

They must be selling snacks outside.
Red bean cakes, candied berries, grilled rabbit, puffed rice . . .
My husband and I saw a public execution when we were very young.
When the condemned man was brought out, the crowd roared and
Pelted him with rocks and rotten vegetables.
My husband's eight-year-old boy part stiffened
As we screamed and hurled moldy melons.
Maybe I will have the same effect on men in this audience
Perhaps the sight of Dou Yi flying, then falling, will make women wet
And watching me die will make you lust for life.
Afterwards, will you go home
Shove your bodies together and try to forget
That you—
And you—and you—
And you, and you, and you, and you
And even you—
Will vanish
Without a trace?
Erased.
Everything ends.
Doctor Lu gave me a blue pill to take with my last meal.
How strange to already feel like I'm drifting down
Towards King Yama's house
Away from you and this fleeting, temporary body.
What can be made of this short, wretched life?
Heaven and Earth fear the strong and oppress the weak
Earth fails to discriminate between good and evil—
Heaven mistakes the wise man and the fool—
Both leave me nothing but two streams of tears.

She recognizes a woman in the audience.

Mother Cai—
I didn't want you to see me like this.
I confessed to save you.
If I don't die, how can I save your life?
A thousand beatings and ten thousand punishments
One blow, one streak of blood, one layer of skin.
They beat me 'till pieces of my flesh flew out
And I was dripping with blood.
Mother Cai, from now on,
When it is the winter solstice and the new year festival,
And on the first and fifteenth day of the month, if you have rice pulp and
Water left, leave a half bowl for your daughter to eat.
If you have spirit money left unburnt, burn a wad for Dou Yi. Please—
Think of Dou Yi, who was sold by her mother

And can no longer conjure her face.
Think of Dou Yi, who tended your son's grave when
His life was taken building this town's factories.
Think of Dou Yi, who was framed for murder,
Betrayed by a lecherous judge
And executed for a crime she didn't commit.
Mother Cai, don't cry,
Don't get angry or curse the sky
Maybe Dou Yi is not fit for this time.
My husband once told me about a loyal official framed for murder;
As he howled at Heaven before his execution,
Frost flew from the sky even though it was May.
If we still live on a planet that hates injustice,
Snow will fall from the clouds and shield my remains.
May that snow be the last water that falls on New Harmony until
Justice is brought to Dou Yi.
Officers—
Do you see the white flag flapping overhead?
If I am innocent,
Not a drop of hot blood will spill onto the green earth or
Stain my clothes, no matter how many bullets pierce this flesh.
My blood will fly towards the Blue Sky and
Stain the white flag flying above.
This has happened before when wrongs were suffered by honest women.
Now it will happen here,
Where the good suffer poverty and a short life
And the wicked live long and make lots of money.
Because officials are heartless and choose to
Close their eyes and fill their pockets,
And men in this town were born with mouths
That can right wrongs with a few words—
But you are all too timid to speak!

The sky darkens. **Dou Yi** *takes in her surroundings.*

This floating world dims for me
A cold wind spins
Officers, I promise you—
It is the hottest time of the year,
But soon snow will tumble down like cotton
And New Harmony will experience the wrath of a drought for three years.
They say Heaven has no sympathy for the human heart—
The Blue Sky will answer my prayers.
Mother!
Wait until snow falls in June and drought lasts three years.
Only then, will my innocent soul be—

CRACK CRACK CRACK!

Bullets hit **Dou Yi**'s *head and neck. She flies sideways, and collapses onto the ground, dead. The white flag flying above them turns red and heavy with fresh blood.*

Three People's Armed Police Officers enter. **Officer 2** *and* **Officer 3**, *the younger officers, carry a stretcher.*

Officer 1 *takes a few cell phone pictures of* **Dou Yi**'s *body—including a "thumbs-up" selfie with him and her bullet-ridden head.*

When he is done, the other officers transfer **Dou Yi**'s *body to the stretcher.*

Officer 1   Who hit her neck?

Officer 2   Who do you think?

Officer 3   It wasn't me!

Officer 2   Horse shit. You drank too much coffee.

Officer 3   Says who?

Officer 2   Your twitching left eyelid.

Officer 1   The bullets have cauterized her wounds. There's not a drop of blood anywhere.

Officer 3   There's not enough girls as it is. Why get rid of a perfectly good specimen? They should have let me marry her and keep her under house arrest.

Officer 1   That would be considered a "cruel and unusual punishment."

Snow starts to fall in thick white clumps.

Officer 3   I'm a beast in the kitchen. Any woman I cook for would be on her knees—

Officer 2   Dying of food poisoning.

Doctor Lu *enters, dressed in surgical scrubs.*

Officer 1   Move.

Officers 2 and 3 *pick up the stretcher with* **Dou Yi**'s *body.*

Doctor Lu   The van unit's prepped.

Officer 3 *notices a necklace on the ground. He tosses it on the stretcher.*

Officer 3   She lost her necklace.

Officer 1 (*reading characters*)   "Double Happiness." Maybe in the next life.

Officer 2 (*off snow*)   What the—

Officer 3   It's ashes from the incinerator.

Officer 2   Fuck me. It's snowing. How strange—

Officer 1   It's called "climate change."

The men start to exit. The snow follows **Dou Yi***'s body, accumulating on top of it, covering it completely.*

Officer 3   When we kill on any other day, the ground is full of fresh blood. Look at the flag—it's bright red and soaking wet. This death sentence must be unjustly sent.

Doctor Lu   Oh dear. My tomatoes aren't going to like this.

Officer 2   Your spinach will.

Officer 3   Cabbages like cold too—

Doctor Lu   We don't have time to talk about vegetables. Move faster. I have patients from seven countries waiting on this harvest.

They exit. It continues to snow.

Scene Nine

A spacious loft, hours later. **Rocket** *packs a suitcase.* **Handsome** *rushes in.*

Handsome   Sorry I'm late. There were oceans of traffic.

Rocket   (–)

Handsome   How are you, darling? How is your heart?

Rocket   (–)

Handsome   We closed the deal. The funds will be released tomorrow. We're finally free.

Rocket   (–)

Handsome   Please. I've been frantic. Say something.

Rocket   Where do our cards go?

Handsome   Cards?

Rocket   That we send to the teenager's family.

Handsome   My assistant sends them off.

Rocket   To which province?

Handsome   I'd have to check.

Rocket   You don't know?

Handsome   My mind is muddled. I've been so worried.

Rocket   What was the boy's name?

Handsome   We agreed to avoid details—

Rocket   I changed my mind.

Handsome   It was Wei—Wei something.

Rocket   Are you sure?

Handsome   What's this about?

Rocket   I have a feeling it might be more—feminine.

Handsome   The boy's name?

Rocket   Something more like . . . Dou Yi.

A long pause.

Handsome   You were—

Rocket (*interrupting*)   That's no excuse—

Handsome   You were inches from—

Rocket (*interrupting*)   My fate?

Handsome   No—

Rocket (*interrupting*)   That was my path.

Handsome   Rocket / please

Rocket (*interrupting at /*)   Are you so petrified by the prospect of solitude you can't face the natural order of things?

Handsome   You weren't even thirty yet.

Rocket *finishes packing up his suitcase, zips it up and prepares to leave.*

Rocket   I'll send for the rest.

Handsome   Where are you going?

Rocket   Home. To my family.

Handsome   No!

Rocket   Am I your prisoner now?

Handsome   I'm your home. I am your family.

Rocket   I won't waste my life with a man who spent three years inventing idiot stories.

Handsome   Why should you be denied a full life simply because organs are not—

Rocket (*interrupting*)   Because it's my right to choose what goes in my body.

Handsome   You signed that right over to me.

Rocket   Fuck you.

Handsome   You did.

Rocket   Handsome—

Handsome (*interrupting*)   You gave me medical power of attor—

Rocket (*interrupting*)   To exercise my will. My choices.

Handsome   You were barely conscious. How could I ask you?

Rocket   Did you, even in your weakest, most sniveling moments, believe there was a world in which I'd want the heart of an executed woman stapled into my chest?

Handsome   She took my father. She owed me a life.

Rocket   That explains your first lie. What about the hundreds of others?

Handsome   You would have done the same thing for me.

Rocket   I would have honored your wishes.

Handsome   I couldn't lose you. I'm sorry I lied.

Rocket   That's it? (*Yells out the window.*) Handsome Zhang is sorry! He's sorry for fucking me over in this life and most likely the next!

Handsome   You belong in this world.

Rocket   Take it back.

Handsome   What?

Rocket   I reject your gift. Take it out of me!

Handsome   Look me in the eye and tell me that if I was on my death bed and it was in your power you wouldn't have done the same thing.

Rocket (*not looking*)   I wouldn't have done it.

Handsome   Look at me and tell me you would watch me die and spend what time you had left knowing you'd had a chance to save your best friend—your true family—

Rocket   I shouldn't be here.

Handsome   That woman is not dead because of you. If you had not received her heart it would have gone to the next highest bidder. We are so close to finally getting the future we've fought for. The one we deserve—if you still want to share it with me. Please, Rocket. Forgive me.

Rocket   What else are you hiding?

Handsome   There's nothing else.

Rocket   Are you sure?

Handsome   On my father's grave—I swear it.

Rocket   No more lies, Handsome. No more tricks. Do you want what I want, or what gives you the life you wish to be living?

Handsome   I want what you want. I want only your happiness.

Rocket   There are more important things in this life than me being happy. No more lies.

Handsome   I swear it.

Rocket   Take me out of this desert.

Handsome   As soon as you're well.

Rocket   Doctor Lu says there's nothing wrong with the heart.

Handsome   Then what—?

Rocket   Stress.

Handsome   Let's leave tomorrow. First thing.

Rocket   After I put out offerings for Dou Yi.

Handsome   Offerings, for the woman who murdered my father?

Rocket   Offerings for the woman who saved my life.

They exit.

Scene Ten

The Temple to the Goddess of Mercy. The next morning. **Tianyun** *and* **Fei-Fei** *stand before an altar covered with flowers and fruit.* **Tianyun** *drops pieces of spirit money one by one into a red metal can full of burning paper. There is a stone statue of the Goddess of Mercy behind the altar.*

Fei-Fei   What is she holding?

Tianyun   A jar of pure water and a willow branch, which she uses to beat away demons.

Fei-Fei   Dou Yi's not a demon.

Tianyun   Now that we know her story and have given her offerings, she can leave this world and join Buddha. And if there are any demons to beat on that path, the Goddess of Mercy will help her. (*Addressing altar.*) Goddess of Mercy, please watch over Dou Yi and help her leave this world safely. (*She bows three times to the altar.*) Now, bow three times to the altar and send Dou Yi your best wishes.

Fei-Fei *bows three times to the altar.*

Fei-Fei   Person Who Hears Sounds, help Dou Yi get what she wants. If she's hungry and needs cookies and crackers, please share some with her.

Tianyun   Don't forget her new clothes.

Fei-Fei *pulls out a joss paper clothing set that she has drawn, colored and cut out of construction paper.*

Fei-Fei   Dou Yi, I'm sending you nice clothes like the ones from my stories. I hope they keep snow from chilling your bones.

Tianyun   I'm sure she'll be very comfortable.

Fei-Fei   Now you give her something.

Tianyun *removes the Double Happiness necklace from around her neck.*

Tianyun   Dou Yi, I'm returning your necklace.

Tianyun *drops the necklace into the smoldering red bucket full of ghost money.*

Fei-Fei   No!

Fei-Fei *lunges towards the can to pull out the necklace, but* **Tianyun** *is fast and pulls her backwards, so she doesn't burn herself.*

Tianyun   What are you doing? You'll burn yourself—

Fei-Fei   You promised!

Tianyun   It's over. We helped her. She just needed food offerings so she wouldn't be a hungry ghost.

Fei-Fei   Not enough!

Tianyun   We've done all that we can.

Fei-Fei   Then why isn't it raining?

Tianyun   It's time to go home.

Fei-Fei   Help my sister!

Tianyun   You don't have a sister.

Fei-Fei   Liar!

The sky darkens. A swarm of locusts and a brown swirling cloud of dust approach.

Fei-Fei   You did this.

Tianyun *and* **Fei-Fei** *exit the temple. The red can full of offerings continues to burn. The fire inside grows brighter.*

Scene Eleven

A balcony in **Handsome** *Zhang's house.* **Rocket** *has set up an altar full of offerings for* **Dou Yi***. He drops sheets of ghost money into a red canister.*

Dou Yi *sits beside the altar, eating food offerings. She wears the clothes* **Fei-Fei** *sent her—long, flowing winter robes you might see in illustrated stories about ancient China.*

Rocket *doesn't see her.*

Rocket

Ghost of the woman Dou Yi—
My name is Rocket. Your heart beats in me.
If I could do it over I'd have refused your heart,
Left this flesh and moved into a new form.
Life on earth must change with the seasons—
Death should be as normal as birth.
We bid farewell to some and welcome others,
With arms flung open to embrace what
Earth and the Blue Sky might bring.
I held on too tightly and let my love for one man
Cloud my ability to see clearly
Missing my one chance to leave this body with dignity.
Ghost of the woman Dou Yi
Forgive me
Forgive me
Forgive me.
I hope this food gives you strength
And finds you resting in peace.

Rocket *falls silent. He continues to burn paper money.*

Dou Yi

My hands were packed in dry ice
Flown across the Pacific and
Stitched onto a man who lost his overseas.
My palms open doors to
Rooms my feet haven't walked through and
Caress a woman my eyes will never see.
It doesn't snow there but my
Nails ache when they touch ice and
Scratch strange characters onto that
Soldier's skin while he's sleeping.
His doctors call it post-traumatic stress but
He knows they're words from a
Language his tongue never learned
Justice.
Justice.
Justice.
Across the East Sea a yam farmer
Uses my corneas to see.
She dreams of snow but thinks
It's ashes from a childhood fire bombing.
On the far side of the Atlantic my stomach digests
Food that never passed through my lips
Food my teeth didn't chew

Food my tongue hasn't tasted
Food that could have made this spirit stronger
And act sooner if someone offered it to Dou Yi.
But my heart—
My heart beats in this town,
Pumping blood through a man
Loved by the son of an official,
A son who moved Heaven and Earth for
His Happiness
His Future
His New Harmony.
These offerings have given me strength
I feel my spirit reviving.
Justice
Justice
Justice.
Justice and burial for the widow Dou Yi.
Justice
Justice
Justice.
But how can you bury a woman whose butchered body's still living?
Justice.
Justice.
THAT IS MY HEART.
IT SHOULD BEAT INSIDE ME!

Dou Yi *thrusts her hand into* **Rocket**'s *chest and retrieves her heart from his chest cavity.*

Rocket's *eyes widen as he sees* **Dou Yi**, *opens his arms to embrace her, then collapses onto the floor, dead, his chest soaked in blood.*

Dou Yi

I'll put it away for safe keeping.
If she clears my name
Mother will find it
And bury me.

Dou Yi *parades her heart around the stage as a dust storm and swarm of locusts hits the house, consuming all light, engulfing the town in darkness.*

End of Act One.

Intermission.

Act Two

Scene One

Outside **Nurse Wong**'s *bar. Sunrise. Two days later.*

A thick brown haze, the result of ongoing dust storms, hovers, obscuring the sun and surrounding buildings. Mounds of dust and dead locusts have been swept into piles. Dozens of funeral wreaths, circular signs ringed with silk flowers that bear calligraphy-ink written messages of condolence, surround an extravagant funeral altar. The altar is laden with three-dimensional joss paper objects—reproductions of houses, cars and fancy electronics which cover the table, alongside gift baskets brimming with food, alcohol and cartons of cigarettes.

Perched on the altar are the **Ghosts of Rocket Wu** *and* **Dou Yi***. Both are dressed in colorful new clothing—fully realized versions of joss clothing burned by* **Handsome** *and* **Fei-Fei** *respectively.* **Rocket** *smokes a cigarette and holds a half-empty bottle of imported beer.*

A loud emergency tone sounds over the town's emergency intercom system. A message blares through outdoor speakers.

Intercom   Citizens of New Harmony. Emergency evacuation procedures go into effect at 1300 hours. Ground forces from the People's Liberation Army will execute the evacuation order by sunset.

Raucous, upbeat marching band music plays from an unseen funeral band leading a procession of mourners through town. The living, who are dressed in traditional funeral garb of white hemp clothing and white hemp head hoods, file past the altar to pay their final respects to the deceased.

The procession is led by **Handsome Zhang***, who wears a dust mask over his nose and mouth, and sunglasses to hide his puffy eyes. He holds a framed portrait of* **Rocket***.* **Nurse Wong** *is beside him, also wearing a dust mask. She holds a bouquet of lilies. They pass the altar, bow, then exit in the direction of the marching band, which is playing something jarringly Western, as the music is meant to scare away evil spirits.*

Arriving next in the funeral procession are **Worker Fang***,* **Worker Zhou***,* **Worker Chen** *and* **Worker Huang***, all in hemp clothing. Their dust masks hang around their necks, as they are mid-conversation.*

All workers face the altar and bow.

Worker Fang   Let's split.

All but **Worker Chen** *start to exit.* **Worker Chen** *drops to the ground, refusing to leave.*

Worker Huang   My folks don't want to leave either.

Worker Zhou   They will when there's a gun pressed to their heads.

Worker Chen   How the fuck am I going to dig up twenty generations of Chens by sunset?

Worker Huang   I'd worry more about fitting them into one suitcase.

Worker Fang   The allowance is twenty kilos per person.

Worker Zhou   Per living person, you shit-for-brains ninny.

Worker Chen   I'm the eldest grandchild. Those graves are my responsibility.

Worker Huang   Save yourself and sneak back for tomb sweeping.

Worker Chen *ignores him and stalks off, refusing to leave.*

Worker Fang   Fuck this planet. If Earth's going to be such a punishing little bitch we should evacuate to a space station and end this abusive relationship.

Worker Zhou   Worker Fang wants to be the first peasant in space.

Worker Fang   My parents were migrants from the far western territories. Their parents came from Central Asia. What if it's my destiny to carry the Fang line away from this godforsaken place?

Worker Zhou   It won't be easy.

Worker Fang   Do you think that when the first fish flopped onto land to start the long march towards life on two legs he expected it to be easy?

Worker Huang   Space travel's a young man's game. If this planet's sinking I'm going down with it.

Worker Fang   Where's your sense of adventure? We Chinese are the world's most daring migrants. We can survive anywhere—

Worker Zhou   That's not cursed.

Tianyun *and* **Fei-Fei** *enter, also wearing hemp clothing and dust masks.*

Worker Huang   Hey Little Warrior!

Worker Fang (*singing*)   Happy birthday to you, happy birthday to you, happy birthday dear—

Fei-Fei *kicks* **Worker Fang** *in the shin. He stumbles backwards, trips over his legs and falls.*

Worker Zhou   Nice work!

Worker Zhou *holds up a hand, attempting to give* **Fei-Fei** *a high five. She ignores him and stares at the altar.*

Tianyun   I'm so sorry—she's not been herself. She hasn't said a word in two days.

Worker Huang   Don't worry, Boss Lin. We don't like his voice either.

Worker Fang   There's no point calling her Boss Lin. The deal didn't go through.

Tianyun   I'm afraid that's not true. You're looking at the new owner of ten thousand tons of broken, dust and locust clogged machinery.

Worker Zhou   Aiyah! What are you going to do?

Tianyun   I had natural disaster coverage. I'll be reimbursed for the losses.

Worker Chen   Stop the evacuation.

Tianyun   I'm afraid I can't. Not unless it rains by sunset and conditions reverse.

Worker Chen   So make it rain. Fix this!

Fei-Fei *stands by* **Worker Chen**, *allying herself with him.*

Tianyun *grabs* **Fei-Fei** *by the hand and starts to exit.*

Tianyun   We need to go home.

Worker Chen *drops to his knees.*

Worker Chen   Please—I beg you. Save our home.

Tianyun   I don't have the strength.

Fei-Fei *kneels beside* **Worker Chen** *in a similar entreaty.*

Worker Zhou   My cousin works for the coroner. This was no natural death. How do you know she won't go after your little one next?

Tianyun   My daughter is an innocent. Why would she hurt her?

Worker Huang   Nobody's innocent. We might all be cursed.

Worker Fang   Nurse Wong's bar is an evacuation point. We'll wait for you there.

Tianyun (*to* **Fei-Fei**)   You have a beautiful voice. Please think about using it.

Worker Chen   She'll speak when you fix this.

Fei-Fei *and* **Worker Chen** *remain on their knees, entreating* **Tianyun**. **Tianyun** *puts on her dust mask and exits into the haze.*

Worker Huang   Let's go.

Worker Chen   Come on, little warrior. I'll make you fried dumplings.

Worker Fang   Dumplings! Good idea. Funerals always make me hungry.

Fei-Fei *exits with the workers, leaving the Ghosts of* **Dou Yi** *and* **Rocket Wu** *alone on the funeral altar.* **Rocket** *lights a cigarette, takes a long drag and exhales lustily.*

Rocket   Will there be torture?

Dou Yi   Everyone's tortured.

Rocket   Everyone?

Dou Yi   Some for a few seconds, others for centuries. When it's done, Ox-Head and Horse-Face will feed you soup and you'll forget everything.

Rocket   Do I have a say in what I come back as?

Dou Yi   Did you die peacefully?

Rocket   I didn't resist.

Dou Yi   Did you eat meat?

Rocket   Mostly organic.

Dou Yi   Did you take more than you needed?

Rocket   Define "needed."

Dou Yi   Focus on good deeds in the next life. Maybe you'll have a say after that.

Lights and sound shift. The sound of the ocean swelling, the earth opening up, ten thousand Buddhist monks chanting in unison.

Rocket   Is it time?

Dou Yi   Put on better shoes.

Rocket   What's wrong with Italian leather.

Dou Yi   You'll be walking for forty-nine days.

Rocket *changes into a pair of high-top sneakers. He's not wearing socks.*

Dou Yi   Where's your socks?

Rocket   He didn't send any.

Dou Yi   Then you're going to get blisters. Take some snacks too.

Rocket *stuffs a backpack full of sandals and food offerings and slings it over his shoulder.*

Ox-Head *and* **Horse-Face**, *guardians of the Buddhist underworld, enter. They are very tall and official-looking.*

Rocket   Shall we?

Dou Yi   The wrongs committed against me have not been addressed.

Rocket   They might make an exception.

Dou Yi   I won't return to a world that permits massive injustice.

Rocket   I'll look for you in the next life.

Dou Yi   I wish you peace with every step.

Rocket *bows to* **Dou Yi**, *then joins* **Ox-Head** *and* **Horse-Face**. *They exit.* **Dou Yi** *is alone on stage.*

Scene Two

Town bar. **Handsome Zhang** *and* **Nurse Wong** *browse a catalog full of urns. The ground is completely covered in dead and dying locusts.* **Nurse Wong** *flips to the final page of the catalog.*

Nurse Wong   This is their Presidential Suite. One-hundred-percent jade, with a certificate of authenticity.

Handsome   I should have had the courage to let him leave this world when he wanted. He had a chance to depart with dignity. I robbed him of it.

Nurse Wong   Because you loved him.

Handsome   I loved the happiness I felt in his presence.

Nurse Wong   Do not let grief destroy your good memories.

Handsome   He knew where his heart came from.

Nurse Wong   Your intentions have been pure from the very beginning.

Handsome   He didn't kill himself.

Nurse Wong   The townspeople are traumatized. Suicide is the right story.

Handsome   Where is his heart?

Nurse Wong   The evacuation notice is causing enough panic. We'll say we've cremated it with his body. We don't have the strength to endure another murder investigation.

Handsome   I don't have the strength to endure a week without Rocket.

Nurse Wong   In time, you'll find another reason for living.

Handsome   Go to the crematorium. Bring him back in the suite.

Nurse Wong   The jade is a generous choice. You are giving Rocket a wonderful home.

Handsome   That's all I ever wanted to do.

Nurse Wong   Your fates weren't aligned in this lifetime. They will be in the next.

Handsome   My father was right when he said I was wrong from the very beginning.

Nurse Wong   I was there. I caught you with these hands. The boy who emerged from his mother was innocent and sweet.

Handsome   Is it because I didn't burn enough incense in my last life that I must suffer so much in this one?

Nurse Wong   Though you own many stocks, you have not cornered the market in suffering. Pack your things. I'll buy the jade suite and have them put Rocket in it. We'll take him out of this wretched town by sunset this evening.

Nurse Wong *exits with* **Handsome.**

Dou Yi

> Heaven and Earth, I thought you could be counted on.
> Why haven't you answered my prayers?
> I struggled to the end and fought to the finish,
> Yet daily I still weep at the Home Gazing Terrace,
> Awaiting the confessions of my enemies.
> Who will clear the criminal charges of the wrongly executed one
> Who confessed under blackmail then torture?
> I thought officials would reexamine my case
> How could I know they would execute me?
> My own vows have been comprehensive
> The widow Dou Yi kept all her promises.
> First, I said my blood would stain the white silk
> Flying on the flagpole above me,
> Second, that snow would cover my corpse.
> Third, I promised a three-year drought would visit as divine punishment.
> People today are not virtuous
> They are wanton, and lacking in purpose.
> How much longer must I wait?
> Is it my fate to be trapped here for all eternity?
> Must my drought burn this town to the ground
> Before the living bring justice to Dou Yi?

Scene Three

A stall behind the Temple to the Goddess of Mercy. **Mother Cai**, *a blind woman with weathered, sun-damaged skin, folds towels in a dimly lit room. She wears drab, utilitarian clothing.* **Tianyun** *enters.*

Tianyun   You must be the woman they call blind Mother Cai.

Mother Cai   I am she.

Tianyun   I was told I could get a massage / here

Mother Cai (*interrupting at /*)   I charge forty for feet and shoulders, one-hundred for full body.

Tianyun   Feet and shoulders will do.

Mother Cai   Remove your shoes and have a seat on that stool. I'll prepare the herbal soak.

Mother Cai *pours a steaming kettle of herb-infused water into a metal basin then lowers* **Tianyun**'s *feet into the herbal water.*

Tianyun *winces and pulls out her feet.*

Mother Cai   If you don't try to escape the pain your body will accept it. Relax. Stop resisting.

Tianyun *lowers her feet into the steaming water.*

Mother Cai *starts to massage* **Tianyun**'s *shoulders.*

Tianyun   Gentler, please.

Mother Cai   This is the pressure you need.

Tianyun *falls silent, and breathes through the discomfort.*

Tianyun   I'm not usually this tense.

Mother Cai   There are decades of grief locked in these shoulders.

Silence. **Mother Cai** *massages* **Tianyun**'s *shoulders, neck and jaw.*

Tianyun   My daughter turns seven today.

Mother Cai   If fate is kind, she'll care for you when she's older.

Tianyun   If fate is kind I can care for myself.

Silence. **Mother Cai** *massages* **Tianyun.**

Tianyun   Do you have children?

Mother Cai   I did. And for a time, they walked under the Blue Sky.

Tianyun   Where are they now?

Mother Cai   Fate was not kind.

Tianyun   Are you a native of this town?

Mother Cai   I'm from Bamboo Mountain. It's five hours from here.

Tianyun   What brought you to New Harmony?

Mother Cai   My son had a job building Master Zhang's factories. My daughter and I came along. I adopted her at a young age to be a wife for my son.

Tianyun   Are you alone in this town?

Mother Cai   I brought my son's ashes home to the family plot. I see him every tomb-sweeping.

Tianyun   And your daughter?

Mother Cai   Release. Let the tension flow out of your body.

Tianyun   Where is your daughter?

Mother Cai   Do not speak unless you're improving the silence.

Tianyun   What happened to Duan Yun?

Long silence. **Mother Cai** *runs her fingers along* **Tianyun**'s *face.*

Tianyun   Why didn't you burn offerings for her? Why wasn't she buried?

Mother Cai   You must be a Lin.

Tianyun   You guess correctly.

Mother Cai   I sensed your dishonesty the moment I laid my hands on your meat.

Tianyun   Why did you change my daughter's name to Dou Yi?

Mother Cai   You lost the right to call her your daughter when you sold her to me.

Tianyun   I was fifteen when I had her. How could I know anything about being a mother? You swore you would care for her as if she was your own bones and flesh.

Mother Cai   I did not shirk from that duty.

Tianyun   I scoured the cemetery records. Why wasn't she buried?

Mother Cai   The state claimed her remains. Nothing was wasted.

Tianyun   She spoke to you at the execution grounds. She begged you to care for her spirit.

Mother Cai *dries* **Tianyun**'s *feet and starts massaging them roughly.*

Tianyun   Softer.

Mother Cai   This is your liver channel. If it's tender, it might mean you're directing your anger in the wrong direction.

Tianyun   What direction do you suggest?

Mother Cai   Towards self-knowledge. Towards seeing yourself for the woman you are. Not who you wish you could be. I've learned many lessons from the school of poverty and suffering. Things a woman with your soft, pedicured feet could never fathom.

Long silence.

Tianyun   I was attacked by my unit manager.

Mother Cai   The secret emerges. The heart channel loosens.

Tianyun   I was fourteen. My grandmother would not help me get rid of the pregnancy.

Mother Cai   So you dumped the girl with your granny, then sold her to me.

Tianyun   I was lost. I could hardly take care of myself. I thought I had found her a good home.

Mother Cai   (—)

Tianyun   Why did you change her name?

Mother Cai   To give her a chance to be more than a bastard rejected by the woman who named her.

Tianyun *reaches into her purse and hands her a one-hundred kuai note.*

Tianyun   Keep the change.

Mother Cai   It must be nice to have money.

Tianyun   It beats being poor.

Mother Cai   Does it beat a living daughter?

Tianyun *raises her hand to slap* **Mother Cai**, *then restrains herself.*

Tianyun   Forgive me. I know you have lost not one but two children to the will of the Zhang family.

Mother Cai   Will is one word for it.

Tianyun   Which would you use?

Mother Cai   Greed.

Tianyun   Do you think she's innocent?

Mother Cai   The Zhangs always want more than what's theirs.

Tianyun   How can I help her?

Mother Cai   I'm not an oracle. For answers like that you should go to the temple.

Tianyun   Your children have been dead for years. Why remain here? Why don't you go home?

Mother Cai   You don't have much time. This town will be empty by sunset. Go to the temple. Ask the Goddess for help.

Tianyun *exits.* **Mother Cai** *folds towels.*

Scene Four

Town bar.

Worker Chen, **Worker Fang**, **Worker Huang** *and* **Worker Zhou** *enter with* **Fei-Fei**. **Worker Fang** *carries* **Fei-Fei**, *who clutches her dragon kite.* **Worker Huang** *lugs three beat-up suitcases.* **Worker Chen** *holds a small willow seedling in a pot wrapped with birthday themed paper.* **Worker Zhou** *lugs an overstuffed suitcase and wears many, many layers of clothing.*

Worker Fang (*to* **Worker Zhou**)   You've gained weight!

Worker Huang   You saw him this morning!

Worker Fang   I'm impressed! Have you been stuffing yourself with pork belly?

Worker Zhou   Take all the clothes in your closet and wear them at once. This leaves room in your suitcase for sentimental things.

Worker Fang   A sound packing strategy.

Worker Hang *neatly arranges his three suitcases in a corner.*

Worker Huang   All I need now are a few soldiers to drag my parents out of the house.

The sound of a distant rumbling.

Worker Fang   The ground forces are arriving!

Worker Chen   Hide me!

Worker Huang   We'll stash you in your family plot—

Worker Chen   I'm too young to be buried!

Worker Zhou   He means wait in a tomb.

Worker Huang   It's how my folks lived through the dark years.

Worker Zhou   The soldiers will be too superstitious to look for you there.

Worker Fang   Stay here, little warrior, we'll be back in a few minutes.

Worker Chen *offers* **Fei-Fei** *the potted seedling.*

Worker Chen   Little Warrior, take care of this for me. It's a willow seedling my cousin brought from the South. It might be the last living plant in New Harmony.

Fei-Fei *accepts the plant.*

Worker Fang   Move!

The workers exit, leaving **Fei-Fei***, alone with the willow seedling.* **Dou Yi** *enters.*

Dou Yi   Thank you for the clothes. I'm much warmer now.

Fei-Fei   (–)

Dou Yi   Did you know we have the same mother?

Fei-Fei   (–)

Dou Yi   Do you know what that makes us?

Fei-Fei *nods.*

Dou Yi   Sisters should stay together, don't you think?

Fei-Fei   (–)

Dou Yi   Come with me. Let's be snow girls together.

Dou Yi *takes* **Fei-Fei***'s hand.*

They exit together.

Scene Five

The Temple to the Goddess of Mercy. The ground is covered with locusts and dust.
Doctor Lu kneels in front of an altar laden with citrus fruit and pink sponge cakes.
He chants Buddhist sutras through a dust mask.

Doctor Lu (*chanting*)   Amitofo amitofo amitofo amitofo . . . (*Continues.*)

Tianyun *enters.*

Doctor Lu (*continues chanting*)   amitofo amitofo amitofo . . .

Tianyun   I didn't expect you to be Buddhist.

Doctor Lu   I've been a vegetarian for twenty years and open this temple each
morning. It's not much, but it keeps my spirit from abandoning me. I've spent
more time in front of this altar than inside my own home. Where will I pray
tomorrow? How long will it take before this place is buried by dust, like one of the
lost cities?

Tianyun   It seems the world has gone crazy.

Doctor Lu   No matter what madness existed out there, I could come here and find
some measure of peace.

Tianyun   Are there many temples in this town?

Doctor Lu   Not anymore.

Tianyun   Not enough patrons?

Doctor Lu   This is the only one that didn't burn.

Tianyun   From the drought caused by Dou Yi?

Doctor Lu   Lord of the Blue Sky. Do you think she caused it?

Tianyun   I think you know how to bring back the rain that would water your
vegetables.

Doctor Lu   Do you know what I do before every organ harvest? My assistants and
I face the body on the operating table, bow three times and thank that person's spirit
for their contribution to the living and the reduction of suffering. I chant sutras while
I'm operating. "Infinite light, infinite life, infinite wisdom."

Tianyun   That's surprising.

Doctor Lu   Most prefer to picture us cackling wildly as we dig our scalpels into the
condemned and dismantle them, part by part, like a prize car.

Tianyun   Is it hard to remain optimistic when your work is so dark?

Doctor Lu   I focus on the lives being saved instead of the one taken. I've been in
this line of work for so long death is an old friend who visits frequently. A friend who
very soon will come calling for me.

Tianyun   How do you deal with the possibility that some of the executed might not be guilty?

Doctor Lu   A lotus grows in muddy waters, yet its flowers remain spotless.

Tianyun   What does that mean?

Doctor Lu   I may live in this town, but I am not of it. And a doctor in this country does not choose his specialty. It is assigned to him. Alas—fate gave me steady hands.

Tianyun   What would you have picked?

Doctor Lu   Something to do with the ear. It's a miracle we stand on two legs at all. It's all about balance. The stuff in the inner ear keeps us from toppling.

Tianyun   That would have been a very different calling.

Doctor Lu   In other places people donate their bodies freely. Here we're more superstitious, which is why in the past we've resorted to more dubious moral ground. But, I am an optimist. Hearts and minds are changing, along with the law.

Tianyun   But why, with Dou Yi, did everything work out so neatly?

Doctor Lu   She had type O blood—the universal donor. Type O inmates on death row surface once in a blue moon. When they do—vultures swarm.

Tianyun   Vultures?

Doctor Lu   People with agendas and timelines. It's a free market enterprise.

Tianyun   Did Handsome bribe the judge?

Doctor Lu   (–)

Tianyun   Doctor Lu. Did Handsome Zhang manipulate the execution date so Rocket could have Dou Yi's heart?

Doctor Lu *packs up the altar offerings.*

Tianyun   Handsome arranged all of it, didn't he? Everything leads back to the Zhangs.

Doctor Lu   The lotus grows in muddy waters, yet its flowers remain spotless.

Doctor Lu *bows to the Goddess of Mercy statue, then exits.* **Tianyun** *bows to the statue, then starts to exit when* **Worker Fang**, **Worker Huang**, *and* **Worker Zhou** *enter in a panic.*

Worker Fang   Boss Lin, Boss Lin!

Worker Huang   Where is she?

Worker Zhou   I see her!

They sprint towards her.

Tianyun   What is it?

Worker Huang   We just stepped out for a few minutes—

Worker Fang   I told her not to go anywhere—

Tianyun   Where's Fei-Fei?

Worker Zhou   We've looked all over town—

Worker Huang   The guest house, the factories, the hospital—

Tianyun   Where's my daughter?

Worker Fang   The ghost took her.

Worker Huang   Shut your voice.

Tianyun   Why do you say that?

Worker Fang   Our suitcases were covered in snow.

Tianyun   Keep looking.

Worker Zhou   The evacuation's underway. The sun sets in three hours.

Tianyun *starts to exit. The workers follow her out.*

Worker Fang (*shouting offstage*)   Little Warrior!

Worker Zhou   Birthday Girl!

Worker Huang   Where are you?

Scene Six

Funeral altar. The altar now has **Rocket***'s portrait on it.* **Handsome** *faces it, holding a jade urn.* **Tianyun** *enters, lights a stick of incense, and faces the altar.*

Handsome   I know every inch of his body. Every scar, birthmark, and mole.

Tianyun   That's not him. It's just pulverized bone.

Handsome   It's the middle of summer. Why is he cold?

Tianyun   Only the finest jade stays cool in hot weather.

Handsome   When I first saw this land, before it became the town of New Harmony, it was so lush it looked like something out of a story.

Tianyun   What was it called before?

Handsome   Cloud Forest. There were herons and cranes. Rivers, lakes. And trees, as far as the eye could see.

Tianyun   Perhaps it's time you and I worked together to restore this land to what it was before factories came to town.

Handsome   This will be a ghost town by sunset.

Tianyun   It isn't night yet. We could bring back Cloud Forest.

Handsome   With what water?

Tianyun   The water that will fall from the sky and water new seeds when we clear the name of Dou Yi.

Handsome   The town gossips have poisoned your ear.

Tianyun   I was with Rocket when Doctor Lu told him the truth about his heart.

Handsome   I will spend the time I have left in this body regretting my decision to keep that truth from him.

Tianyun   Did you influence the date of Dou Yi's execution?

Handsome   I did what a woman in your position has done countless times to get what she wants.

Tianyun   Dou Yi was my daughter. I gave her up when I was very young.

Handsome   Then you are the most wretched of mothers.

Tianyun   She was innocent.

Handsome   The court found her guilty.

Tianyun   A court you've informed me can be bought.

Handsome   Please, let me grieve.

The **Ghost of Dou Yi** *enters. She looks stronger and more alive than ever before. She is dressed in vibrant Yuan dynasty robes.* **Tianyun** *hears her but doesn't see her.* **Handsome** *can't hear or see her.*

Dou Yi   Don't give up.

Tianyun   She was a very sweet girl. She didn't deserve what I did.

Handsome   I know what it's like to be raised by a narcissist. She may not have my forgiveness, but she does get my pity.

Dou Yi   He knows more than he's saying.

Tianyun   Now Fei-Fei, my second daughter, is also missing.

Handsome   Then you have my pity too.

Dou Yi   You'll get her back when you bring justice to me.

Tianyun   Did you ever speak to Dou Yi?

Handsome   I never laid eyes on her.

Dou Yi   Liar.

Tianyun   Tell me the truth. What happened to my daughter?

Handsome   She was poor, young and female in a town owned by my father.

Tianyun   I'm sure you know more.

Handsome   I have no words left for the mother of a murdering whore.

Dou Yi *swipes* **Rocket***'s urn off the altar. The contents spill out.*

Handsome   Rocket!

Handsome *rushes to push the contents back into the urn and discovers that what he thought was powdered bone is fluffy white snow.*

Handsome   Where are his ashes? Where are his bones? Why is there snow inside Rocket's home?

Dou Yi   Men in this town were born with mouths that can right wrongs with a few words. Why are you too timid to speak?

The sky darkens. Stars appear in the sky. The sound of a bubbling brook, bullfrogs and nightbirds can be heard.

Handsome   What is this? What's happening?

Dou Yi

> Mother—
> Snow fell in June
> Drought lasted three years
> Now my innocent soul will be revealed.

Scene Seven

The same location, three years earlier. **Master Zhang**, *a brawny, straight-backed military official in officer's clothing enters. There is a holstered gun strapped to his belt.*

Handsome   Why is my father here? What's happening—am I awake or am I dreaming?

Master Zhang (*singing*)

> "You ask my love how deep it runs
> How much do I love you?
> My feeling's true
> My love is strong
> The bright moon stands for my heart."

Handsome   Ba. Welcome back.

Dou Yi *and* **Tianyun** *fade into the background as the lights shift.*

Master Zhang   I fell in love with your mother on a night like this one.

Handsome   I didn't think you could see stars in Beijing.

Master Zhang   Don't look up for too long. You might get lost.

Handsome   That's no longer possible.

Master Zhang   What changed?

Handsome   I'm happy.

Master Zhang   Happy enough to start running our factories?

Handsome   If I can split my time between Shanghai and New Harmony.

Master Zhang   You don't know how happy this makes me. You're going to be a great leader. Are you as hungry as I am?

Handsome   There's something I want to go over.

Master Zhang   There's ten thousand things to go over! Surely this can wait until we're stuffing our stomachs with grilled lamb.

Handsome   I need a loan.

Master Zhang   For what?

Handsome   The only home I'll ever need.

Master Zhang   Is my son Handsome in love?

Handsome   He is.

Master Zhang   Lord of the Blue Sky—YES! Where are you hiding her? Don't be coy. Where's my new daughter?

Handsome   Ba—

Master Zhang   You're right. My apologies. How much do you need?

Handsome   Three million.

Master Zhang (*whistles*)   You always had expensive taste. I guess I'm to blame. My friend Henry deals in luxury properties—

Handsome   I said a home. The kind you find with the right person.

Master Zhang   What's the cash for—some destination wedding?

Handsome   A heart transplant.

Master Zhang   My boy! Are you not well?

Handsome   It isn't for me.

Master Zhang   You're twenty-two. Surely you can find someone healthy—

Handsome   He will be healthy once he has surgery.

Master Zhang   Would that not make people laugh until their mouths split?

Handsome   I have searched Heaven and Earth for happiness. Now that I have it there is no mountain I won't move to hold onto it.

Master Zhang (*bursting into laughter*)   You're pulling my leg. This is a joke. A bad dream.

Handsome   My life until I met him was the bad dream. He has woken me from it.

Master Zhang *slaps* **Handsome***, hard. He reels.*

Handsome   Let me be who I am.

Master Zhang *hits him again.*

Master Zhang   The Zhang line demands an heir.

Handsome   I will not live in your shadow any longer.

Master Zhang   You are a blackness that has plagued me since birth. You were wrong since your first step on this earth.

Handsome   If what I'm feeling is wrong I never want to be right.

Master Zhang *continues beating his son.*

Master Zhang   I planned and plotted for you. I set up factories. I was full of hopes for you. I thought and I worried.

Handsome (*sarcastic*)   Poor father. Have all your thoughts and pains been for nothing?

Master Zhang (*stopping himself*)   A body as thin and weak as yours won't withstand these beatings. You break my heart, boy. You destroy me.

Master Zhang *rushes out.* **Handsome** *lies still on the ground. A long pause, then* **Nurse Wong** *rushes in.*

Nurse Wong   Sweet Handsome!

Handsome   This is why I always end up swallowing my voice, and holding my breath.

Nurse Wong   This old body knows your sorrow.

Handsome   Life on Earth holds no meaning if Rocket's not in it.

Nurse Wong   Of the thirty-six stratagems, escape is supreme. Let's leave, precious Handsome, take what assets we can and start over in a new place.

Handsome   Where can you find a man who would weep down the Great Wall at his lover's funeral? Where can you find a man who would throw himself into the river? Where can you find a man turning into stone awaiting his beloved's return? Here. Here. That man is me.

A very drunk **Master Zhang** *enters carrying a terrified* **Dou Yi***, over his shoulder. His free hand carries a fistful of* **Dou Yi***'s woven flying creatures.*

Master Zhang (*singing*)

"You ask my love how deep it runs
How much do I love you?

My feeling's pure
My love is firm
The bright moon stands for my heart."

Dou Yi *struggles, trying to free herself.*

Master Zhang   I found this lonely widow selling "crafts" on the street. She's too shy to haggle but I know there's only one way she's making ends meet. Young lady—consider yourself commissioned to make a one-of-a kind piece for the Zhang family.

Dou Yi   LET ME GO!

Master Zhang *dumps* **Dou Yi** *at* **Handsome**'s *feet.*

Master Zhang   Handsome, this craftswoman needs a collaborator. Take off your pants. Give me an heir.

Dou Yi   No no no no no no no no—

Master Zhang   Shut your voice, you little wench.

Handsome   A human life is tied to Heaven and Earth. How can you treat it like dirt?

Master Zhang (*training gun on* **Handsome**'s *temple*)   Do what you want in the dark! Far away from the light of the Blue Sky, you can see whomever you please, as long as you guarantee you will not be the last of the Zhangs.

Handsome   Remarry and give this burden to another.

Master Zhang   That "burden" is a privilege that belongs to the first son. Give me an heir and I will pay for that surgery.

Handsome   Do you swear it?

Master Zhang   A small fee for restoring the respect of twenty generations. Nurse Wong! Give these lovebirds some room.

Nurse Wong   Master Zhang, I don't think—

Master Zhang *smacks her, HARD. She reels.*

Master Zhang   You sideways prick in the bone. I didn't ask you to think.

Master Zhang *and* **Nurse Wong** *exit.*

Dou Yi   Let me leave.

Handsome   I can't.

Dou Yi   I have been faithful to my husband. I don't deserve this.

Handsome   Who said anything about deserving it? He won't stop. He'll never stop until he gets what he wants.

Dou Yi   I can tell you're not like him.

Handsome   I am like him. More than I ever wanted to be. Take off your pants.

Dou Yi   I won't.

Handsome   Then I will take it from you.

He advances towards **Dou Yi***. She motions to the double happiness necklace around her neck.*

Dou Yi   Look at my necklace. "Double Happiness." Do you know what this character means?

Handsome   I have spent my days searching for a life that contains that character. Your happiness is dead. Mine isn't—but he's fading.

Dou Yi   My happiness lives. It comes from the honor I bring to his memory.

Handsome   Shut your voice.

Dou Yi   It comes from keeping my word. And refusing to be seduced by the treasures and gold of this floating world.

Handsome *lunges towards* **Dou Yi***, rubbing her clothes in the dirt, mussing up her hair. He doesn't notice* **Master Zhang** *and* **Nurse Wong** *approaching.*

Dou Yi   Swine—stay away!

Handsome   If we are to honor our happinesses we must make my father believe I put his heir in your belly.

Dou Yi *rips and soils her dress even more.*

Dou Yi   How's that?

Master Zhang   Not very convincing.

Handsome   *Ba—*

Master Zhang   You pathetic worm. Must I show you how it's done?

Master Zhang *hands* **Nurse Wong** *his gun and advances towards* **Dou Yi***.*

Handsome   *Ba, no—*

Master Zhang   You had your chance. Now you'll settle for sloppy seconds—

Master Zhang *lowers himself onto* **Dou Yi***.*

Master Zhang (*singing*)   "Softly, this gentle kiss—"

Handsome   Stop.

Master Zhang (*singing*)   "It has touched and moved my heart. Deeply, this sweet romance—"

Dou Yi   GET OFF ME!

Handsome   I said STOP!

Nurse Wong *gives* **Handsome** *the gun.*

Nurse Wong   Again, with the strength of this steel—

Master Zhang   Beautiful women I have had by the thousands. Not one has been as stubborn and prickly as you, little wench.

Handsome   How can I cut off my roots?

Master Zhang   Nurse Wong, are there not worse things than giving your body and flesh to the Zhang family?

Nurse Wong   Finish it. It's time to be your own tree.

Master Zhang   Handsome, watch closely. This is how you make a son—

Nurse Wong   Now!

BANG! **Handsome** *shoots* **Master Zhang** *in the back. He collapses on top of* **Dou Yi***, covering her in blood.* **Dou Yi** *screams and pushes him off her.*

Handsome   I have searched Heaven and Earth for happiness and have finally found it. Why can't that be enough?

Master Zhang   You can't finish it—

Handsome   Father, you are truly grand and mighty.

Master Zhang   You don't have the spine!

Handsome   Please accept this deep bow from your son Handsome Zhang.

BANG! **Handsome** *shoots* **Master Zhang** *again. He dies.* **Handsome***, destroyed, weeps by his father's body.*

Nurse Wong *makes a call on her cell phone, retrieves the gun from Handsome, and wipes his prints off it.*

Nurse Wong   He was not your family. For a time you knew each other, now he is dead and gone. He was never the father you yearned for. The day is breaking. Return to Rocket. Your inheritance will pay for his surgery. I will move Heaven and Earth to buy the heart that he needs.

Handsome *turns to* **Dou Yi.**

Handsome   Forgive me. I was never going to hurt you.

Nurse Wong   You are in shock. Sleep. I'll handle the girl.

Handsome   Thank you.

Handsome *exits.*

Dou Yi   My mother-in-law is very sick. If you'll lend me fresh clothes—

Nurse Wong   If you say anything about what you saw tonight I will make sure your mother-in-law spends the rest of her remaining minutes wishing each one was her last.

Dou Yi   Don't hurt Mother Cai.

People's Armed Police Officers *enter.*

Officer 3   Who reported a disturbance?

Nurse Wong   This peasant has killed an army official.

Dou Yi   No!

Officer 2   Hands in the air!

Dou Yi   Tell them the truth!

Nurse Wong   This woman may be young but she is stubborn and cunning. Not even a beating would frighten her. Confess your crime—for the sake of your mother-in-law.

Dou Yi   I confess.

All Officers   Hands!

Dou Yi *raises her hands. She is handcuffed.*

Nurse Wong   You'll find her grubby prints all over his body.

Dou Yi   Woman, could it be that you don't know shame?

The police officers exit with **Dou Yi.**

Scene Eight

The inside and outside of **Nurse Wong**'*s bar. One hour before sunset. Uniformed* **People's Liberation Army Soldiers** *patrol the exterior of the bar and carry piles of suitcases to offstage buses and evacuate the citizens of New Harmony. Inside the bar,* **Nurse Wong**, *wearing rubber gloves, squirts a bottle of rat poison onto pieces of bread and lays the poisoned bread along the perimeter of the wall.*

Intercom   Citizens of New Harmony, the mandatory evacuation is underway. Proceed immediately to your nearest evacuation point. Ground forces from the People's Liberation Army are waiting to transport you out of the region.

Handsome *enters.*

Handsome   The town's shutting down. Why are you baiting traps?

Nurse Wong   So that if it becomes safe to return I won't find my pension's been ravaged by rodents.

Handsome   Are you that optimistic?

Nurse Wong   I am sensible and pragmatic. Are you ready to leave this dry land behind us?

Handsome   Such a fate does not belong to a man who's lost his mate.

Nurse Wong   We're survivors. Love always comes with a risk.

Handsome   Did you assume two men growing gray together was rare and unlikely?

Nurse Wong   Have a seat. Let's drink to his memory.

Handsome *sits at the table.* **Nurse Wong** *removes her gloves, retrieves two glasses and pours them each a glass of wine.*

Handsome   Have you ever regretted what you—what we—did to Dou Yi?

Nurse Wong (*lifting glass in a toast*)   To Rocket.

Handsome *drains his glass and pours himself another.*

Nurse Wong   Easy, my love. We have a long night ahead.

Handsome   Answer my question.

Nurse Wong   I do not for a minute regret defending that girl from your father.

Handsome   Is that what we did?

Nurse Wong   You were there. You saw what he was going to / do.

Handsome (*interrupting at /*)   I saw you hand me his gun and tell me to shoot him.

Nurse Wong   To protect her.

Handsome   Were you protecting her when you framed her for murder?

Nurse Wong   That was for you.

Handsome   You protected me, with lies, told in my name.

Nurse Wong   Just as you did for your Rocket.

Handsome   Oh, my sweet man. What devastation have we wrought in your name?

Nurse Wong   There is no worse fate than being born into a poor, female body. Who's to say we did not do her a favor by helping her escape that karma quickly?

Handsome   Woman. Can you hear what you're saying?

Nurse Wong   How many nameless faces with silent fates have given their vitality to the Zhang family?

Handsome   We sent a woman to her death then bid on her body.

Nurse Wong   You bought three years of happiness. You'd do it again for more time with him.

Handsome   As a courtesy I should tell you officers of the law are coming.

Nurse Wong   To help get us out?

Handsome   To arrest me for the murder of my father, and us both for false testimony in the case of Dou Yi.

Nurse Wong   What do they know?

Handsome   Soon they will know everything.

Nurse Wong   Keep your wits about you. Who does this help?

Handsome   Everyone who has paid the price for my happiness.

Nurse Wong   Handsome, calm yourself. You've gone mad from grief.

Handsome   If I am mad it is because I was raised by a mad woman who taught me to defend my own interests over everyone else's.

Nurse Wong   I taught you how to live in a world that operates by those principles and you have flourished within it.

Handsome   I have not flourished. I am the destruction of this town.

Nurse Wong   Listen to me. We are cut from the same cloth—

Handsome (*interrupting*)   You are a servant. I was a fool to bind my life to you.

Nurse Wong   Everything I've ever done has been out of love.

Handsome   Your duty was not love. It was service, in exchange for a salary. I'd be better off if you'd left when I'd finished draining milk from both breasts.

Nurse Wong   Let me tell you something I've been hiding in my heart for a very long time.

Handsome   Save it for the judge.

Nurse Wong   You are my flesh.

Handsome   What?

Nurse Wong   You come from this body.

Handsome   Would that not make people laugh until their mouths split?

Nurse Wong   The woman you called "mother" was barren.

Handsome   Will you say anything to stay out of jail?

Nurse Wong   I gave birth to you alone in a room full of rats. Mistress Zhang pulled you out of my arms and claimed you as her own moments after you emerged. She could not bear a child no matter how many times she tried and as you know, when your father wants an heir, he will be forceful.

Handsome   Do you expect the sound of pipes and song to accompany the reunion of mother and son?

Nurse Wong   That is the truth, plain and white.

Handsome   Why wait until you're facing prison to share it? Who, peasant, are you really protecting? Whose will did you serve when you made me your weapon?

Nurse Wong   You were about to wound a woman, like your father had, to the very core of her being. I kept you from becoming him. I liberated you from the karmic trap of the Zhang family.

Handsome   You must be relieved the Zhang line ends with me.

Nurse Wong   Have faith, my love. You will find another.

Handsome   You say I was born in the company of rats. Why are you murdering my brethren?

Nurse Wong   You are not a rat, Handsome. You may be meek, but you are good.

A long pause.

Handsome   My suitcase is in my bedroom, *mother*. Fetch it for me.

Nurse Wong   Hearing you use that word brings joy to this tired body. Are you ready to leave this terrible desert?

Handsome   Of the thirty-six stratagems, escape is supreme.

Nurse Wong   Yes, my son. That's the spirit. Your mother will take care of everything.

Nurse Wong *exits.* **Handsome** *paces around the room, and refills his wine glass.*

Handsome   Where can you find a man who can erode the Great Wall with his tears? Where can you find a man with the will to sleep in a grave? Where will you meet a man who will carry winter clothes over thousands of miles and turn into stone awaiting his beloved's return? Here, Rocket. That man is me.

Handsome *drinks from the bottle containing rat poison. The* **Ghost of Dou Yi** *enters.*

Handsome   Ghost of the Woman Dou Yi. I see you. Do you see me?

Dou Yi   You were born with a mouth that could right wrongs with a few words. Why didn't you speak?

Handsome   I cared more for my happiness than yours.

Dou Yi   Maybe in the next life you'll learn to let go.

Handsome   Tell Rocket to wait. Tell him I'm coming.

He dies. **Nurse Wong** *enters with a suitcase. She does not see* **Dou Yi.**

Nurse Wong   Let's hurry now, darling. The last buses are about to—(*Sees his body.*) Oh Handsome! No. No, my boy. My heart. Come back to me.

Nurse Wong *cradles* **Handsome**'*s limp body in her arms.* **Dou Yi** *remains in the room.* **Police Officers** *enter with* **Tianyun.**

Officer 2   Old woman! What happened to this man?

Nurse Wong   My son drank rat poison. This world means nothing if Handsome's not in it. I confess. I goaded this sweet boy to murder his father, who had violated me to the depths of my being. To protect him and myself I framed the woman Dou Yi.

The **Police Officers** *arrest* **Nurse Wong** *and carry her off. Several others move* **Handsome***'s body onto a stretcher and carry him out of the bar.*

Tianyun *and* **Dou Yi** *are alone in the bar. Red, purple and orange light streaks across the sky as the sun sets over New Harmony.*

Mother and daughter face each other, but do not move towards each other. A long pause.

Tianyun   Duan Yun.

Dou Yi   Mother.

Tianyun   I've been looking for you.

Dou Yi   You haven't found me.

Tianyun   Where is your beautiful, precious body?

Dou Yi   You could spend the rest of your life collecting the pieces.

Fei-Fei *runs on, carrying a fist-size burlap parcel tied together with a double-happiness necklace.* **Fei-Fei***'s hair, clothes and the burlap parcel are covered in snow.*

Fei-Fei   Hello mother.

Tianyun   My love. Where have you been?

Fei-Fei   Playing in the snow with my sister Dou Yi. We made snow angels and built snow girls and we made a snow fort!

Tianyun   A snow fort?

Fei-Fei   And a snow bed and look what I found under my snow pillow!

Fei-Fei *hands* **Tianyun** *the burlap parcel.*

Dou Yi   Bury me, mother.

Fei-Fei *starts to dig a hole in the ground.*

Tianyun   What are you doing?

Fei-Fei   Put her heart in the dirt and I'll put my little tree on top of it. Worker Chen said it's the last living plant in New Harmony.

Tianyun *places* **Dou Yi***'s heart in the pot.* **Fei-Fei** *puts her willow seedling on top of it. They smooth the dirt around so it covers the heart and the roots of the seedling.*

Dou Yi   Do you have a birthday wish?

Fei-Fei   Yes. Should I say it out loud?

Tianyun   You have a strong voice. Use it.

Fei-Fei

Sister, we buried your heart and planted a seedling on top of it.
It's small, but with water could become a big willow tree.

Please send rain so it grows tall and strong
And has long branches I can use to beat back demons
Like the Goddess of Mercy.

Fei-Fei *and* **Tianyun** *bow to the pot and* **Dou Yi.**

Thunder rumbles. Lightning flashes.

It starts to pour. It's the hardest rain the region has ever seen.

The world of the living recedes.

Dou Yi

Do not make the excuse that natural disaster occurs every generation
The will of one woman can make the Blue Sky repent.
Make the world right for your children
Make sure no child needs wings
Or you may wake to find your own bones and flesh
Mutilated by the world you turned your back on
And have no choice but to mourn her
And the chance you missed to fight
For justice for every being
Here now
And yet to visit
This floating, fleeting world.

Ox-Head *and* **Horse-Face**, *Guardians of the Land of the Dead, enter.*

Dou Yi *joins them. They exit to the underworld.*

It continues to rain.

Watering the soil that contains **Dou Yi**'s *heart and a young willow tree.*

End of Play.

Afterword

Joshua Chambers-Letson

How do you stage the beginning of the end of the world? "A thick brown haze, the result of ongoing dust storms, hovers, obscuring the sun and surrounding the buildings. Mounds of dust and dead locusts have been swept into piles," writes Frances Ya-Chu Cowhig in a stage direction at the beginning of *Snow in Midsummer*'s second act. Cowhig emphasizes the cumulative, mutually implicated nature of ecological and manmade disaster throughout *Snow in Midsummer*. The near-rape and murder of an impoverished woman (Dou Yi) is the result of collusion between a wealthy family and the state. A chain of ecological oddities and disasters (a freak snowstorm in June, three years of drought, a plague of locusts and dust storms) proceed from this act, accumulating to make life in the region unliveable. After Dou Yi's murder, and fulfilling her oath, snow blankets the June ground as her blood accumulates in a white flag flying overhead. "The snow follows Dou Yi's body," Cowhig writes, "*accumulating* on top of it, covering it completely." In turn, the drought worsens over the play's duration as eventually "mounds of dust" and dead locusts become so dense that "the ground is covered with [them]."

Surprisingly, the play concludes *not* with a cessation of ecological catastrophe, but with yet another incidence of it. After Dou Yi's mother, Tianyun, uncovers and avenges the injustice of her daughter's death, the world of the play is not restored to the ecological and social balance that reigned before. Rather, the drought ends by way of a new storm: "Thunder rumbles. Lightning flashes. It starts to pour. It's the hardest rain the region has ever seen. The world of the living recedes." Does "the world of the living recede" because audience attention is focused on Dou Yi's journey towards the underworld, or is this because the world of the living is to be buried beneath the flood waters? Concluding the play on a hopeful note, with water quenching the parched soil where Dou Yi's heart is finally laid to rest, the stage directions ("it continues to rain") still posit two questions: when and if the rain will stop and what will grow from Dou Yi's buried heart?

Based on Guan Hanqing's thirteenth-century Chinese play *The Injustice to Dou Yi that Moved Heaven and Earth*, Cowhig draws on the conventions of Yuan era drama, as well as the ghostly revenge tragedies of the early modern English stage (such as Shakespeare's *Hamlet*) to define the world of *Snow in Midsummer*. But, alongside recent works by writers including Octavia Butler and N.K. Jemisin, we might also situate the play within the contemporary tradition of speculative, Black feminist and feminist of color, ecologically-centered literature. Such authors center the stories of women of color, as well as feminist of color epistemologies and social practices, to approach the question of how we are to inhabit an impossible present, if not labor to produce new worlds and new ways of being in the world.[1] Cowhig's play, and Jemisin's

---

1   Octavia E. Butler, *Parable of the Sower: A Novel* (New York: Seven Stories Press, 2016); N. K. Jemisin, *The Fifth Season* (New York: Orbit, 2015), *The Obelisk Gate* (New York: Orbit, 2016), and *The Stone Sky* (New York: Orbit, 2017).

and Butler's novels, all tell the story of dying worlds rich with the (however faint) hope that new worlds may come into being through feminist praxis. All three occur against a landscape of ecological catastrophe and suggest that any attempt to give birth to a world worth living in will require a reconciliation with the forms of racial, gender, sexual, economic, and geographic injustice that characterize the world we presently occupy. Similarly, all gesture to practices of reparation between femmes of color, and mothers and daughters in particular, as critical to a vision of such new worlds and worldings.

The accumulation of dust storms in *Snow in Midsummer* recalls the California of Butler's *Parable of the Sower*, which is set in the near future in the midst of ongoing political and economic breakdown. There, dust storms, manmade fires, and other ecological catastrophes ravage what's left of U.S. civilization. Cowhig's mounting piles of dust and dead locusts also resonate with the piles of ash that accumulate across the landscape in Jemisin's *Broken Earth* trilogy. Set in the Stillness, a massive, single-continent world wracked by constant seismic activity, Jemisin's series begins when a manmade rift along an equatorial fault line sets into motion a nuclear winter that threatens to engulf what scraps of life and civilization have survived the earth's rage against humanity. As Jemisin's narrator states at the beginning of the series, the book tells the story of the world's end, but "the ending of one story is just the beginning of another . . . When we say 'the world has ended,' it's usually a lie, because *the planet* is just fine."[2] And though, at the beginning of the series, the narrator insists that "*This is the way the world ends.* For the last time," the series concludes as the narrator muses, "This is the way a new world begins," reminding us that the end of the world always carries with it the possibility for the birth of a new one.[3]

Much of my thinking here is indebted to Black feminist theorist Chelsea M. Frazier who notes that Butler's novel is centered around Black women, which is arguably the case in the *Broken Earth* series as well. For Frazier, Butler's novel posits the potential for a Black feminist ecological "ethics that points to new and fundamentally different possibilities and not improvements of existing ones."[4] Butler's and Jemisin's novels materialize what, in Frazier's terms, could be "a truly 'new' environmental politics [that] would render our present world unrecognizable."[5] Giving birth, in other words, to truly new worlds. For Frazier, "Butler's harrowing and seemingly apocalyptic depiction of the future centers the instability of the racial, spatial, and gendered organization of our present world" such that "the most jarring element of Butler's future California is its similarities in aesthetics and patterns to the world we inhabit presently."[6] Mobilizing the conventions of speculative fiction, Butler writes of a nightmarish future that ultimately seems continuous with (and an extension of) the present, whereas Jemisin utilizes the genre of fantasy to draw allegorical connections between the world of *Broken Earth* and that of the reader. While reading either Butler

---

2 *The Fifth Season.*
3 *The Stone Sky*, 398.
4 Chelsea M. Frazier, "Troubling Ecology: Wangechi Mutu, Octavia Butler, and Black Feminist Interventions in Environmentalism," *Journal of the Critical Ethnic Studies Association* 2, no. 1 (2016): 60.
5 Ibid., 40.
6 Ibid., 48.

or Jemisin, one becomes less concerned that the novels' apocalyptic scenarios describe where we are headed, perceiving instead that this is the world in which many of us already live.

As Frazier insists, it is the particularity of a Black feminist praxis and the centering of Black women that opens up the potential for new worlds to emerge in *Parable of the Sower*. By drawing a comparison between Cowhig's play and Butler and Jemisin's work, I do not mean to displace the Black feminist particularity centered in Frazier's analysis. Instead, I am interested in what we might learn when we think the Black feminist eco-ethics of Frazier's work and Butler and Jemisin's novels alongside what we could provisionally call the Asian/American eco-feminism of *Snow in Midsummer*. After all, there are many formal and political resonances between the three pieces: all are concerned with human-made ecological catastrophe and all explore how the centering of feminist and woman of color epistemologies and practices can open up the possibilities for new worlds and new ways of being in the world.

If Butler and Jemisin place Black women at the center of their worlds, Cowhig's play is uniquely interested in Chinese women (mothers, daughters, and sisters), their (albeit fraught) relationships with each other, and their relationships with queer men. Setting her play in contemporary China, Cowhig subtly appropriates the conventions of Orientalism in a fashion that functions similarly to Butler and Jemisin's critical deployment of the conventions of sci-fi and fantasy. That is, just as Butler and Jemisin mobilize the alternative times and spaces of future or fantasy worlds to ask critical questions about the reader's present, Cowhig mobilizes the play's Chinese setting to invite audiences in Britain and the U.S. (where the play was first staged) to make critical connections to their own surround.

In the U.S., both historically and in the present, "China" regularly figures as a constitutive Other against which Euro-U.S. political and racial identity is defined. As Rey Chow observes, on the one hand, after the Communist revolution in China, the U.S. developed a melancholic imperialist attachment to China, which functions as "a symbol of the United States' loss of guardianship over the most populous area of Asia."[7] On the other hand, China surfaces as threat to be feared, insofar as it is represented "as the other of all the positive values embraced by the United States."[8] Not only a geographic, moral, and racial Other, "China" is ultimately also figured as a temporal other. As Petrus Liu notes, following Johannes Fabian, "modernity's colonial production of racial others operates through the 'denial of coevalness,' whereby cultural differences between actually coexistent societies are understood as temporal differences in degree of development. The denial of coevalness conveys an impression of a time lag between actually contemporaneous cultures."[9] "China" thus regularly surfaces in the Euro-U.S. imaginary as a paradigmatic example of the racial, temporal, political, sexual, and moral Other.

By setting the play in the overdetermined elsewhere of "China," Cowhig consistently deconstructs the "denial of coevalness," while reminding the audience of the ways in

---

7 Rey Chow, "King Kong in Hong Kong: Watching the 'Handover' from the U.S.A.," *Social Text* 55 (1998): 94.
8 Ibid.
9 Petrus Liu, "Why Does Queer Theory Need China?," *positions: east asia cultures critique* 18, no. 2 (2010): 297–8.

which "China" and "America" (or "East" and "West") are less distinct and coherent identities than mutually implicated, co-constitutive, overlapping, and deeply integrated systems of national, economic, political, ideological, racial, sexual, territorial, and discursive practice. The sexual objectification and violence against the women in the play is not framed as a uniquely Chinese problem, nor does the play root the problem in Orientalist stereotypes of "backward" Chinese sexual and cultural differences. Instead, the scenes of sexual harassment and violence that occur throughout *Snow in Midsummer* bear a striking resemblance to the use of money, law, and other official and private forms of power that facilitate and protect the sexually predatory (if not violently murderous) behaviors of powerful men. In other words, Master Zhang stands alongside figures like Donald Trump and Harvey Weinstein. While the crimes of the Cultural Revolution haunt the margins of the play, its atmosphere is entirely contemporary (complete with female CEOs and gay marriage) and its crises are predicated upon crimes that occurred *not* in the revolutionary socialist or feudal past, but in a present characterized by China's central place in the capitalist global economy. The fact that the patriarch (Master Zhang) is already dead at the beginning of the play, or that the narrative's outcome is primarily shaped by empowered queer and female characters (Tianyun, Handsome, and Rocket), might lead us to question whether the rise of women and queer men into tiers of economic and political power (whether in China or the U.S.) will not simply perpetuate the world of stratification and injustice to which Dou Yi is violently and callously sacrificed.

It ultimately becomes clear that (with the exception of Dou Yi's sister Fei-Fei and possibly her birth mother Tianyun) *everyone in the play, and possibly the entire world, is implicated* in the injustice done to Dou Yi. Not only does Dou Yi's heart end up in Rocket's unwitting body, as a result of Handsome's privileged machinations, but her flesh is torn apart and transformed into commodities that are consumed by the world market. Her hands are "packed in dry ice / Flown across the Pacific and / stitched onto a man who lost his overseas," as her murder is extended and stitched into the flesh of a (presumably) U.S. American soldier who (it is implied) lost his hands during one of the U.S.'s adventures in military imperialism. The sundering apart and dispersal of Dou Yi's body across the globe suggests that the entire world system—including all of us caught up within it—are implicated in her death.

As with Butler and Jemisin's novels, Cowhig's play gives her audience a vision of the shape of things to come and a sense of the powerful force that a feminist of color praxis may play in giving birth to the world that begins in the wake of this world's ending. Dou Yi's curse will only end by heeding her call for "justice." But by the play's conclusion there still remains a question as to whether justice is possible. "Where is your beautiful body," Tianyun asks her daughter's ghost, to which Dou Yi replies, "You could spend the rest of your life collecting the pieces." If the entire world is implicated in the death of a forgotten, subaltern Chinese woman, it only seems right that the world is not restored to its previous order when the injustice done to Dou Yi is finally recognized. The threat of the flood ("the hardest rain the region has ever seen") recalls the biblical flood of the Old Testament. But Dou Yi's flood is founded less on the patriarchal and punishing violence of God the Father's wrath and fury, so much as it emerges from the restoration of ties between mothers, daughters, and sisters, and the other feminist practices of mutual care, recognition, and restitution performed by the women of color (and in Rocket's case, queer men) at the play's center. It is in this way that *Snow in Midsummer* also resonates with Butler and Jemisin's work insofar as all three attempt to imagine the path towards (and, to some extent, the impossibility) of repair in the relationships between mothers and daughters as an element of the making of new and better worlds. In Butler's *Parable* series, a daughter must grapple with the personal, often painful effects of her mother's evangelical vision to transform the world for the better. In *Broken Earth*, a mother sacrifices everything (including her body) to save her daughter, and the world, in the same moment. As with Cowhig, reparation is never complete and full up with the rending forces of loss and grief. But it is, yet, a path towards new growth and new life.

In Dialogue with Frances Ya-Chu Cowhig, Christine Mok, and Joshua Chambers-Letson

The following conversation was composed online between November 20, 2020 and January 30, 2021.

CM & JCL   Your writing and development process is deeply physical and grounded in the kinds of relations, improvizations, and engagements that occur within (and out) of the time space of theatre making. Can you talk a bit with us about the process of how each of these works came together? How do you construct these worlds, both on the page and collaboratively in the realm of production and development?

FYC   I'd be happy to. I try to keep the writing process tactile and physical by writing the first few drafts of each scene by hand and spending as little time in front of the computer word processor as possible. I find sitting in front of a glowing screen draining and unpleasant, not to mention endlessly distracting when an internet connection is also present, which makes it not a conducive creative space for me. The way I keep myself writing and brainstorming is by making the journey as pleasurable and delicious as much as possible, which for me most often means writing by hand outdoors under trees or beside bodies of water, or inside by a sunny window or crackling fireplace.

Β The hardest part is getting to the end of the first draft. I typically rework the first thirty pages until I feel I have laid the right foundation for the rest of the dramatic experience. This means I have figured out how I am rendering character—in terms of description, dialogue and physical behavior. By this point I also want to have a sense of the storytelling work the physical objects are going to do, what the physical and social environment of the play is, how transitions between scenes can operate, and how sound can be used to specify setting, which then makes it easier to move quickly between scenes because the set can do less work. I ascribe to the adage that a play is a conflict between what you see and what you hear, and keep this in mind as I develop the various layers of storytelling—movement, sound, visuals, dialogue—that together make up the architecture of a script.

Sometimes I collect my own versions of physical objects I want to use in the script, so that I can spend time manipulating the objects and investigating the ways they can be altered visually and used to create visual metaphors that support nonverbal storytelling. Occasionally I make little sketches and storyboards that help me keep track of where my characters are in a scene and imagine what is possible in terms of physical actions and social dynamics. I often mutter under my breath as I write, and tend to hear the rhythm and sound of a line percussively first, then use the musicality of what I hear to inform word choice.

Before I begin a play I read a lot of nonfiction and watch a lot of documentaries. This helps me to understand the worlds I am exploring and the types of people (or nonhuman entities) that move through them. I consider myself a collage artist in my approach, in that I do research with an eye towards finding both areas of similarity and overlap and also points of dissonance and counterpoint in the material I am exploring—and also try to approach the material with curiosity and an open mind.

CM & JCL   What is the most pleasurable part of this process?

FYC   Collaborating with designers, and ensemble work with actors. One of my favorite directors to work with is Tea Alagić, because of how generative and fearless she asks actors to be. For example, in the first developmental workshop of *The King of Hell's Palace*, which was hosted by East West Players in Los Angeles, as soon as the play was read through once, Tea asked the actors to put away their scripts and improvize the whole play from memory. She then did another exploration where the actors had to sing the whole script as if it was an opera, and accompany their singing with heightened, gestural movement.

After spending what is often years alone with the script, it feels magical to surrender the story and characters into the bodies and minds of capable actors and watch it come alive. If the actors know their characters extremely well and are comfortable with improvization, I sometimes use this way of working to generate the first draft of a missing scene. For example, I might give a pair of actors their objective in the missing scene and a couple things that need to happen, and then ask them to improvize a few different ways such a scene could unfold. I don't take notes or record the improvisation, I just watch the scene closely and absorb the pacing, emotional palette and manipulation tactics the actors offer during the improvizations. I use this information to inform the scene I then write very quickly, either immediately after the improvization, or before the next day's rehearsal.

CM & JCL   And the least pleasurable?

FYC   There are two parts of theatre-making that I find more draining than others. One is the social labor of making sure I have enough input into and oversight of certain early aspects of the production process, such as costume design, marketing, casting and publicity, often with theatres that are used to staging the work of dead playwrights. Much of this is due to the fact that individuals working on my plays often have very little experience with the worlds the plays are depicting and haven't done adequate research, so they make choices in costume or graphic design that place an orientalist and archaic frame around the work. These choices are often unconscious and have to do with prior depictions of China on stage and attempts to make the worlds seem "other" or "exotic" in an attempt to bring in audiences. I often feel exhausted by the amount of advocacy I have to do in all these avenues outside the rehearsal room, and also disappointed in how engagement with marketing and publicity on behalf of the play sometimes results in my being labeled "difficult" by employees of theatres that produce my work—a word I have frankly only ever heard being applied to female theatre-makers.

The other dispiriting part of theatre-making has to do with how bad many artistic leaders in institutional theatres have been in communicating with me about work I have been commissioned to write for them. I have been in many situations where the institutional dramaturg or literary manager responsible for communicating with me about the status of my work at the theatre makes promises to me about when I will hear back from them, and then not only does not follow through on it, but also subsequently ignores my follow-up queries for months and months. The complicating factor is that in many cases my institutional "advocate" is someone who is relatively powerless at the theatre, and may not even be in regular communication with their own artistic director. Though my socialization leads me to try to be kind and forgiving with these individuals, being repeatedly ignored and not responded to in a timely manner by theatres who have asked me to create work for extremely low pay is soul-crushing, and often leads me to feel as if I am in an abusive relationship with these commissioning theatres.

CM & JCL   What is your process once a play is open and running, when the directors and designers have flown home, and the work is given unto the audience by actors, stage managers, and crews to perform night after night?

FYC   I usually fly home the day after opening night and do not see the production again. I typically move on to a different project, and don't work on the play again until there is another production lined up. This also gives me time to "forget" a particular production or interpretation of my work, which makes it easier to get back into the script. I like to be present for the development and rehearsal of a play through its first two or three professional productions. After that I consider the script finished and move on.

CM & JCL   One of the elements that runs throughout these plays are questions of familial relation. Families, in your plays, are messy and are often compromised by the economic and political conditions various family members navigate. Yet in other places, as in *Snow*, kinship and the relationships between mothers and daughters, in particular, can be sites of regenerative power. Can you talk to us a bit about families and relationships in your plays? How do you arrive at these relations in your process as you develop characters?

FYC   One reason I like to tell stories through familial relation is that it allows complicated histories and big ideas to play out in a way that is intimate and intergenerational. Often stories lauded for their "epic" structure tend to feel less emotionally impactful and therefore less memorable to me, because I lose the experience of individual people inside these larger narratives. By setting the dramatic conflict of my plays within the fabric of intergenerational family structures, I am trying to use the familiar and accessible lens of intimate family relationships to reveal larger tensions within the world of the play. I am also looking at how things like family loyalty get in the way of individuals trying to live in accordance with their values. Because the family, rather than the individual, is traditionally the core unit in East Asian societies, the social pressures and shame cultures that uphold it are more potent than what you might typically find in an Anglo-American family drama.

CM & JCL   Can you talk a bit about the relationship between the familial and the Chinese setting of the plays?

FYC   Sure. On one level, I'm very interested in writing about areas of Chinese history and culture that are vulnerable to erasure and forgetting due to censorship and how information is controlled in the People's Republic of China (PRC). On another level, I'm interested in looking at how the pressures and conflicts in specific situations in the PRC are a bellwether for where we are headed globally, in regard to things like the rise of surveillance capitalism, the manipulation of the press, the management of perception by national and corporate interests, and how those same entities are leading us into chaos and ecological collapse by privileging profit and social control over the longer term well-being of individuals, communities and ecosystems.

In terms of how I find my way into story through orchestrating character—given that the rural/urban class divide in China has been called a form of internal apartheid—I chose to lean into and explore this divide in all three plays by having characters from both rural and urban China. Because there remains such a major divide in today's China between individuals who were alive during the Cultural Revolution and consequently have lived memories of the "chaos," and those who were born in the "New China" and have no memories of famine or social unrest, it was important to me in these plays to represent in each one at least three generations of society—youth, working adults, and elders.

JCL & CM   While your plays drill down into the darkness and light of the family and complicate the couple form (whether a duo of brother-sister, mother-daughter, or a romantic couple), the relationships in your plays always gesture outwards to much larger communities. Producers would probably be happier if your plays were just two-handers or remained enclosed within the nuclear family. How do you approach scale and scope—from the individual to the collective, human to humanity—in crafting your worlds?

FYC   My first playwriting class was housed within the Africana Studies department at Brown University. It was taught using what my professor, Elmo Terry-Morgan, calls the "Research-to-Performance Method." This is a way into dramatic writing that begins with inquiry into the world of the play and the tensions and conflicts that exist in it. From the very beginning of my playwriting journey, I have been working with an eye towards looking to how one could use dramatic writing to explore and illustrate larger tensions in society. Beginning with the first play I wrote in Professor Terry-Morgan's class, I have been interested in creating story scenarios in which someone who is going against the grain of their society is doing so at the expense of both their own personal happiness and physical safety, and also the wellbeing of someone close to them who is trying to play it safe and stay on the right side of power. I like using the family as a unit for storytelling because the stakes are clear and the pressures and consequences can be felt. I think this allows big social questions to play out in intimate ways that are relatable because they feel human-sized—provided, of course, that I enter the play with the right dramatic question, and orchestrate the right set of oppositional characters around that dramatic question.

CM & JCL   How do you begin to search for that question?

FYC   Usually the dramatic question is related to something I am struggling with existentially. Despite the epic nature of the plays in this volume, the questions the characters face are the same questions I struggle with, tensions that I also see echoes of at the community, national and international level: When can I live for myself and when should I live for other people? How far downstream and upstream should I look to understand the consequences of my choices and actions? Who and what has shaped the ideas that form my understanding of "reality"—and what hidden agendas might be there? I like to spin out ideas broadly during the research stage, and then make specific choices with an understanding of both practical production constraints and the kinds of storytelling strategies the audiences coming to my plays are familiar with. As I search for the right constraints for my dramatic narrative, I'm looking for ways to make abstract ideas concrete enough to be manipulated through physical space in real time, through the journeys of bodies and objects onstage.

CM & JCL   Is this connected to the theatrey-ness and theatricality of your plays, which calls upon the materiality of bodies and objects on stage and in the audience, as opposed to the solitary reader hailed by print?

FYC   I think about this through the lens of production constraint: How can I create the storytelling equivalent of a symphony with the resources of a chamber orchestra? One way into this is through double casting, and having, for instance, a cast of six actors play seventeen characters. Again, this also can mean embedding a lot of storytelling into the journeys of physical objects on stage, so that actors don't have to do all the heavy lifting.

CM & JCL   There are any number of "afters" that occur within the worlds of your plays, and oftentimes these come *after* catastrophe, both historical and personal: after the massacre of democratic activists in Tiananmen Square, after the most violent excesses of the Cultural Revolution, after the devastating effects of neoliberal reform in the People's Republic's transition to a "socialist market economy," after a government covers up its failure to contain a viral outbreak (of HIV—and, now, COVID-19), or what comes after the betrayals of friends and family. There are distinct but overlapping questions of what comes after, whether its seismic, economic, reorganization; personal betrayal or literally our betrayal of our stewardship of the planet? How do we reflect upon the questions of what comes after that each of these three plays is posing to us?

FYC   What I love about Norse mythology, and also Taoism, Buddhism and Chinese folk religion, is that endings are necessary so that they can be followed by new beginnings. "Each of the plays in this trilogy tracks a central character enshrouded in a veil of deception. Sometimes this deception is willful ignorance, other times it is a structurally supported amnesia that benefits business and government. Common to all three plays is pressure on characters to keep up the facade that everything is okay, that the world the character is inhabiting is normal—or at least the best one can hope for. By the end of each play, one or more characters has gone on a journey of dis-illusionment, by which I mean that the illusions they were under, illusions they used to justify their existence and life choices, have been shown to be false or hollow or corrupt in a way the character cannot forget or distance themself from. For these characters, to continue in the face of this new knowledge would require a life of wilful self-deception and a descent into cynicism, which for reasons specific to each character would make life unliveable. At the end of each play one or more central characters has to choose whether to make a choice that benefits themselves and the operations of a world they now understand to be built on a foundation of exploitation and deceit, or they can choose otherwise—which comes at the cost of their own personal safety and material comfort—and their family's.

CM & JCL   One of the consistent—and consistently horrifying—themes to emerge in your plays are these very "operations" of a world built on deceit and exploitation. People are bought and sold, stripped to the flesh and transformed into commodities for trade in local and global markets. Can you talk a bit about the place of capitalism and neoliberalism in these works? What does it mean to describe these plays as "three parables of global capital." And what is it about theatrical form that opens up and allows you to explore these questions as you do?

FYC   To me this means thinking about these stories as allegories and not just the literal narrative in terms of character and plot. To live in the modern industrial world is to consume daily—if not hourly—products, goods and utilities constructed, mined, moved and delivered by a largely invisible underclass. In all three of these works I am attempting to illuminate the entanglements and complicated relationships between producers and consumers, and also look at ways specific ideas are used as forms of social control—both to keep the underclass an underclass, and also to make it extremely difficult and personally costly for members of the managerial/ruling class to challenge the system. Effective writing for the stage often requires the playwright to externalize thoughts and ideas and embed them into objects and characters in conflict. Live theatre can be a potent place to examine the invisible relationships we have with workers and products, as everything can be compressed and made to unfold before your eyes in real time.

CM & JCL   You are writing in English, developing and mounting plays in the U.S. and U.K. with Asian diasporic actors, and addressing a western audience, while staging "China." China has long been a subject for the American theatre. However, there is often an intermediary frame of a "Western" character as either a stand-in for the audience or as a way to metaphorically hold a (white) audience's hand. Can you talk a bit about this dynamic and about the dramaturgical move that you make by eschewing the traveler (whether it's Nixon, René Gallimard, or the Asian American characters in a text like David Henry Hwang's *Soft Power*, Hansol Jung's *Among the Dead*, or Mia Chung's *Me for You for Me*) or other such "Western" presences?

FYC   Because China's industrial revolution happened later than it did in the United States or the United Kingdom, by setting these stories in China I am choosing a setting that allows relations of power and exploitation that are present everywhere to be illustrated clearly and starkly—not because they don't exist elsewhere, but because they have not yet become as effectively hidden from view.

Instead of employing the convention of having a character that represents an Outsider or Other in these plays, I chose to link this figure of the "Western traveler" to ideas traditionally linked to Western Civilization, and make these ideas central to the way in which social control and personal aspiration operate in each of these plays. For example, in *The World of Extreme Happiness*, the central idea/attitude I link to the character of Sunny is the self-help fantasy of "boot-strapping," which is core to the American Dream. I chose to follow this idea after researching the lives of young migrant workers in Shenzhen and learning how popular self-help classes and books are, most of which are translations of American texts like *The Secret* and *How to Win Friends and Influence People*. By following the cynical, self-serving behaviorist strategies learned from these texts, Sunny is able to achieve gains in material wealth and status—for herself. These come at the expense of other people in her community, as she is moving up in a social hierarchy that she knows to be corrupt and baseless, out of a desire for personal safety and material comfort.

CM & JCL   We began preparation for this volume in the early months of a new pandemic (COVID-19) and amidst a tumultuous reorganization of U.S.-China relations. Can you offer some reflections on how these recent historical forces affect your reflection on this body of work?

FYC   Dr. Shuping Wang, the Henan public health official who was the whistle-blower in the Henan AIDS crisis, and whose experiences inspired *The King of Hell's Palace*, was on my mind a lot in January and February of 2020, when the COVID-19 pandemic was causing the city of Wuhan to go into lockdown. Although Dr. Wang passed away several months before the Wuhan lockdown, I'm sure she would have seen a lot of parallels between her own experiences as a Chinese whistle-blower in the nineties and the recent struggles of Dr. Li Wenliang, the Wuhan ophthalmologist who had tried to warn his colleagues about the then unknown disease and was reprimanded by the police for spreading "rumours" about the disease that would eventually take Dr. Li's life. There are a lot of parallels between how the Chinese government tried to suppress vital information regarding the Henan AIDS outbreak and their attempts to suppress information during the COVID-19 pandemic. I am glad that Dr. Li has been recognized by millions inside China for his courage and heroism and hope that one day Dr. Wang will also be widely recognized inside her home country for her bravery and sacrifice in response to the Henan AIDS epidemic.

CM & JCL   Having created this trilogy—did you set out to write three?—what comes next for you? Where does your pen go; your mind wander? What worlds are you exploring during this theatrical pause?

FYC   I did want to write three plays set in contemporary China that used a cast of all Chinese characters. Beyond thematic linkages, I didn't have specific stories in mind at the outset, besides a general interest in exploring rural/urban migration and the lives of a factory workers. I also wanted help the family friend I just mentioned, Dr. Shuping Wang, tell the story of how the Henan government ran for-profit plasma collection centers that caused a rural AIDS epidemic and resulted in the deaths of tens of thousands of Chinese farmers. I hope that someday this trilogy will be produced in rotating rep by a single cast of actors—and that the production schedule will make it possible to experience all three plays in a single day.

Now that my work on this trilogy is complete, I am making a deliberate move away from work set in mainland China, towards Asian America, and the Chinese diaspora. I continue to be very interested in and inspired by the myths and folk customs that developed in China over the millennia, but am now more interested in how they might be adapted and harnessed in relationship to the Chinese diaspora worldwide, rather than within the geographic and ideological boundaries of the People's Republic of China, which, after all, is not even eighty years old yet.

Thematically, I'm interested in stories that examine the industrial human's relationships to nonhuman worlds, in hopes that they might help to envision paradigms that move humans away from the ideological center of the universe. I've become very interested in looking to stories from Chinese folk religion centred around ecological deities and cyclical relationships to the natural environments. I'm interested in thinking through what moral and existential alternatives might be suggested by religious frameworks that envision us returning to earth again and again, in both nonhuman bodies, and human bodies that are nothing like the ones we have previously known. If our culture was built on the mythos of our continual return to Earth, and continual re-engagement and re-investment in the ecological and social communities of both human and nonhuman worlds on this planet, might our behaviour and investments be different than they are in social and economic systems based on a Christian, Jewish, or Muslim imagining of Earth as a place we only occupy for one lifetime, in a single human body, and then never return to again?

Acknowledgments

The author and editors would like to thank the following for their assistance with bringing this volume into the world: Nathan Lamp provided invaluable editorial support in the final period of this manuscript's compilation. We are additionally grateful to the team at Bloomsbury including Dom O'Hanlon and Meredith Benson. We would also like to thank the theatre agents who helped advocate for the commission and production of the plays contained within this volume: Antje Oegel, Rachel Viola, and Harriet Pennington-Legh. We are also grateful to the dramaturgs who advocated for the production of these plays and helped them find their form during early stages of development: Tanya Palmer, Ben Power, Pippa Hill, Nic Wass, and Amrita Ramanan. Gratitude is also owed to the directors who first staged these plays in readings, workshops and world premieres: Tea Alagić, Justin Audibert, Jonathan Berry, Michael Boyd, Michael Longhurst, and Eric Ting. Finally, for those who have chosen to be entangled with us: Eldon Grant Porter, Victor Gonzalez, Joshua Rains, and Brian.